The Necessity of Poetics

ALSO BY ROBERT SHEPPARD (* *published by Shearsman Books*)

POETRY
The Flashlight Sonata
Transit Depots/Empty Diaries (with John Seed [text] and Patricia Farrell [images])
Empty Diaries
The Lores
Tin Pan Arcadia
Hymns to the God in which My Typewriter Believes
Complete Twentieth Century Blues
Warrant Error *
Berlin Bursts *
The Given
A Translated Man *
Words Out of Time
Unfinish
History or Sleep — Selected Poems *
Twitters for a Lark (co-authored) *
Micro Event Space
Bad Idea
The English Strain *
British Standards *

FICTION
The Only Life

EDITED
Floating Capital: New Poets from London (with Adrian Clarke)
News for the Ear: A Homage to Roy Fisher (with Peter Robinson)
The Salt Companion to Lee Harwood
The Door at Taldir: Selected Poems of Paul Evans *
Atlantic Drift: an anthology of poetry and poetics (with James Byrne)
New Collected Poems of Lee Harwood (with Kelvin Corcoran) *
Selected Poems of Mary Robinson *

CRITICISM
Far Language: Poetics and Linguistically Innovative Poetry 1978–1997
The Poetry of Saying: British Poetry and Its Discontents 1950–2000
Iain Sinclair
When Bad Times Made for Good Poetry *
The Meaning of Form in Contemporary Innovative Poetry

ON ROBERT SHEPPARD
The Robert Sheppard Companion, ed. Byrne & Madden *

Robert Sheppard

The Necessity of Poetics

Shearsman Books

First published in the United Kingdom in 2024 by
Shearsman Books
PO Box 4239
Swindon
SN3 9FN

Shearsman Books Ltd Registered Office
30–31 St. James Place, Mangotsfield, Bristol BS16 9JB
(this address not for correspondence)

www.shearsman.com

ISBN 978-1-84861-952-4

CONTENTS

Introduction: Gathering from the Past

Alongside the poetry I write, there is a poetics, and this I have articulated in a variety of forms. At the same time, I have tried to interrogate the nature of poetics itself, both in my own practice, and in others'. This selection aims to pair articulation with interrogation.

For many years I have put at the centre of my poetic practice, my teaching and pedagogy of creative writing, and – latterly – my literary criticism, the production and/or study of writerly poetics. I say 'writerly' to distinguish it from other uses of the term – some critics use it to describe their unpacking of the packaging of literature – because I want to limit it to the writings that writers write about writing, which are (still) curiously misread. Even more curiously, I've never managed to produce a *definitive* essay on the topic. However, I have (repeatedly) *defined* poetics as the 'product of the process of reflection upon writings, and upon the act of writing, gathering from the past and from others, speculatively casting into the future'. I have recently, in my opening contribution, 'Poetics as Anticipation', decided that the activity is best thought of as 'anticipatory' rather than 'speculative', though it strikes me now that it might be best to call it *both* 'anticipatory', for its excited forward-thrust, and 'speculative', for its sense of exploration. Excitement *and* exploration. It looks as though another definition is forming itself.

Perhaps it is not surprising that something that I wish to remain protean and unfinished should evade my attempts at a single essay, or rather, that my attempts should become as protean and unfinished as the activity itself. Outside of this book, I have compiled lists of poetics from the ancients to our contemporaries (they ended up on my blog). I have co-edited and introduced a transatlantic anthology of poetry and poetics, *Atlantic Drift,* where the reader may find a variety of contemporary examples. I have written literary critical essays about particular writers' poetics, which have appeared in most of my academic volumes; there is one such essay in this book, because of its centrality to the enterprise. I have written my own poetics to further my own writing. They are 'essays', in the true sense of the word, though not in style, since hybridity seems the mode for these 'attempts'.

I have presented this book broadly in reverse chronological order, so that one moves from blooms to roots. Part one contains my recent poetics, the culmination of several decades of testing and trying, tending to be personal in their focus, towards the bodies of poetic work I have produced, am producing and anticipate producing. Part three contains some of my first attempts at poetics, often of a communal nature, aimed at creating a poetics for a poetry scene or group, mostly now, but not wholly, of literary historical interest. Part two concentrates on works that attempt to define the discourse of poetics critically, explore its nature experimentally, and display its discriminations, forms and major themes, both for myself and for others (both established and emerging writers). Issues resonate between the pieces, and appear as pre-echoes, or repetitions and insistences, in this arrangement.

Rather like poetics itself, then, my conceptualisation of poetics keeps developing, but it also keeps returning to its central occasion, the text that lends its title to this volume, 'The Necessity of Poetics', which heads section two. Of course, this 'central occasion' involving definition, wasn't the first, since I had long developed my own poetry in the nexus of the innovative British poetries, in which poetics was an essential part of its communal development. Early documents relating to practice and community are found towards the end of this book, dating as far back as the 1980s, though I also can be found complaining about the *lack* of poetics. The most egregious part of 'The Necessity of Poetics' is my attempt, first drafted in 1999, to offer multiple definitions of poetics – I remember pieces of paper scattered across the floor – and to present them as a performance piece (at a Creative Writing conference). The over-determination of multiple definitions has a propensity to confuse, but it also has the potential to enthuse. At various times, I have published them as part of a series of re-edited and supplemented booklets called *The Necessity of Poetics*, which really were handouts for students. (Creative Writing as an academic discipline, with a methodology of its own, haunts my work *on* poetics, but not my works *of* poetics.)

Later, I began to think of poetics as a discourse, as a particular practice that developed its own rules (and history), and a section of 'The Necessity of Poetics' focuses upon this thought. Another important qualification for me was that poetics' 'truths' were provisional, not universal (though they might have been thought of as such by their authors), that the discourse was developed specifically with the aim of furthering literary work, the anticipation and the speculation (as I now see them) working together. Whenever I refine my sense of poetics (if that is what I am doing in my restlessness) I find that the definitions I assembled in 1999 usually prefigure my later ways of thinking – and *making* (for making is at the root, etymologically, as well as practically, of poetics). The one that resonates most as I write now is my assertion that poetics is not a blueprint but a thumbnail, and the associated suggestion that the writing produced may not be *described* in the poetics (that the writer was deluding herself, or that something else happened in poesis). That this qualification extends to the poetics of my own work marks each utterance I make as provisional, even in a piece such as 'Pulse', which takes the form of a processual 'treatise on metre', or 'A Voice Smears Across the Screen', which tests out the critical stance manifested in my volume *The Meaning of Form*, as does 'The Formal Splinter' in a much more impacted way. The tendency of critics to read writerly poetics as deficient literary criticism must be vigorously resisted, as I argue in 'Speaking Differently'. My inaugural lecture, 'Poetics as Conjecture and Provocation', attempts to strengthen that resistance, as well as to defend the provisionality and flexibility I robustly define elsewhere, through argument, poetry and poetics, though I also offer a reading of the work of Christopher Middleton.

I would hope that, from those essays attempting to capture the evanescence of the discourse in others' poetics, such as 'Speaking Differently', which considers the works of Pierre Joris and Adrian Clarke (and Maggie O'Sullivan), to those that offer the thumbnail projections of the poetics of my own creative work, like 'Poetics as Anticipation', these pieces will display a variety of approaches in a variety of forms. My own poetics ranges from my most recent anticipations of my 'English Strain' sonnet project, presented differently in several pieces, including 'Hanging Out Inside Sonnets' and 'Era il giorno ch'al sol si scoloraro', which may be thought of as 'practice-led research', to the earliest reproduced here, *net/(k)not//-work(s)*, which attempted to encapsulate the linguistically innovative poetics that developed in the London literary field of production in the 1980s onwards, which I outline in 'Took Chances in London Traffic', and I hope they will appeal to readers (and writers), critics and historians, of poetry and poetics. (They also specifically relate to my long network of texts *Twentieth Century Blues*.) Pieces like 'Negative Definitions', 'Working the Work', and 'Incite! and Ignite!' were attempted public rallying-cries from within that literary field. I would hope that, from my generalising formulations about form itself as a cognitive instrument, in 'Formal Splinter', to more homely accounts of my practical uses of images (in 'Ekphrasis and Anti-Ekphrasis') or of various textual techniques (in 'MATERIALS + PROCEDURE') or even of the pervasive use of radio as a metaphor for writing ('Critical Tuning'), in section two, my work may prove of *use*, and enter the various debates and the many material artistic practices to which they speak. Most of all I hope that these, often occasional, pieces will offer illumination and inspiration, for writers (and also for teachers, pedagogues and students of Creative Writing). From the early 'Linking the Unlinkable' to the recent 'Poetics in Anticipation', consideration of technique opens towards ethical and social levels of intervention, and even to a hesitantly utopian politics.

Textual Notes and Acknowledgements

Nearly all of these pieces were written for particular occasions and publications, and their styles vary enormously. Readers may enjoy that variety as it is encountered, but the more fastidious may find my inconsistent formatting irritating. However, each piece is internally consistent; many carry footnotes and some endnotes, while others carry bibliographies though some don't. I have only emended the texts where I felt the formatting incongruous. Where it has bedded in, I have left it, such as in my inaugural lecture, where footnotes counterpoint the oral delivery. Passages in square brackets indicate additions to the text made for this volume.

I would like to thank the initial organisers and audiences who heard some of these pieces, and the editors who published some of them.

'Shifting an Imaginary: Poetics in Anticipation', appeared as part of the 'New Defences of Poetry: Celebrating the Bicentennial of Shelley's "Defence of Poetry"', Newcastle University website, July 2021.

Parts of 'Pulse' were first published in *Edge Hill University Poetry and Poetics Group Journal*, Volume 1 (2019), and in *Tentacular 5*.

'The Formal Splinter', appeared in ed. HL Hix, *Counterclaims: Poets and Poetries, Talking Back*, McLean, IL/Dublin: Dalkey Archive Press, 2020.

'A Voice Smears Across a Screen: Material Engagement with Form, Forms, and Forming', appeared in Nathan Jones' and Sam Skinner's collection, *Torque 1: Mind, Language and Technology* (web), 2014.

'Hanging Out Inside Sonnets: A Text and Anti-Commentary,' first appeared in *The Lincoln Review 2*, May 1st 2021, and was reprinted in the *Edge Hill University Poetry and Poetics Group Journal*, Volume 2 (2021).

'"*Era il giorno ch'al sol si scoloraro*": A derivative dérive into/out of Petrarch's Sonnet 3', first appeared in: eds. Carole Birkan-Berz, with Guillaume Coatalen and Thomas Vuong, *Translating Petrarch's Poetry: L'Aura del Petrarca from the Quattrocento to the 21st Century*, Oxford: Legenda, 2020. My thanks to Legenda, and to Dr Graham Nelson in particular, for issuing permission to republish this item.

'The Necessity of Poetics' first appeared as 'The Poetics of Writing; The Writing of Poetics', in *Creative Writing Conference 1999, Proceedings,* Sheffield Hallam University, 1999. A shorter version, emphasising practical uses for students, was published by Ship of Fools in 1999 solely for distribution amongst Writing Studies MA students at Edge Hill College of Higher Education (later University), Ormskirk, Lancashire, UK. Another – emphasising poetry – was published in *Pores* (2001). Updated versions were amended, expanded and abridged in various ways – a Ship of Fools booklet was published in 2002 and was re-printed a number of times until 2016 – but the chief addition is the section 'Poetics as Discourse' which was written in 2009. Certain sections have been removed for this republication.

'Speaking Differently' originally appeared as 'Poetics and the Manifesto: On Pierre Joris and Adrian Clarke', on *Jacket 2* (web) August 2014.

'Poetics as Conjecture and Provocation: an inaugural lecture delivered on 13 March 2007 at Edge Hill University', then appeared in *New Writing: The International Journal for the Theory and Practice of Creative Writing,*. Vol 5: 1, 2008.

'Critical Tuning: Radio Interference and Interruption as a Poetics for Writing' appeared in *VLAK* 1 (1), 2010.

'Took Chances in London Traffic', appeared in eds. Robert Hampson and Ken Edwards, *Clasp: late modernist poetry in London in the 1970s.* Bristol: Shearsman, 2016.

'Negative Definitions: Talk for the Subvoicive Colloquium, London 1997', was read at the colloquium, and then published in *Sulfur* 42, May 1998.

'Linking the Unlinkable', first appeared in *Pages* 362-380, January 1996, reprinted in *Generator* 7 (Vol 2), April 1996, manifested first in book form in my *Far Language* (1999), and also forms part of *The Poetry of Saying: British Poetry and its Discontents 1950-2000*, Liverpool: Liverpool University Press, 2005.

'Working the Work' appeared in *First Offense* 3, 1988.

'Invite! and Incite! SubVoicive One Day Colloquium, 30th July 1991, University of London' first appeared as 'No One Listens to Poetry', *RWC Extra*, Summer 1994.

net/(k)not//-work(s) first appeared as a booklet from Ship of Fools, 1993. As the pamphlet itself explains, the original 'acknowledgements' list constituted 'part of a larger network' of its text and context, partly acknowledgements of first appearances and partly further reading bibliography. Though I have updated it a little, I thought it best to leave it where it was: at the end of that network, though it is a kind of endless beginning to the present volume.

'The Necessity of Poetics', 'Ekphrasis and Anti-Ekphrasis' and 'MATERIALS + PROCEDURE: on writing "The Given"' have at some time appeared on my blog *Pages*.

The cover features a detail of an untitled painting by Patricia Farrell. Thanks, as so often, for her work on this image.

One

Poetics in Anticipation:
Shifting an Imaginary, towards *British Standards*

A more compassionate world, inspired by the great sacrifices of NHS frontline staff?

Or a crueller world, of people, *some* people more than others, sacrificed to the greater good: Dominic Cummings' 'few pensioners', the Governor of Texas' improbable opinion that 'there are more important things than living'? Not levelling up, but whacking down.

Defund the police or defend the statues? Even Extinction Rebellion seems deflated, though not defeated.

We could be 'drunk with open-mindedness' at this point, as Louis Aragon puts it. (Aragon 1987: 151)

After The Hungry Years The Drowning Years The Age of Irony Warrant Error The Age of Immiseration, a hope for a worldlier world, one more ecologically fragile, but fluid, worldlier in is inter- (and outer-) nationalism.

'I'm transfigured into a bigger idea/ shifting an imaginary where I'll/ remain for all eyes to behold', in the valetudinary words of Idea. (Sheppard 2021b: 96)

In the poem, a lower case 'bigger idea' in opposition to a singular capitalised 'Big Idea'. In the world, the smaller the ideas are, the more focussed they become, doable, durable.

'Neurologically speaking,' writes Lee Ann Roripaugh, 'I would suggest: challenge a reader's perceptions, assumptions, modes of thinking, pre-conceived histories, and ideologies; foster attentiveness (to language, to others, to the surrounding world); create new neural pathways in the brain in lieu of neural ruts developed in response to sociocultural clichés'. (Roripaugh 2020: 28)

Blah blah blah media voices saying poetry must be harnessed to the restorative necessities of the post-Covid world (one big assumption there), as if compensation is what art offers, like a negligent government department. Art's formal splinter, its promise of a partly uncontrollable aesthetic encounter, may not necessarily yield a positive or 'therapeutic' response.

Utopia that embodies our hopes lies beyond any representation. 'Hope is the opposite of security,' Ernst Bloch hopes (Lagapa 2017: 8). It is an 'anticipatory consciousness', a creative 'forward dream', but a lucid one, in opposition to the constructions of 'blueprint utopians' (Lagapa 2017: 119).

Bloch's 'not yet' chimes with Nathaniel Mackey's 'not yet', as Jason Lagapa puts it: negatives, negations, particularly formal ones, constitute the poetics of this gesture (Lagapa: 55).

Put in these terms it is (almost) enough it is never enough.

Utopian hope is as anticipatory as our 'rhythmising consciousness', to use Nicolas Abraham's term for one important phenomenological 'impulse' (as outlined in *Pulse*) (Sheppard 1). A relationship between instinctive intentionality as immediate action and utopic figuration linked in the active forming of the poem.

Poetics as a luminous phrase, a catalytic particle. Less a slogan or a buzzword, than a *koan*. Poetics is another anticipatory activity. I've hitherto called it 'speculative', but is it not better thought of as 'anticipatory'? That has me sitting at the edge of my seat, alert, 'speculative' sinking back into a thousand cushions.

In Lee Harwood's 'Notes of a Post Office Clerk' we read the words, 'a list of simple, practical, and just acts/ moves towards a real "socialism"', but not the list itself (Harwood 2004: 253). The list is excised (though published separately in a magazine), disproportionately long for notational form, maybe. Perhaps too programmatic. In any case, promised 'just acts' are enough to read the poem (as poem).

Also unaccountably excised from Harwood's poem (at a later stage of republication), this visionary account of 'process': 'Changes that produce changes. The action simultaneous, not linear. The action chemical in that one change transforms the whole into a completely new set of references' (Harwood 1977: 57).

Just as aesthetic encounters must be open to potential negative affect (though moderated by forms of reception), political and cultural ideas, and their transformations, must be open to negative effects (though constrained by social institutions).

The danger is the move from the NHS being 'powered by love' to 'there are more important things than living', from *Black Lives Matter* to 'I need a haircut', from declarations of human rights to the extermination of human 'rats'.

We need to defend rights that have no ground to them, other than recognised common humanity, 'the human covenant' (Sheppard 2007: 41).

Boosterism is the poetry of Brexit. Political ideas, to work as poetry, have to be registered corporeally, on the human frame, with its anguished and ecstatic voice, as in the writing of Sean Bonney.

A young woman holds up a homemade banner: 'I'm really not happy about this.' Homemade *form*: homemade *refusal*. Like a poem?

'2020,' Steve Hanson states, 'whether we like it or not, is the start of an acutely painful transformation of the world…', poised against a Randean 'libertarian Conservative clique', aided by 'capitalist realism', now we witness 'a planned economy of crisis' (Hanson 2020: np).

Hanson quotes Will Davies as counterclaim: 'Utopia is … something that emerges among all of us as a need in the face of some lack' (Hanson 2020: np). Lagapa quotes Levitas: 'Concrete utopia … is anticipatory rather than compensatory. It reaches forward to a real future, and involves not merely wishful but wilful thinking' (Lagapa 119). The utopian emergence is *both* communal and real, to conjoin these two definitions. That doesn't diminish the carefully distanciated formulations of a poem's utopianism, the biggest ideas in the smallest letters.

There are questions that have no answers but there may always be responses.

You might think that you couldn't build something that you can't imagine or present, but isn't that what writing a poem often feels like? A genuine literary work cannot be imagined by a reader before it comes into being, as Derek Attridge attests in *The Singularity of Literature*. (Of course, it has been anticipated by the writer's poetics, though as thumbnail not blueprint.) This is another link between (a specialised version of) phenomenological intentionality and the utopian impulse.

It's not that the explorative motion of writing – the feeling that all writing is improvised – is itself directly utopian. It is that this mode of making shares its anticipatory vectors with the 'anticipatory consciousness' of utopian aspiration. The pulse with the impulse.

It is almost (like) a representation of a non-representation, an image of a non-image, but it is to be savoured.

'The utopian moment,' Norman Finklestein is quoted, from his book *The Utopian Moment*, 'stands revealed [in] that very moment when the text most strenuously resists thematic or interpretative closure' (Lagapa: 125). And *formal* closure, I'd say (as the author of *The Meaning of Form*). And liberation of the *said* in the *saying*, I'd add (as the author of *The Poetry of Saying*).

> I hang out inside *these* sonnets, punching
> echoes into new shape, because I take
> poetry as the investigation
> of complexity through the *means* of form,

I sing (as the poet of *Bad Idea*), (Sheppard 2021b: 13) in this *English Strain* project. (Sheppard 2021a; Sheppard 2021b.) Activating a force field *between* text and transposition.

'Transposition' (in preference to 'translation', even to 'intralingual translation' in Jakobson's witty term) is borrowed from Rosi Braidotti. In her musicological derivation, it's an 'in-between space of zigzagging and of crossing: nonlinear and chaotic' (Braidotti 2011: 226). 'Transposable moves,' in genetics, she explains, 'appear to proceed by leaps and bounds and are ruled by chance, but they are not deprived of their logic' (Braidotti 2011: 226).

These poems are 'new shapes' until they become old shapes. Then I shall anticipate other forms.

Form. Re-form, not reform. De-form, un-form, in-form, out-form. Etc. All the forms of forming. All forms of forming. Not just Form, not ever form, but form*s*.

Not just forms, but all the forming and re-forming the social can form.

A listening happens after saying. I cannot say what comes next *and* I'm saying it now.

17 June –2 July 2020

WORKS CITED

Aragon, Louis, trans. Simon Watson Taylor. *Paris Peasant.* London: Picador Classics, 1987.

Attridge, Derek. *The Singularity of Literature.* London: Routledge, 2004.

Braidotti, Rosi. *Nomadic Theory.* New York, Chichester: Columbia University Press, 2011.

Hanson, Steve, review of Davies, W. *Economic Science Fiction* in *Manchester Review of Books,* 3, 2020.

Harwood, Lee. *Boston-Brighton.* London: Oasis Books, 1977.

Harwood, Lee. *Collected Poems.* Exeter: Shearsman Books, 2004.

Lagapa, Jason. *Negative Theology and Utopian Thought in Contemporary American Poetry.* Cham: Palgrave Macmillan, 2017.

Roripaugh, Lee Ann, in ed. Hix, H.L. *Counterclaims: Poets and Poetries, Talking Back.* McLean, IL and Dublin: Dalkey Archive, 2020.

Sheppard, Robert. *Warrant Error.* Exeter: Shearsman, 2007.

Sheppard, Robert. *The English Strain.* Swindon: Shearsman, 2021a.

Sheppard, Robert. *Bad Idea.* Newton-le-Willows: Knives Forks and Spoons, 2021b.

Sheppard, Robert. 1. 'Pulse: All a Rhythm' (see next chapter)

Pulse: All a Rhythm[1]

Two women
come splashing towards us with the breaking
waves, holding hands, laughing,
neat in their single-piece bathing suits,
hair awry in the wind
that combs the waves. There is 'pulse' here,
there is even 'groove', if we were to re-
construct the scene as pure sound. A wave crest
beyond them, a little horizon, pours over
its own rim, cresting, and readies itself
to dash past the thighs of these dancers
and crash at their feet as they land on the
seaweedy littoral.

*

'Pulse': my chosen metaphor was of fluctuating emissions from a star, but that seems too distant, now. I think instead of radio waves on an ancient short-wave wireless, where the active listener (the radio enthusiast) can *feel* the power of transmission, the varying strength of the signal, forcing and retreating in a rhythm of alternations.

Ranjit Hoskote, reading at Bluecoat, Liverpool, used the word 'surge' to describe his metrics, the push and pull of language along a line.

---

[1] The first draft of this piece was made by 'writing-through' Tiger C. Roholt's *Groove: A Phenomenology of Rhythmic Nuance*. New York and London: Blooms-bury, 2014, between August 2016–February 2017. My previous overt uses of 'writing through', applied loosely, as here, to admit interruptions and interpolations (including superimpositions of parallel texts), include the processing of 'Superman' frames in 'Utopian Tales' (1986) in Sheppard 2008a, and the more procedural 'Reading *The Reader* of Bernard Schlink', excerpted in Sheppard 2015. Throughout this process, contingency is its rhythm, a pulse that matches the varieties of montage, de-montage, that I attempt in my own practice, with interruption as structure, with transformation and transposition, formal resistance, creative linkage, 'imperfect fit', near-perfect fit, all kinds of multi-form unfinish (Fisher 2016: passim). Later drafts were subject to the usual processes of revision and editing, in the light of that poetics.

Or Juliet Troy:

>   rainforest pulse through the medicine cabinet
> pulse under the pavement (Troy 2016: 23).

There is wholeness in motion when a rhythm is in you, neither theory nor sound. Intention folded upon extension. As in walking, as in running, as in repetition.

Which philosophy of mind touches the body? Are you of sound mind? Is there a 'sound-mind'?

We know it's there and we want to talk about it! Present-ing. Surging. And when we're talking about it, we're talking about many other things as well:

>   It is all a rhythm,
>   from the shutting
>   door, to the window
>   opening…   (Creeley 1978: 163)

in Creeley's words. Timbers on a treadmill. The method is step-by-step. But we're dancing.

Take a dictionary definition and lean it like a shovel against the wall. *Pulse*: a beating, a throbbing: a measured beat or throb: a variation: a single beat or impulse: a signal of very short duration (that's the radio definition): the beating of the heart and the arteries:
(here's a figurative one): *a thrill.*
Like the word 'writing', pulse is both noun and verb.
Which definition is Terry Day using, when he says, proliferating unlicensed synonyms for his unlicensed playing, 'I developed a pulse, a texture, a wash, a dialogue, form of drumming over which a soloist could be free from the restrictions of time and metre'? (Toop 2016: 166).

A beat so near its expected moment of appearance, we need micro-ears to sense it, it seems, micro-tongues to produce it. It bristles and prickles.

Rosmarie Waldrop says '…impossible to pin down. It is the truly physical essence of the poem, determined by the rhythms of my body, my breath, my pulse' (Duffy 2013: 68).

That much we've learnt already, yet she has more: 'But it is also the alternation of sense and absence, sound and silence. It articulates the between, the difference in repetition' (Duffy 2013: 68).

The opposite of sense is *not* nonsense or non-sense in this reading.

Waldrop says: 'I gave up stress for distress … the unstructured space of prose' (Duffy 2013: 93). She gave up verse for its apparent obverse. She sacked the old drummer. Or: 'The rhythm of prose is an important automatizing element; the rhythm of poetry is not … Poetic rhythm is … disordered rhythm,' as Shklovsky says (Shklovsky 1965: 24).

Heather McHugh turns etymological: '[poetry] is the very act of turnings, toward the white frame of the page, toward the unsung, toward the vacancy made visible, the worldlessness in which our words are couched' (Duffy 2013: 93).

Verses: ploughlines. Boustrophendonic.

Only one leg pushes at the ground, as he lands, the other kicking back, body twisted, and arms raised towards where the head turns in anticipation. This is a momentary prayer to the gods of bodily rhythm, the perfect ballet of the highly tuned.

It's a matter of primal cognition down there. 'For meaning itself is grounded in repetition: the never-before experienced, the wholly other, is meaningless, not even available to perception,' as Derek Attridge reminds us (Attridge 2013: 48).

Percepts are finer than concepts, the 'non-conceptual content'. The cognitive content of form registers without accompanying summary, as it were. Forms think or form thinks (as I've put it elsewhere).[2] Perhaps all

---

[2] In Sheppard 2016: implied in every sentence of the book, including its first:

poems are secretly, formally, mantras.

'*Bija* mantras are monosyllabic mantras considered to be sound without meaning; they have no etymological root and no semantic value,' says Nisha Ramayya (Ramayya 2016: np).

'Mantras occupy a domain that is situated between ritual and language,' writes Fritz Staal; 'The similarity between mantras and bird songs is due not to common function, but to common non-functionality...' (Ramayya 2016: np).

After the 'invention' of 'free verse', 'Poetry did not leap gratefully out of its bonds, but discovered new ways to bind the protean substance of language' (Attridge 2013: 220).

These variations that push and pull, could they amount to an intervallic signature? Joe Luna notes: 'British poet, Douglas Oliver ... *believed* that the stresses in lines of poetry were the actual sites of fleetingly lived inter-subjective encounters between poet-author and reader' (Luna 2016; italics mine). But we live in a world in which too many people *believe* too many things but don't *know* enough, post-factual, post-Brexit.

There can be no definition without the existence of prose, its theoretical obverse, even as Agamben defines poetry as 'the discourse in which it is possible to set a metrical limit against a syntactic one', enjambment options from zero to ... whatever is the opposite, or full extension, of zero (Agamben 1995: 39). And pauses and halts. Definition is not measure(ment), of course. Flicker hardly registers on the scale.

You could provide information in foot-prosody terms. Free iambics. Varying trochaic. Shifting between the two. Lost in the fixities of metre. 'To the ear, however,' notes Attridge, 'even to the ear responding to the poem some eight centuries after it was composed, it has an immediately recognizable rhythmic form that goes with a distinctive swing' (Attridge 2013: 149). It is perceived, recognised, received. Performed.

'Poetry is the investigation of complex contemporary realities through the means (meanings) of form' (Sheppard 2016: 1).

We're back to cognition again, to the idea that form knows something, that forms know something, that form, as Adorno contends, may be sedimented content, though is not readable as such. Yet form – and that includes rhythm – is revealed in tracing forms on the page and in reading as event and act.

Hugh MacDiarmid knew 'the kind of poetry' he wanted, and wrote 'The Kind of Poetry I Want' to tell (but not demonstrate to) us; nothing could be farther from the deft ease of Fred Astaire's dancing that he eulogises therein, than his, nevertheless, fascinating erudite lists of world-cultural facts. Thinking of the Welsh, he wants

> A poetry full of *cynghanedd*, and hair-trigger relationships,
> With something about it that is plasmic,
> Resilient, and in a way alarming – to make cry
> 'I touched something – and it was alive.'
> (MacDiarmid 1985: 1017)

He knows what he wants but it is 'something' beyond immediate category. The dedicatee of MacDiarmid's 'Third Hymn to Lenin', Muriel Rukeyser, also notes an elusive 'something' in *her* poetics-poem, 'Poem White Page White Page Poem':

> something is streaming out of the body in waves
> something is beginning from the fingertips

which brings us back to rhythm as energy, waves, pulses, surges and, as in MacDiarmid's poem, it engenders life:

> the small waves bringing themselves to white paper
> something like light stands up and is alive
> (Rukeyser 1994: 268)

Streaming. Waves. Plasma. Pulses. Resilience. Surge.

Split description into two parts. Like knowledge.

There is verifiable knowledge, indeed 'propositional'.[3] There is another kind of cognition, which we cannot name. It is indirect. Unfolding. There is knowledge and there is truth. So it is with description.

'There is the world,' states Merleau Ponty (Merleau Ponty 1962: xvii). 'Perception is never *finished*,' he adds elsewhere (Merleau Ponty 1962: 56).

On the one hand, rhythm is elusive, at least in part, eludes description; on the other, 'rhythm must be interpretive', as Pound says (Allen and Tallman 1973: 42); it is 'a form cut into time', or better: form cut into time (Allen and Tallman 1973: 65). Or forms cut into time (or times). A lot of (my) time was spent on form (and form*s* and form*ing*); now I must conceptualise what threatens to resist conceptualisation. (See Sheppard 2016 for how that time was spent.)

Is it the description that we will not remember, or the effect of moulded sound itself that we will not recall long enough in the immediate, continuous present of unfinish to begin to describe? In any case, a communiqué about rhythm is not the rhythm, not that one, there, ever-present but incomplete, uncompleted, *there.*

I'm dancing around the rhythm, not dancing to it, stamping on its toes.

Nuance wins over metre. It's only about whether the effect works. The relations between elements of poetic artifice. 'An unavoidable accessory after the fact,' opines William Carlos Williams of 'measure' (Sullivan, 1970: 121). No, it is *in* the fact, could even *be* the fact. It is projective pulse, not retrospective measurement.

Indirection is our direction. Part of a 'dynamization of emotion into a separate form,' as Williams says of the poem, rightly it seems to me (Williams 1970: 133).

What form knows is not an apolitical apprehension of beauty. We have been carried by artifice too far for that. 'Paraphrase', of course, 'is amnesia of form' (Sheppard 2016: 21).

---

[3] See Sheppard 2016: 12-13.

'Negative capability' to one side for a moment, the reception of the artwork, the perception of rhythm in it, as it, is an act as much as it is an event, as Attridge says (Attridge 2015: 3). I must do something with what is done to me; I must work with what has worked upon me, receiving what is given. Remember, Keats didn't extol the virtue of 'neutral capability'. 'Positive capability' was what Keats supposed Coleridge to suffer from, an invariant grasping after reason that he couldn't shut off: the noise of his table-talk, a mind clogged with the opiates of abstraction.

A record of grunts, the passage of air between lips, the degree of moisture in spittle emitted, would not provide the data, the calibrations we'd need.

There is an alarm bleeping incessantly in the street, slicing into my brain as I write. Its periodicity is exact, its insistence relentless, unhuman, inhumane. 'You can have a situation in which everything is constant and very boring,' Robert Creeley told me, paraphrasing Pound. You are undergoing periodic onslaught. 'Or,' continued Creeley, 'you can have a situation in which everything is variable and that's equally – that's chaos' (Creeley and Sheppard 1984: 45).

I see now why Dewey's aesthetics appeals to Attridge, for an active-passive model of aesthetic experience, analogous to his own sense of the 'act-event' of aesthetic cognition (Attridge 2015: 3).

The bleeping has stopped and the silence swells. Unpulsed. I probe it for sounds. Constant and variant. With my sound-mind.

Creation is in the ear of the beholder. Perception in the tracking attention. Participation in engaged enactment, re-enactment, embodiment. Climbing into the skin of a poem and dancing around in it, 'animated by the rhythms of a unique formal vision,' as Christopher Middleton *hopes* of the artificer poet (Middleton 1980: 169).

Here is a syllable. It is heavy (hear also a metaphor). Here is another, weak this time. A foot is declared. Here is yet another syllable. Is it heavy, as heavy – or heavier? Or lighter? Is it weak as well, weaker than the weak, heavier than the weak, yet still weak? Ish?

These are comparisons that belong to unshifting categories. Measure its strength, and it ceases to be the heavy syllable in an iambic foot: it's framed, taken out of the surge. It doesn't *sound* – or sound like anything at all.

In addition to constant and variant (that's audial), there's figure and ground (that's visual), but the Necker Cube fluxing before our eyes teaches our ears to behave. 'In short,' writes Merleau-Ponty, 'I organise the cube' (Roholt 2014: 48). I hear the rhythm as I go, figuring it out against the soft ground of the poem.

Everything becomes a figure if you listen analytically, detached. Yet it is only as a sequence that it can be experienced and each new figure constructs its new ground.

'The time of the poem,' writes Robert Duncan, 'is felt as a recognition of return in vowel tone and in consonant formations, of pattern in the sequence of syllables, in stress and in pitch of a melody, of images and meanings. It resembles the time of a dream…' (Mottram 1977: 12-13).

I cannot focus using terms like 'demotion' and 'unrealised', separate from the 'psychological and physiological *experience* of periodicity', for example (Attridge 2013: 112). Those words block my ears, fill my mouth, stuff my nose. Pulse is in the wash (and it's not periodicity alone we experience). The terms are useful only in their relationships. Re-focusing re-forms. The second syllable doesn't 'clarify' or 'resolve' the first. It's something new. There is an uncertain difference because the third syllable belongs to a different perception. And so on.

Yet hearing it in performance: intuitive act-event.

When we feel it, that 'break of syntax to produce the rhythm … energy in production', in Allen Fisher's words (Fisher 1985: 225), or any other contemporary way of producing 'pulse', we're apprehending something like the backs of our heads, which we cannot see. An indication of 'disturbance and indeterminacy', predicated on the way we see the front of our heads in mirrors (Fisher 1985: 236).

Read Steph Burt on Lucia Perillo's oddities: 'And when they stop, the quiet means something, like the dropouts in reggae or rock music, when you hear nothing but the repeated pattern that holds up the rest of the song' (Burt 2016: 23). To show that a 'repeated pattern … holds up the rest of the' poem is an operation of *form*, its actualising, its *forming* (Sheppard 2016). I've never held an oscillator up to a voice, like Douglas Oliver, partly because a microphone is not a reader. It's a recorder. *Rewind*. Listen, in an act of attention, close listening. Respond responsibly.

Beating with unbeatable nuance. We've found a different way into difference. To say 'It is all a rhythm' is not just phenomenological; it is social and political too. As Edith Sitwell realised: 'The rhythms of life *have* broken down: you are entirely right – slackened, loosened, like a pulse that is ceasing to beat … Inspired by what you say,' she writes to Jack Lindsay, 'I have started practising again, like a pianist – (I did that when I was young, practised technical experiments each day)' (Lindsay 1968: 60). Technique is not craft, but cognition. Patterns we find in the world. Daily, if possible.[4]

The being of the poet is co-dependent and interwoven with the becoming of the poem, as Lambros Malafouris didn't quite say (Malafouris 2013: 212).

'For active externalism, marks made with a pen on paper are not an ongoing external record of the contents of mental states; they are an extension of those states' (Malafouris 2013: 74).[5]

Cognition is located everywhere: in the mind, in our artefacts; in their rhythms, therefore.

We can only experience the pulse when we are not listening for it.

Isolated, the other tracks fade, as on a mixing desk. There's just a beat, irregular or not. The heart has gone out of it; the living form is hushed, the form that 'stops us in our tracks of thinking, and asserts itself in that moment of stillness,' as Angela Leighton puts it, as if a music dropout (Leighton 2007: 21).

---

[4] 'Daily, if possible', also stands as a description of the attempted method of the original 'writing through' of Roholt's *Groove* out of which this text formed.

[5] In an email to me Lambros Malafouris expressed pleasure that his 'theory of material engagement' was finding literary uses.

Don't listen to the pulse as a thing; it will only surge, losing form, taking form, once the other tracks are mixed back in.

We know the human metronome *feels* what we feel. Close encounter, bringing the other into a proximity where it loses just enough of its otherness to be heard.

'Announcing with the poem that we are about to change,' as Muriel Rukeyser says, might be a way to stay with this feeling; its fluidity becomes our fluidity. Its rhythms become our rhythms (Rukeyser 1994: 166).

In drowsy numbness I began forming words, not noticing the rhythms, the occasional rhyme, in my sound-mind. Though breaking the spell to collect some paper to scribble in the dark, I let any facility I have assemble the words into rhythmic sequences, adding as they came; first unbidden;

then bidden: controlled and contrived. Conscious. Semi-amnesia of content. Turning on the turn, 'the dry shells of dream open as' I 'wake', this sonnet co-becomes with my rising consciousness, my surprise (for this is not a common process of composition for me).

Pulse, literally, taken in one of those little clips over my fingertips. Nothing wrong there, apparently. A normal pulse rate. But sinking into the slippery pool of my own sweat, it's my heartbeat I can hear, as I slither around with it: it's pounding at times, relaxed at others, and I'm aware of it persisting almost like time itself, or like little ice-pick rhythms tapping across the gigantic rockface of Time. A miniscule journey across vastness.

I'm freezing, I'm burning, as in a Wyatt version of Petrarch.

Infected. I'm no metronome; I'm a chaos of rhythms.

'Poetic rhythm *is* ... disordered rhythm.' (Shklovsky 1965: 24;
    italics mine)

I used to witness Adrian Clarke at the Writers Forum Workshop every fortnight, stepping up to embrace (and sometimes battle with, figure out) the surge. There's no other way. I remember Tom Raworth sitting down, picking up 'Writing' and launching into its relentless short-lined measures (with interruptions) at a patter, his face scarlet by the end of twenty minutes. Other writers, two lines in, stopping, apologising, returning to the beginning, the re-negotiation of the silent *Hwaet!* that kicks off every poem (in various ways). To re-calibrate the surge. Like Parker and Gillespie breaking down on recordings, repeating, strengthening the riff, building be-bop out of swing's swing, the *idda-bop idda-bop bop bop bop bop* of the apposite kick off.

The thing is, as Robert Kaufman puts it aphoristically: 'To make thought sing and to make song think' (Kaufman 2005: 212).

*

Nicolas Abraham's essay 'Rhythmizing Consciousness: An Essay in the Temporality of Rhythm' (1952), is one that I'd missed, his *Rhythms* picked up in a Chester charity shop, and read on the train home. An appropriate place (or succession of places) since he uses the experience of train rhythms to elucidate his concept of 'rhythmizing consciousness', 'apprehended as activity, as spontaneity' (Abraham 1995: 71): 'I was perceiving the monotonous sound of the wheels, and my body was receiving the same periodic jolts; but in the interval between the sounds, I was taken hold of by a tension, an expectation, which the next shock would either fulfil or disappoint' (Abraham 1995: 70). Separate from ordinary perception (the mere measure of simple periodicity), rhythmising consciousness 'creates itself in creating the world' in true phenomenological co-creation, in perpetual expectation, as in the intentional intervals between 'jolts' that Abraham experiences mentally and corporeally – and describes (Abraham 1995: 72). Though the world often crushes its effectivity, it is capable of grasping that world: '*It is always possible to identify the object of our expectation, and this alone is what permits the inexhaustible temporal play of rhythmizing consciousness*' (Abraham 1995: 78).

There must be a disposition that allows the apprehension that 'it is all a rhythm' both in the world and inside a poem, and this term will do as well as any to describe what thus far I have called the sound-mind.

But when Abraham turns to *poetic* rhythm, he doesn't. He predictably turns to *metre*, despite a distinction he draws between objective metre and 'an emergence, whether continuous or discontinuous, that is projected by rhythmising consciousness' that he calls a 'term' (Abraham 1995: 79).

The 'term is a dynamic, vectoral unit, characterized by increasing tension, and oriented' – like all good little phenomenological concepts – 'towards completion', all of which could be used to delineate the metrics that I am stuttering towards – so long as we pass over the adopted or adapted quasi-metrical analyses to which he then proceeds (Abraham 1995: 80). (The interactions between the *teleutē* and the *prosteleutē* to pick out two words, the first directed toward the endings of metrical feet, the second motioning projectively, are typical; this sounds like 'objective', if not conventional, metrics to me.) He enslaves himself to various classical quantitative metres and their ancient rules.

Here I part company and I'm reminded of – and need – the way John Hall, for example, wisely relates close analysis (which is not the same as close reading or listening) to a homely, writerly view of creative process, which offers an account of rhythmising consciousness in a form to which I may subscribe, in his account of Peter Hughes' poetry:

> Finding careful prosodic judgements in an analytically slowed-down reading, does not mean, necessarily, that these effects were very deliberately planned in: it does mean, though, that there is very careful poetic listening and judgement going on within the composition, and that this has much to do with the wish to keep more than one register in play within every few lines (Hall 2013: 82).

I re-read passages of *Chapters on English Metre* by Joseph B. Mayor, published 'Cambridge: At the University Press' in 1901 (a blue-stamped copy once belonging to the Bombay Branch of the Royal Asiatic Society), wondering at the supposed intricacy of metrical invention, inversion, substitution, metamorphosing. Tables, charts, parsings, scanning. A whole imperial exercise to show the assumed mechanisms of Shelley, Milton, William Watson, as though their listenings and judgements had been fully conscious.

But even allowing for the prosodist's methodology of its day, the bourgeois period of Aestheticism, the imperialist era of appropriation and exoticism – he does talk of Whitman metamorphosing prose into poetry, and Dickens, in places, doing the opposite – I have never accepted with my mind, body or ear a single demonstration of a metrical pattern in the book.[6]

Rhythms, in the rhythmising consciousness we all possess, need to be perceived in context, anticipated pulses in the surge, not as isolated elements of an assumed system. Peter Brötzmann speaks of 'free' music in a way we might think of 'free' verse.[7]

> I mean all this talking about free is a bit rubbish now after all these years. Nothing is free, as we know as some elder gentlemen – nothing is free, not in the arts, not in daily life. You have to make your space and use what you have and you have to explore what you don't know yet and that's what it's about (Brötzmann and Leigh 2017: 24).

The analytical approach misses the poetic potentiality in our rhythmising consciousness, with its projective expectation, 'which the next shock would either fulfil or disappoint', as we explore what we don't know (yet) (Abraham 1995: 70).

Art and life may exchange their properties (or try to) but they must also transform, shuttling linkage. That counts. Listen to the beat, the lilt, the sway, the surge, the pulse, the wash, the last shock, the next shock, where it belongs, in its anticipating tension, as Abraham would say. But when we measure the measure, it dies.

There is always mis-description in description, but there is often also the moment 'when the text takes form before our senses in our actual interaction with it' (Sheppard 2016: 223). It emerges as the rhythmising consciousness expectantly probes futurity. It is there, however metaphorical,

---

[6] Neither would most *contemporary* prosodists, I should add.

[7] See my contentious entitling of the first section of my pedagogic piece, 'Taking Form: Experimental and Avant-Garde Forms', 'What *was* free verse?' (Mc Loughlin 2017: 76). Curiously, another chapter in this volume talks about how substitutions of metre are made, an opening iambic becoming a kick off trochaic, for example, to avoid the monotony of regular metre. Maybe there is no regular metre, just a regularity haunting the irregular pulses in the surge of the line, the surging of lines, guided by our sound-minds, our rhythmising consciousnesses.

however we figure out this ground, however indeterminate we are in our determination to musicate experience.

The plea is simply to listen, but not to listen simply.

Reading *The Wolf* I find a similar idea in two places. A review of the Faber annexation of Bunting's poems quotes Bunting himself, in 1972, comparing his poesis to Eliot's supposed critically controlled method: 'My matter is born of the form – or the form of the matter, if you care to think that I just conceive of things musically. There's no fitting, at least consciously. Whatever you think I am saying is something I could not have said in any other way' (*The Wolf* 34: 76).

In Sandeep Parmar's 2016 interview with Vahni Capildeo, the latter rebuffs a barrage of literary critical definitions of lyric: 'When I am writing poems, I am not able to reflect like a critic or' – worse – 'academic', and comments: 'Poems quite often arise musically for me, in a rhythm or a voice that are not the rhythm or voice I would myself "naturally" use. When a poem arises like this, I feel more like a composer than a writer. I am not sure what gives me access to this zone, or whether the things I bring out of it will "work" when my editorial brain takes back control, or when I have to perform such pieces out loud' (*The Wolf* 34: 55).

Prosody leads away from that music, not towards the critical (which Bunting abjures and Capildeo re-admits only as editorial and performative quality control), but towards detachable elements. There are exceptions, such as Derek Attridge's work, which teaches us that *form* is not an arrangement of *forms* but is the act-event of *forming* (Attridge 2004; 2013).

A rhythm that gathers rather than controls, a rhythmising consciousness of expectation and discovery.

*

Where there are rhythms we find bodies, or parts of bodies, moving (even minimally). The feel of a rhythm is – in part, at least – a bodily thing, an embodied rhythmising consciousness. The antique metaphors of 'feet' point to dance, rather than to music (or through music to dance). Metrics are petrified choreographies. Lyric points towards the lyre as instrument for musicating the self, or its versions of itself. Drama unites music, dance, and poetry in bodily presence (though often masked).

However it is produced, pulse is received and perceived viscerally, a matter of kinaesthetics rather than aesthetics. Just as a man at a dance, toeing the twisting line with polished brogues, responds to music with elements of dance, so the reader of a text (to use the dullest word for the language arts) responds, even if minimally, in bodily movement, whether in the flickering saccades inside the eye, up and down and all over the page, or the tapping of a foot, a slight sway.

In production, observe the scale that runs, mini to max, from Geraldine Monk's 'Unvocalised (private)' performance,

> Corpus in repose. *Corpus in almost repose-us.*
> Eye-orbs fly-wink. *gzz.* Mini-zigger-*jit* (Monk 2003: 215)

to the 'Max somatic dynamics' of the public poetry reading where 'the bodied poet' is 'broke on the back of phonemes' and 'body mass is conduit' (Monk 2003: 219/220).

The bobbing pulse-rattle that we hear (and see) whenever Ulli Freer reads.

A mouth moves to make a poem, even silently, even imperceptibly on the edge of stillness. 'Unutterings sucked in silent/ body folds' (Monk 2003: 215). Lips and tongue shaping, ghosting the written word. From head-voice to whisper to murmuring ('mutterance') to phoneme-release to phrasal recitation (Monk 2003: 217). Through to the unlikely 'cry of a cantor, a triumphant pleading', to quote a late poem by Roy Fisher (Fisher 2016: 15). The mouth moves the poem on, and the rest of the body aligns itself, with gentle support, with defensive tension, to this bodily language. The rhythm of the poem is partly in these gestures, as in the poem, the intentional rhythmising consciousness. 'Something is streaming out of the body in waves', as Rukeyser puts it (Rukeyser 1994: 268).

Henri Meschonnic wants to raise the question of rhythm to re-insert it into the living, breathing body. To re-inscribe history so that rhythm is historically shaped but is nevertheless ahistorical, beyond ideology, resistant. A politics, yes, but Talmudic mysticism draws us away from embodied mind.

Upper limit: Rhythm is the total articulation of the poem.

Lower limit: Metre is replaced by paradigmatic relationships of sound (of all sorts: alliteration, consonance, rhyme, etc.) not syntagmatic metrical markers (Hugill c. 2007).

There are no non-meaningful elements of poetic artifice (Sheppard 2016: 29-46). They are all potential instruments of critique.

Visual poetics is a silent spanner in the sound-box of total articulation. Do not annunciate white space mechanically.

'Rhythm,' writes Meschonnic, 'is the language-organisation of the continuum of which we are made,' and who can disagree, except to think of the pull of the bodily? (Meschonnic nd: 2). But it's not just the patting of your foot to the metre; it's the use of the full articulatory apparatuses of the body. Or the anticipatory imagining of such in use.

It's also a politics, as Meschonnic knows: 'We need poems, again poems, always poems. Rhythm, again rhythm, always rhythm. Against the generalised semiotisation of society' (Meschonnic nd: 2). And worse, I'd say!

We're beginning to understand rhythm, 'the ethics in action that is this listening, whence the politics of the poem,' as Meschonnic says (as far as we'll throw him) (Meschonnic nd 7).

Merleau-Ponty for embodied perception. Malafouris for embodied cognition. Meschonnic for reminding us that 'with each voice, Orpheus changes and starts anew… Orpheus was one of the names of the unknown… What he designates continues in each and every one of us' (Meschonnic nd 8-9).

The things I make, from a cup of tea to a poem, a form or a rhythm, are part of my extended mind, impressing cognition into the realm of things. Minting the world around me as it moulds me. The interobjectivity of mind and world: 'Our ways of thinking are not merely causally dependent upon but *constituted* by extracranial bodily processes and material artifacts,' argues Malafouris (Malafouris 2013: 227).

'My body has its world,' notes Merleau-Ponty, dryly (Roholt 2014: 93).

'Consciousness is being turned toward the thing through the intermediary of the body,' asserts Merleau-Ponty, rhythmising consciousness included (Roholt 2014: 95).

Not a reflex, but an intention or response.

But when I extend my hand *through* pen *onto* paper *into* writing that is cognitive extension.

I want to hold these two apart, without mutual denigration for a moment; rhythmising consciousness conjoins the perceptual and the cognitive.

The instruments sometime slip from one's hands, deliberately, *breaking*, we say, the line, 'this sublime hesitation between meaning and sound' (Agamben 1995: 41).

'A mismatch, a disconnection between the metrical and syntactic elements, between sounding rhythm and meaning, such that ... poetry lives ... in their inner disagreement,' in 'the versura, the turning point which displays itself as *enjambement*', as Agamben says (Agamben 1995: 40/41).

> There's no end to it line-
> Break its little one (Sheppard 2011: 61)

Thinking with the things that, beyond doubt, exist. Caesura, 'the anti-rhythmic interruption', says Hölderlin, blocks 'the enchanting succession of representations at its height in such a way as to make manifest ... representation itself' (Agamben 1995: 44). But only because we are in, and of, the world, may we represent it. 'The world is not what I think, but what I live through' (Merleau-Ponty 1962: xvi-xvii). Experience is – bad pun – as *qualitative* as the metres the French use. Perhaps it is not so bad a pun, since the *quantitative* in the non-metrical sense is eluded here in favour of 'a certain equilibrium between the interior and exterior horizons', as Merleau-Ponty recommends (Roholt 2014: 97). 'The rhythmic transport that gives the verse its impetus is empty, is only the transport of itself,' concludes Agamben, caesura seen as non-musical dropout, the little one's little one (Agamben 1995: 44).

Perception as a rhythmic orientation, 'meant for a world which it neither embraces, but towards which it is perpetually directed' (Merleau-Ponty 1962: xx). Bodily posture and position become, pre-cognitively perhaps, but cognitive none the less, tensed. As the body extends itself, part of the rhythm that it all is, 'the dynamic couplings of brains, bodies and the material world', ensue (Malafouris 2013: 249).

The spatial spanner: a general visuality in the culture absorbed into poetic artifice as typographical line length, word count, page-space, distribution of text, the rediscovery of concrete poetry, *and* of those white spaces that seem unemphatically rhythmic; all these '*resisting* the expectation that poems occur in time' (Attridge 2004: 72).

But temporality remains the vehicle of rhythm and pulse, its primal scene, as it were, whenever we perform what Attridge calls 'the distinctiveness of poetry', with '*a sense of its real-time unfolding*' (Attridge 2004: 71). Time, 'the continuum of which we are made,' as Meschonnic calls it, embodied in a fleshly embrace with space (Meschonnic nd: 2).

Oxford graduates in the late nineteenth century linked arms and swung along, intoning Swinburne. The metre as metronome. What about an audience listening to Linton Kwesi Johnson *a cappella*, performing 'Bass Culture'? The rhythm a reggae beat, approximated, accommodated. Or Maggie O'Sullivan incanting Buntingesque heavy syllables, sprung rhythms out of Hopkins, sprung again to the level of the syllable, absorbed into her bodily performance, and gifted outwards. (See Sheppard 2005: 233-249 for an account of that embodiment.) Or a film of Frank O'Hara, chatting, smoking – 'I don't even like rhythm, assonance, all that stuff. You just go on your nerve' – giving voice to verve, with studied nonchalance, a sick body all nerves, awaiting the fatal beach buggy (O'Hara 1974: xiii). The body is present here, not as authorising centre (the authoritative author) but as a principle of rhythm, 'body mass is conduit', the actualising of the embodied rhythmising consciousness (Monk 2003: 220). It's for other performers, other listeners, too, whether their bodies are visibly moving or not, or know it. Or don't.

Bodies deal with, think into, things. Rhythmising consciousness is one small part of this, intending through time, extending in space. 'The spoken word is a gesture, and its meaning, a world,' notes Merleau-Ponty (Merleau-Ponty 1962: 214). Part of that gesture, in and out of poetry, is rhythm. And part of the world that it means is also rhythm. From the womb, where the rhythm world begins – listening to heartbeats, pulses – according to percussionist Evelyn Glennie, onwards in time, outwards into space (Glennie 2017).

*

Feeling the rhythm of a poem is – in part – understanding it. Understanding the metrical apparatus of the poem, however descriptively useful, will not access the experience of the feel.

Addicts of metre – limerick freaks, manic rappers, bar room doggerelists – can't hear rhythm when it swings free of regularity. No feel for it, no sense of how its parts inhere. No use telling them, 'Just concentrate on the heavy beats and string them together in their variety, variability,' (which is as far as I go *metrically* in teaching poetry. It's the only way to perform Thomas Wyatt's poems now without confusion; 'In this view Wyatt is writing in the tradition of stress or accentual verse dating back to Anglo-Saxon poetry,' writes R.A. Rebholtz, except that I am thinking about the per*form*ance of form by a reader reading, not of Wyatt counting syllables with his podgy fingers) (Wyatt 1978: 46).

Mostly, there remains the complaint that a certain structure of words and sounds is not a poem at all. In extremis, it is dismissed as meaningless, as though metrical tedium is the guarantor of sense. (This is an old battle, I know, but it rages at the fringes of culture, where some of us teach.)

To say 'It is all a rhythm,' is no use to them, though I suspect enjoining them *through* the act-event of bodily performance of the pulses of Creeley's poem 'The Rhythm', its emphatically enjambed articulations, may enlighten some. It's time to re-read it: 'The rhythm which projects/ from itself continuity' (Creeley 1978: 163).

At that point, the performer-listener is standing at the right point.

Poems are explored by mind and body, and we are forever learning, balancing equilibrium and disequilibrium, in trial and error, a struggle to 'get' the rhythm right, push-pull, across the lines' smooth ride or bumpy breaks, zero enjambment or maximum enjambment, until there is just the beat, the pulse, patterned or not, marked out for us.

When we 'get' a rhythm, we tense against a metrical norm, if there is one, against and with the pulse if there's not (and also if there is).

It is all a rhythm, of course, but when it's in a poem (or any other aesthetic object) it's a matter of form. It's one matter of form, in fact. And the critical function of the poem is asserted by its being art, by its having form (See Sheppard 2016: 213-239).

Keston Sutherland suggests, thinking of Agamben's notions about enjambment and caesura at least: 'Prosody is implicit cognition ... manifest in poetic language as the technical and unending dialectic of transgression and reconciliation' (Sutherland 2004: 53-4).

Feeling the rhythm *is* comprehension, and rhythm is cognitive, '*an act of thought* – that is, a cognitive process that criss-crosses the boundaries of skin and skull, since its effective implementation involves elements that extend beyond the purely "mental" or "neural"', as Malafouris puts it (of knapped flints) (Malafouris 2013: 19).

But bodily metaphors – pulse itself, 'feet' even – that haunt any exploration of rhythm (and sometimes of metre) bring us back to the (right) point where rhythmising consciousness locates and produces, feels *and* comprehends, rhythm.

It keeps reappearing, the spatial turn, that begins in 'the kind of dance-like saccades recorded in eye-tracking experiments', as Eleanore Widger says, when we encounter 'a fairly extreme dispersal of syntactic elements', such as in Elizabeth Bletsoe's poem 'Here Hare Here' ((Widger 2016: 378; Tarlo 2011: 108-110). 'We cannot progress through this poem from top to bottom,' she claims, 'but must, in a sense, go back in time (or re-trace our footsteps, as it were) to re-read certain parts in order to build meaning through making connections' (Widger 2016: 378-9), a progress that would, at least, complicate the '*sense of ... real-time unfolding*' of poetic encounter, which also grounds poetic rhythmising as an act-event (Attridge 2004: 71). Widger quotes Joseph Frank, who goes further: 'Word-groups must be ...

perceived simultaneously,' he says (Widger 2016: 379). Either rhythm is folded back upon rhythm in time, or it is a spatial field of simultaneities. *Seen* like this. It's (another) matter of form.

Rhythmic excitability is underestimated (in poetry). Whether a poly-rhythmic wash no one can 'follow', a wild pulse produced by torn syntax, or one so attenuated as to be barely perceptible, they may lift us into a receptive zone we cannot quite believe we have entered.

The 1968 Christmas Day variations that Bob Cobbing and others produced out of his 'Tan' theme from *The ABC of Sound*, push a regular pulse to the edges of articulation (Cobbing 1970).

While soft-voiced Lee Harwood seems almost to efface pulse through 'the use of speech materials in rhythmic units that fall outside of prosody,' to quote William Rowe: 'In Harwood's early work, it is a question … of how to let the plasticity of speech, its subtle rhythmic and tonal variations, build the poem, without subordination to other orders: i.e. speech as present event … rather than speech imitated … For this, various conditions are necessary: incompletion, especially syntactic, but also semantic; and also a unit of rhythm that is both variable and shorter than the line' (Rowe 2007: 58-9). Read visually: those short white spaces.

The culture of 'linguistically innovative poetry' (to use a widely adopted tag) influences notions of rhythm, to be sure. It inherits the non-metrical verse tradition of the British Poetry Revival and its (largely) American forebears. One reason I feel the need to write this 'treatise on metre' is the lack of contemporary discussion of rhythm, of its no longer seeming a pressing issue of poetic artifice (as though it had been settled decades ago). Again, this may be an effacing effect of the growth of interest in the visual as affect, but that is to ignore its own rhythm.

Rhythmising consciousness is multi-sensual, not just aural.

The question is something like this: what guides Jeff Hilson in both writing and performance? 'Hilson reads with passion and humour, but also with what looks like concern: the furrowed brow, the forlorn, puzzled catch in the voice,' observes Stephen Thomson well. 'The manner is appropriate to verse that is engaged without being clamourous or self-aggrandising' (Thomson 2007: 153). But *verse* it still is, and rhythm part of its formal matter and its observed 'passion'.

And what of the cultures of women writers? Rukeyser, Waldrop, O'Sullivan and Monk (and Glennie) have appeared in this 'treatise' as proponents of the bodily, though nothing might be generalised from this.

Perhaps there is a dialectic *between* the socio-rhythms of cultures (groups, movements and clusters, including gender, race, disability…) which are developed through identity and identification, exchange and development, *and* the idio-rhythms of individuals, the element of pulse, the aspect of the term of rhythmising consciousness, that Pound says may not be counterfeited, however group-inflected.

It matters which part of the 'field of literary production', as Bourdieu calls it, the proponents of a poetics of pulse or a theory of rhythm occupy (Bourdieu 1993). The customary 'habitus' that is received and acquired may be developed to the point of an anti-habitus, which is how 'open field poetics' must have looked (for some) in contrast to 'academic' verse in 1950s America. Remember, 'free verse' itself was associated with other 'freedoms'.

The sociological perspective may obscure as well as illuminate the trajectories of idio-rhythms into, across, and between literary fields.

Variability between people (cultures) *mirrors* variabilities within, and between, rhythms. The dialogic entrainment of metre and syntax, or visible line and legible word, of pulse and surge, of space and time, into complex, indeterminate, polyrhythmic wholes: total articulations. Scott Thurston years ago told me that the rhythms he *heard* in a particular poem were too complex to chart.

Rhythmising consciousness synchronises the patterns of the world, including its rhythms (and its theories of rhythm, and nothing may stand 'proven' by the latter's measures). This is not like clocks being synchronised for railway time in the mid-nineteenth century, in multiple entrainment. The sense of 'real-time unfolding' unfolds as body and mind reach into the world to entrain it, and themselves (Attridge 2004: 71).

'The kind of duration encapsulated in things differs from the kind of duration encapsulated in human bodies and brains,' notes the cognitive archaeologist Malafouris (Malafouris 2013: 247). It isn't in the brain, or even the body alone; it's already extended into the thingy world, where 'human time flows on a number of levels', as Chris Gooden points out, polyrhythmically (Malafouris 2013: 246). Perhaps, as jazz musician-theorist Vijay Iyer conjectures, what we have identified as rhythmising consciousness is part of a forgotten evolutionary stage. (Is it connected to anticipating and predicting danger?)[8] Perhaps, Malafouris suggests, those cognitively drenched 'things act as dynamic attractors, operating in feedback circles that bind the different scales of time together' (Malafouris 2013: 247).

*

Pulse renders sensible the poetic work as it goes, surging, pushing and pulling along a line, a cognitive tool.

What does the poem *intend*, as it is flooded with cognition, and as the reader fulfils its intention, by unfolding it? This is not just a question of the rôle of the reader in completing the poem (which still pertains) but the act-event of 'concretizing' it (as Ingarden might put it), which is arguably a rhythmic 'thing' (See Roholt 2014: 130-1).[9]

---

[8] The 'elegant results' of experiments at Bangor University, 'reveal an electrophysiological response in the brain when participants were exposed to consonantal repetition and stress patterns that are characteristic of Cynghanedd, but not when such patterns were violated,' I read, at about the point I was writing these lines (Anon 2017). How different is this study from the findings I read about later in the day? 'Wild elephants respond to human languages differently depending on which groups of humans have historically hunted them' (Gooding 2017: 15).

[9] I've not written through the whole of *Groove*. Though I approached its end through this method, I was not keen to proceed to, or through, its conclusion. This is partly a rhythmic thing, the feel that something is finished (or best left in a state of unfinish). I have finished, while Roholt has not. I part company with him (for anyone who consults that excellent volume) at the top of page 133, to continue his arguments alone. Here's a final, instructive example: 'Grooves are present in recordings only in an incomplete manner – incomplete in that a listener's activity is required to "concretize" them' (Roholt 2014: 139). It was this kind of statement that drew me to the book in the first place, sending me back to phenomenology, which I had not considered since the early 1980s, and integrating it with the in-

Blast the body with the pulse and its own pulse will quicken (or slow) in response.

Gradually, the pushing and pulling arouses the need for, cognition of, recognition, and this impulse pulls the pulses into its orbit (for everything is in motion). What does the pulse think in its own place? It could be located on the page in the poem, which is out in the thingy world, or in its utterance (actual or virtualised in real-time), which is also in the world, though they are not completely indistinct.

The point is still 'to make thought sing and to make song think,' in acts of poesis, but still we must be specific, as poetics, about the *ways* rhythmising consciousness operates in particular instances[10] (Kaufman 2005: 212).

2016–2018

---

vestigations of Sheppard 2016. When I realised 'grooves' could be loosely substituted by 'rhythms', and 'recordings' could be substituted by 'poems', I foresaw my method, though it is not one of simple substitution, as I hope is apparent.

[10] On poetics, see Sheppard 2008b, reprinted in this volume.

BIBLIOGRAPHY

Abraham, Nicolas, *Rhythms: On the Work, Translation, and Psychoanalysis.* Stanford: Stanford University Press, 1995.

Agamben, Giorgio. *The Idea of Prose,* trans. Michael Sullivan and Sam Whitsitt. Albany: SUNYPress, 1995.

Allen, Donald, and Warren Tallman. eds. *The Poetics of the New American Poetry.* New York: Grove Press, 1973.

Anon. 'We may be hardwired to appreciate poetry: Study', *Indian Express:* indianexpress.com/article/lifestyle/life-style/we-may-be-hardwired-to-appreciate-poetry-study-4532938/ (accessed 19th February 2017).

Attridge, Derek. *The Singularity of Literature.* London: Routledge, 2004.

Attridge, Derek. *Moving Words: The Forms of English Poetry.* Oxford and New York, NY: Oxford University Press, 2013.

Bourdieu, Pierre, *The Field of Cultural Production.* Cambridge and Oxford: Polity Press, 1993.

Brötzmann, Peter (and Heather Leigh), 'Invisible Jukebox', *The Wire 395*: January 2017: 22-26.

Burt, Steph(en). 'Plastigoop', *London Review of Books,* 17th November 2016: 23.

Cobbing, Bob. 'Three Variations on a Theme of Tan', *Sound Texts/?Concrete Poetry/ Visual Texts.* (LP) Amsterdam; Stedelijk Museum, 1970.

Creeley, Robert. *Poems 1950–1965.* London: Marian Boyers, 1978.

Creeley, Robert, and Robert Sheppard, 'Being An Information: An Interview', in ed. Carroll F. Terrell. *Robert Creeley: The Poet's Workshop*, The National Poetry Foundation, University of Maine at Orono, 1984: 35-56.

Duffy, Nikolai. *Relative Strangeness: Reading Rosmarie Waldrop.* Bristol: Shearsman Books, 2013.

Fisher, Allen. *Necessary Business.* London: Spanner, 1985.

Fisher, Allen. *Imperfect Fit.* Tuscaloosa: University of Alabama Press, 2016.

Fisher, Roy. *Slakki: New and Neglected Poems.* Hexham: Bloodaxe, 2016.

Glennie, Evelyn. *Start the Week*, BBC Radio 4: 25th January 2017.

Gooding, Francis, 'Thinking about how they think,' *London Review of Books*, 16th February 2017: 14-15.

Hall, John, 'ET: the missing letters of Peter Hughes' *Behoven'*. In Brinton, Ian, ed. *An intuition of the particular: some essays on the poetry of Peter Hughes.* Bristol: Shearsman, 2013.

Hoskote, Ranjit. Lecture-reading at Bluecoat, Liverpool, August 2016.

Hugill, Piers. *Words Without Measure: Some Readings of Prosody in Contemporary British Poetry.* Unpublished PhD, University of London, circa 2007.

Kaufman, Robert. 'Lyric's Constellation, Poetry's Radical Privilege', *Modernist Cultures* 1:2 (Winter 2005): www-js-modcult.bham.ac.uk/fetch.asp?article= issue2_kaufman.pdf. (accessed 12 August 2013).

Leighton, Angela. *On Form: Poetry, Aestheticism, and the Legacy of a Word.* Oxford and New York: Oxford University Press, 2007.

Lindsay, Jack. *Meetings with Poets.* London: Frederick Muller Limited, 1968.

Luna, Joe. 'Harmless Unnecessary Cat': intercapillaryspace.blogspot.co.uk/2016 /08/ essay-by-joe-luna.html (accessed September 2, 2016).

MacDiarmid, Hugh. *The Complete Poems,* Vol 2. Harmondsworth: Penguin, 1985.

McLoughlin, Nigel. ed. *The Portable Poetry Workshop.* London: Palgrave, 2017.

Malafouris, Lambros. *How Things Shape the Mind: A Theory of Material Engagement.* Cambridge, MA, and London: The MIT Press, 2013.

Mayor, Joseph B. *Chapters on English Metre.* Cambridge: At the University Press, 1901.

Merleau Ponty, Maurice. *The Phenomenology of Perception.* London and New York, NY: Routledge, 1962.

Meschonnic, Henri. 'The Rhythm Party Manifesto', source unknown, n.d.

Middleton, Christopher. 'Notes on a Viking Prow' in ed. Schmidt, M. *British Poetry since 1970.* Manchester: Carcanet, 1980.

Monk, Geraldine. *Selected Poems.* Cambridge and Applecross: Salt, 2003.

Mottram, Eric. 'Open Field Poetry', *Poetry Information.* 17, 1977.

O'Hara, Frank. *The Selected Poems of Frank O'Hara.* New York: Vintage Books, 1974.

Ramayya, Nisha. *Correspondences.* Hunstanton: Oystercatcher, 2016.

Roholt, Tiger C. *Groove: A Phenomenology of Rhythmic Nuance.* New York, NY and London: Bloomsbury, 2014.

Rowe, William, 'Lee Harwood Tristan Tzara', in ed. Robert Sheppard. *The Salt Companion to Lee Harwood.* Cambridge: Salt, 2007.

Rukeyser, Muriel. ed. Jan Heller Levi. *A Muriel Rukeyser Reader.* New York, NY and London: Norton, 1994.

Sheppard, Robert. *The Poetry of Saying: British Poetry and its Discontents: 1950– 2000.* Liverpool: Liverpool University Press, 2005.

Sheppard, Robert. *Complete Twentieth Century Blues.* Cambridge: Salt, 2008a.

Sheppard, Robert. 'Poetics as Conjecture and Provocation: an inaugural lecture delivered on 13 March 2007 at Edge Hill University', *New Writing.* Vol 5: 1 (2008b): 3-26, reprinted in this volume.

Sheppard, Robert. *Berlin Bursts.* Exeter: Shearsman Books, 2011.

Sheppard, Robert. *History or Sleep: Selected Poems.* Bristol: Shearsman, 2015.

Sheppard, Robert. *The Meaning of Form in Contemporary Innovative Poetry.* New York, NY: Palgrave, 2016.

Shklovsky, Victor, 'Art as Technique', in eds. Lemon, Lee T., and Reis, Marion J. *Russian Formalist Criticism: Four Essays.* Lincoln and London: University of Nebraska Press, 1965.

Sullivan, J.P. ed. *Ezra Pound.* Harmondsworth: Penguin, 1970.

Sutherland, Keston. 'Prosody and Reconciliation', *The Gig*, 16, February 2004, 41-55, at 53-4.

Tarlo, Harriet. ed. *The Ground Aslant.* Exeter: Shearsman, 2011.

Thomson, David, 'The Forlorn Ear of Jeff Hilson', in Purves, Robin, and Ladkin, Sam, *Complicities: British Poetry 1945-2007*. Prague: Litteraria Pragensia, 2007.

Toop, David. *Into the Maelstrom: Music, Improvisation and the Dream of Freedom.* London: Bloomsbury, 2016.

Troy, Juliet. *Motherboard.* Newton-le-Willows: Knives Forks and Spoons, 2016.

Widger, Eleanore, 'The "Specific Evidentness" of Contemporary Radical Landscape Poetry: Innovative Form and Spatial Presence in *The Ground Aslant.*' *English*, 2016, vol. 65, no. 251: 363-386.

Williams, William Carlos, *Imaginations: Five Experimental Prose Pieces.* London: McGibbon and Kee, 1970.

The Wolf 34, ed. Byrne, James and Sandeep Parmar. Winter 2016.

Wyatt, Thomas, ed. Rebholtz, R.A. *The Complete Poems.* Harmondsworth: Penguin Books, 1978.

The Formal Splinter

You can't point to form. Form is revealed in tracing forms on the page and in acts of reading as forming. The critical function of the work of art is asserted by it being art, by it having form at all. By being form. The poem doesn't *say*: it participates, it criticises by operating a rigorous critique of itself in self-reflection. Poems – critical in their forms and forming – participate and criticise. Form operates as transfiguration and guilt in the choice of certain materials and in the rejection of others. Form may be sedimented content but is not readable as such. This is not to be confused with the overt content (or paraphrasable content), nor with the forms and formings open to a subtle formalist engagement, with identifiable elements of poetic artifice. That is to be distinguished from material or materials. Form sediments content, subsumes mimesis, becomes material. Form is cognitive, cognition embedded in the sedimentation and in the critical function that is itself called into being by form (and its autonomy). The cognitive content is not a paraphrase of the poem's linguistic content. The autonomy of art enables all of the above, but is itself predicated on the heteronomy of the work of art. Its materials rather than its content derive from the latter, bequeaths its sedimented content as critical form to autonomy, as it were. The autonomous and heteronomous interface results in artists restlessly displaying and playing their formal impulse between three scenarios: art becomes life; life becomes art; life and art exchange properties. None is settled upon and the tension between them drives artistic practice, though not negatively. Dissensus (rather than consensus, both socially and artistically, in relation to heteronomy as well as autonomy) produces the manifold devices of formally investigative poetry (including that poetry now rather widely called linguistically innovative): varieties of montage and de-montage emphasising disruption, interruption, imperfect fit and unfinish, as well as transformation and transposition, creative linkage in other words. They put disorder at the heart of art's order, while simultaneously putting order at the heart of its disruption. Resisting signification within signification is the formal splinter at, and in, the heart of the poem. The critical function of art is born in the instant its form de-forms and re-forms in front of us as precisely a representation of freedom. Political poetry, like all formally investigative poetry, will both say and not say, modified by formal resistance and interruption. If form knows, if forms know, anything they know at least to do these things. (2014)

A Voice Smears Across the Screen: Material Engagement with Form, Forms and Forming

To regard cognition as achieving independent existence outside the brain, inherent in things in general (or in form as a particularity) is not a mystical or magical formulation. I have been wrestling with some notions of the poem (for both my critical and creative work) that express an unproven belief in the cognitive value of form; this can seem pretty ineffable from the materialist point of view I take to be mine. However, cognition can be conceived of as a variety of 'material engagement' in the light of a theory that takes that very name as its own, and my discovery of it was fortuitous. Lambros Malafouris' *How Things Shape the Mind* (2013) contrasts internalist views of mind, where a Cartesian entity computes and calibrates a world it cannot enter, with his own externalist one that recognises 'the intersection between cognition and material culture' (Malafouris 2013: 17), that sees the mind as engaging with, and interacting with, learning from and with, the world, entering it via means of what he calls 'the extended mind' (Malafouris 2013: 17). His presentation at FACT in Liverpool, as part of the Torque symposium, closely followed the argument of his new book which I obtained as soon as I was able, knowing immediately that this work, which struck me as having the brilliance I recall from my first encounter with phenomenology years ago, would provide the instruments of thought (I use the phrase mindfully) that I needed for criticism, poetry and poetics. In fact, its implications for the last two have yet to be drawn.

'For active externalism, marks made with a pen on paper are not an ongoing external record of the contents of mental states' – such as a poem, of course – 'they are an extension of those states' (Malafouris 2013: 74). As Malafouris writes, and may well have said that morning in Liverpool, 'Our ways of thinking are not merely causally dependent upon but *constituted* by extracranial bodily processes and material artifacts' (Malafouris 2013: 227). In short, and in Jonathan Kingdom's differently spelt words, humans are 'artefacts of their own artefacts', and some of those artefacts are the ones we make out of language which then make us (a fact any serious reader must know instinctively) (Malafouris 2013: 231).

Malafouris is an archaeologist and his examples are prehistoric as well as historic. '*Mark-making action and thinking are the same,*' he remarks of early stone inscriptions which, he points out with care, may *not* have originally been depictions; the marks and lines may '*externalize nothing but the very process of externalization*' which would develop into depictions (over breathtaking lengths of time) (Malafouris 2013: 190). Even then, 'those early pictures *bring forth* a new process of acting within this world and, at the same time, thinking about it' (Malafouris 2013: 203).

This is nothing less than a story about how we became human (and how we know we are human), through the agency of this interpenetration of mind and world. Notions of the post-human (rather than post-humanism which strikes me as a different issue) are affected by these nuanced meditations. Arguments for the transformative function of contemporary technologies are both supported and attenuated by this theory. Material engagement affects cognition, as in the modified brains of habitual musicians and taxi-drivers carrying 'the knowledge' and, we might assume by analogy, writers, but it does so in a way that is as old as humanity, from the Greeks to the geeks. Since the making of the first stone inscriptions, men and women – *homo faber* – have always been cyborgs.

But things are also mobile, their affective states largely unrecognised by various social sciences. 'The sensual properties of things and the aesthetic experience of things permeate every aspect of our cognitive activities and permeate our social and emotional relationships' (Malafouris 2013: 87). The uses of objects in mourning, or the uses of religious ikons to access absent beings or to concretize abstract entities, are powerful examples. Arguably a poem might be one of those sensual and aesthetic objects (even agents) and its form – the result of particular *forms* and of acts of *forming* – might be thought of in this way as a material cognitive entity.

As a maker of literary artefacts I wonder about the power of such objects and the analogy between ancient artefacts and the modern artificer. In his 1978 essay 'Reflections on a Viking Prow', Christopher Middleton offers an exhilarating description of the carvings on the prow of the Oseberg ship, traces the way the spirit of the sea, the boat's fickle medium, is carved transformatively as a dragon-like form into the wood, which, it is important to note, remains visibly wooden, foregrounding the medium in its protective animism. 'The ship was protected and guided by marine protoforms,' Middleton notes, emphasising that the work was thereby functional. This material engagement has important implications for the maker of literary works. Middleton concludes that, in distinction to the authors of anecdotal poems with their tendency to 'limp, self-indulgent, and haphazard writing' (Middleton 1990: 287), 'such an artificer' – and the modern artificer poet he lauds – 'is not confessing, not foregrounding his own subjective compulsions, not cataloguing impressions, not hanging an edict from an anecdote' (Middleton 1990: 283-4). The essay is complex, one of the finest poetics pieces by a contemporary poet, but concludes (although these words are at its beginning) with a conjecture that I, for one, would want to live up to as a maker of the cognitive objects we call poems. 'Some poems, at least, and some types of poetic language, constitute structures of a singularly radiant kind, where "self-expression" has undergone a profound change of function. We experience these structures, if not as revelations of being, then as apertures upon being' (Middleton 1990: 283).

Malafouris inspects a potter at work rather than prows, Greeks rather than Vikings, but with some of the same implications. 'The being of the potter,' as Malafouris nicely puts it, 'is co-dependent and interweaved with the becoming of the pot' (Malafouris 2013: 212). The cognition of the potter, and even his or her neural pathways, are changed by the cognitive function of the artefact. Form in a literary work is cognitive through the mechanism of material engagement, through the apprehension of actual forms and perceptible acts of forming. As he says of visual art: 'The artist's sketchpad isn't just a storage vehicle for externalizing pre-existing visual images; it is a tightly coupled and intrinsic part of artistic cognition itself' (Malafouris 2013: 237). The writer's page or screen presents a similar thinking-through that changes the poet as well as the reader (though in lyric forms there is a change of register that makes cognitive language sing).

Trigger Warning

at a love poem
that causes you to think
war with just about anyone
the poem bristles with
implication as you touch
its forms you form it in acts
of forming not
tricks and triggers upon
the wall of cognition for the forms
know a thing or two and not one
might be good for you as
a voice smears across the screen

for my students

There are some unresolved problems with Malafouris' theory and they emerge from his study of the poesis of contemporary potters, where one might have imagined the theory would find its truest fit. Unaware of the 'decisions' made, the potter nevertheless declares that he or she made the pot, as I declare, fairly confidently, that I drafted the poem above. This is an 'agency judgement' and while artificers can conceive of the act as enactive, something happens to us in such an act and we nevertheless claim authorship (Malafouris 2013: 218). 'Unfortunately,' laments Malafouris, 'although a good phenomenological description can pull us inside this seamless flow of activity and agency,' which is what we get accounts of, with increasing intensity, throughout his book, 'when we cut the flow and press the question of agency our inner Cartesian self or "interpreter" wakes up to take control of the situation' (Malafouris 2013: 220). The question of agency in the case of a man plus a gun (a Cartesian 'gun-man') is raised and leaves a perturbing conclusion: 'Action involves a coalescence of human and non-human elements, and thus responsibility for action must be shared among those elements' (Malafouris 2013: 221). It is one thing to say that my poem is responsible for its own forming, even as I formed it. That seems sunnily self-abrogating. But it is quite another to say that the gun is as responsible as the man in a bank robbery.

If Malafouris is to 'put back together' the active and passive parts of a creative act, 'and account for their ongoing and irreducible causal coupling' he admits, 'it remains to be seen whether agency can offer a way to bridge the neural and cultural correlates of our bodily selves' (Malafouris 2013: 226). He remains inspired by a 'vision of the cognitive life of things' which involves 'the distributed and compositionally plastic image of the potter skillfully engaging the clay', rather than by 'the linear architecture of a Turing machine', but admits to not having forged that link in his work so far (Malafouris 2013: 238).

That, of course, is the excitement of reading a thinker in the act of thinking (particularly when that thinker has a novel theory of thinking!). It poses some questions to the poet in me, as regards agency in creative activity. I have long seen choice and chance as essentials in a stochastic poesis, so have little problem with shared agency, but I also follow Derek Attridge in believing that 'authoredness' is something we assume when we read a literary text (and this is not affected by the poetics of appropriation in conceptual writing or other practices) (Attridge 2004: 136). This is the 'agency judgement' we make from the other side. If we assume, in our apprehension of form in acts of forming, that there is *somebody* there, material engagement makes us aware that there is *something* there as well, and that the thing as well as the somebody (or even the body) is doing (some of) the thinking. Although 'cognition has no location', perhaps ethics does; responsibility must lie with the human agent because only he or she can be *answerable* (Malafouris 2013: 85). Perhaps that is a small answer in itself to questions of the bridge between the neural and cultural.

Works Cited

Attridge, Derek. *The Singularity of Literature*. London and New York, NY: Routledge, 2004.

Malafouris, Lambros. *How Things Shape the Mind: A Theory of Material Engagement*. Cambridge, MA, and London: The MIT Press, 2013.

Middleton, Christopher, *Selected Writings*. London: Paladin, 1990.

Hanging Out Inside Sonnets:
A Text and Commentary

The Pataphysical Sonnet

    after Raymond Queneau and Jacques Bens

Returns to the bedroom, out of his head,
Out of tunes fragments come rocking his bed
Between order and chaos, freedom and…?
Ever, I see order's rule in the edge
Riff between sound and silence. Out of hand
The moon in June security has led
So boot if at all to the point of dead
Hope for happiness. For beyond the land,
Every sea must ordain its religions in the edge.
Priscilla leaps from bed, surveys her life
Plus belle qu'une poubelle (just) in a cold sweat.
A certain kind of order, edge-of-knife,
provokes her (13 is unlucky) strife.
DADA was here, but I have no regret.

1977–78 (2020 version)

First published in *Dedicated to you but you weren't listening: Homage to the Soft Machine* (London: Writers Forum, 1979)

COMMENTARY

When my friend Sandeep Parmar asked me whether my younger self would have been surprised to be now re-working the sonnets of the English tradition, as I am, I didn't immediately respond by mentioning this poem. I'd forgotten it. It might not have answered the question, but it is curious that this poem *is* a sonnet, though an odd one, like all of mine. It was written right at the start of my writing career and, although it has not been republished (and neither have its fellow poems from the booklet it shared), it has remained a talisman, as my 'earliest poem' (while slightly later, sounder, but less experimental, poems have occasionally filled that role). My younger self would *not* have been surprised at the re-functioned sonnets of 'The English Strain' project, which now consists of two published books, *The English Strain* (Shearsman Books, 2021), *Bad Idea* (KFS, 2021) and the work in progress *British Standards* (forthcoming, Shearsman Books). Long ago, I modelled a sonnet on somebody else's.

I had found Queneau and Bens in Simon Watson Taylor's anthology *French Writing Today* (1968). I bought my copy in the summer of 1974, when I was continually listening to the Soft Machine, the official orchestra of the College of 'Pataphysics (of which Watson was a part). I might have been surprised how long it took (about a decade) for the Oulipo movement (of which I did not grasp the existence, even, from Watson Taylor's book) to be revealed as a formalist model for British innovative poetry. And about twenty to thirty years for its procedures to become widespread in the alternative poetries. Or even forty years to get into Penguin, as it were. I would have been most astonished to have presaged my inclusion in the 2019 *The Penguin Book of Oulipo* (under the guise of my fictional poet René Van Valckenborch), having been long prepared by the careers of older innovative writers for a life of exclusion and derision. The title of the Writers Forum volume may have been a Soft Machine track, but it was also an unconscious projection of anticipated neglect (which hasn't quite been the case).

What the poem does anticipate is my later contention that formal features may become largely a poem's content. It is a construction of formal constraints. An acrostic on my name (though with a 13th unlucky line, which is what the Oulipo would call a clinamen, a carefully placed spanner in the works, although I didn't know it at the time), the poem uses titles of Soft Machine tracks at the start of most lines. Its rhymes reflect those of Bens, derived from the number π. (I return to this forming in 'For the Numbers' in *Bad Idea*!) 'Pataphysics pointed towards the Oulipo without me knowing, but DADA pointed to the Soft Machine's procedures (and to my contemporary interest in Dada and Surrealist visual art, which again evokes that pre-university summer of 1974).

Of course, the modes of linguistic or formal innovation, experimentalism or the avant-garde, changed between this 1970s sonnet and the work of the 1980s, when 'linguistically innovative poetry' was narrowly defined by Adrian Clarke, Gilbert Adair and myself, to exclude quite a lot of work that is today happily included *in* that category, if it is still used at all. Modes of indeterminacy and discontinuity dominated, not for their own sakes (and certainly not to mime the informational and existential chaos of neoliberalism) but in order to stimulate the reader into becoming an active co-creator of the poem, together with a resistance to, though not a prohibition of, scripts of self-hood. The important self in the poem was that of the reader. There was a definite prohibition of the kinds of socially defined self-hood represented by the limited 'suburban mental ratio' of the Movement poets and their continuing but ever attenuated 'orthodoxy', with its inflexible notions of 'form'. This found its release in certain spoof poems I wrote, gifted to 'Wayne Pratt'; I could thus have my cake and eat it! His reappearance in 'Petrarch 3' at the beginning of *The English Strain* was a surprise.

But 'Petrarch 3' itself was the greater surprise, as, influenced by two contemporary Petrarchan sonneteer versionists, Peter Hughes and Tim Atkins, and one Oulipean, Harry Mathews, and one of the 'anticipatory plagiarists' of that movement, Nicholas Moore (in his *Spleen*), I set this three volume formal investigation going. I've outlined this in detail in '"*Era il giorno ch'al sol si scoloraro*": A derivative dérive into/out of Petrarch's Sonnet 3' (in Birkan-Berz's *Translating Petrarch's Poetry*, Legenda, 2020, but re-printed as the following chapter). I needn't repeat its account of influences, procedures and caprices. Suffice it to say, I've had a fascination with the sonnet, and all of its formal instrumentations of its materials, for a long time. Of course, the interest is shared, as Jeff Hilson's anthology of the innovative sonnet, *The Reality Street Book of Sonnets* (2008), proves. My need to re-investigate the sonnet tradition as well as its form, is part of that, though I have always engaged with the history of poetry – that great repository of formal investigations which shows us where our innovation has come from, and more – usually tacitly rather than overtly. 'The English Strain' is nothing if not overt.

I still believe in the basic orientation of linguistically innovative poetry, but it has broadened out from the necessary closed poetics of a developing writer ('operational axioms' was a term I used, rather stiffly) into a more relaxed sense of poetics (which has become an object of enquiry for me in its own right) as an anticipatory writerly discourse. (In essence, it's just writers talking to themselves, as here!) It provides a set of counters to think with, to test, to reverse, and – wondrous relief – to transgress. One axiom I do have is provided by the opening words of my critical book, 'Poetry is the investigation of complex contemporary realities through the means (meanings) of form' (*The Meaning of Form*, Palgrave, 2016). This is echoed in the dedicatory poem to volume two of this project, *Bad Idea*:

I hang out inside *these* sonnets, punching
echoes into new shape, because I take
poetry as the investigation
of complexity through the *means* of form.

Yes, that's a shadowy 'me' talking. The shifting terms I have adopted for the central mode of these poems ('overdubs' or 'understudies', 'contrafacts' or 'counterfactuals', 'translations' or 'versions') is deliberate, to reflect the restless and various modes of their engagements with their 'originals', to use a word I'd rather avoid. I am happiest now with the term 'transposition' to cover my various processes. Whatever I've called them, I'm activating a force field *between* the 'standard' text and its transposition, which is where active readers will now be located (whether they know the 'original' or not).

I have a resolution to write no further sonnets (and even to avoid 14-line poems). There are enough already, including those in my own invented forms, like the 100 word sonnet, which dates back to the 1990s (2 words + 14 lines of 7 words each), and the 'twittersonnets' featured in my book of micro-poems *Micro Event Space* (14 lines of 10 characters) and a whole previous book of innovative sonnets (arranged in stanza permutations of 5,4,3, and 2 lines) about the war on terror, called *Warrant Error*. (Other forms, such as the half-pint sonnet, I have abandoned before I've used them!) I have already partly abandoned the sonnet frame, while continuing to work my way through the sonnets of Keats (occasionally utilising 28 lines in couplets). I read one of Robert Duncan's 'versions' of Dante's sonnets and was impressed that he didn't mime the frame at all. Projecting ahead to the sonnets of John Clare, I am planning to transpose them as 'quennets'. This has a wonderful circularity, since the quennet form was invented by Raymond Queneau, as a kind of haiku-sonnet. I am represented by Van Valckenborch's quennets in *The Penguin Book of Oulipo*. (Come to think of it, he 'invented' the twittersonnet too.) Like a corona of sonnets, my end is also my beginning, formally speaking. [Update: as characteristic of my poetics, this neat 'circularity' was undercut by contrary formal developments!]

Formalist though I am, 'The English Strain Project' has found its 'complex contemporary realities' in Brexit (and, within the third volume, which I am currently writing, in the Coronavirus pandemic), off which the poems have to feed. Remember, I'm also balancing the 'original' poems *and* contemporary events. Perhaps the satirical mode helps; satire has to take a social view. More fragmented forms of response would make it less possible to accommodate humour, which would be collaged, cut up, chopped out of existence. (I'm not being funny, but I like being funny!) *These* poems have to be close to the grain of experience, which may be an odd claim to make of poems which are also contrafacts of – for example – Michael Drayton's 1619 sonnet sequence 'Idea', which is the case with the poems in volume two, *Bad Idea*. But that is how I see them, until they are finished, finished with, or are finished with me.

Perhaps all poetics should end in the words with which I concluded 'Poetics as Anticipation': 'I cannot say what comes next *and* I'm saying it now.'

October 10–11th 2020

'Era il giorno ch'al sol si scoloraro':
A derivative dérive into/out of Petrarch's Sonnet 3

Petrarch was pretty clear that translation implied more than faithful reproduction of linguistic features. He warned, utilising a conventional metaphor for translation drawn from apiculture, 'Take care ... that the nectar does not remain in you in the same state as when you gathered it; bees would have no credit unless they transformed it into something different and better' (Brigden 2012: 157). This essay involves attempting to trace the transformations involved in the writing of fourteen variations on a 'translation' I made of the third sonnet of Petrarch, *Petrarch 3* (2016), a partly conceptual, partly expressive, sonnet sequence, made under the sign of Oulipo, but informed by earlier poetic interests of my own, even early poems. (It also appears at the beginning of *The English Strain* (Sheppard 2021a).) It is at once impersonal and personal. It is, arguably, both hugely derivative and original, though that last judgement is beyond the scope of my poetics as I define it as a 'speculative, writerly discourse' (Sheppard 2008a: 4). What I can say is that the process was immensely productive, though I would not dare to rise to Petrarch's aspiration concerning the betterment of the original. As a poet-critic, I believe that my literary criticism must inform my poetics – the mercurial writerly conversation that I have with myself in my journal, with others in explicit poetics pieces, and perhaps in this piece I am writing now – but I do not know how particularly, hence my use of the verb 'attempting' above. Indeed, one of the reasons I value writerly poetics is precisely because writers cannot read their own work, or even mislead themselves about what they are doing. I am therefore somewhat suspicious of the kind of practice-led research I am presenting here, but the creative story I have to tell is one that criss-crosses poetics, literary criticism, translation and creative writing itself, and may reveal something about modes of transformation and translational processes.

My acquaintanceship with the innovative sonnet is a long one. I am represented in Jeff Hilson's anthology *Reality Street Book of Sonnets* (2008), which puts an excerpt from *Warrant Error* (2009), my book of 100 innovative poems concerned, as the title suggests, with the so-called 'War on Terror' of the early twenty-first century, alongside the poems of many others, from Ted Berrigan and Tom Raworth, through to my contemporaries Tim Atkins and Adrian Clarke. But my use of innovative sonnet forms, which usually means sonnet aspirant, sonnet approximate and sonnet deviant forms, poems that would not qualify as sonnets under the usual normative 'classroom' description, harks back to earlier work. Indeed, my long network *Twentieth Century Blues* (2008b) contains many 14 line poems and I even invented a new form, the 100 word sonnet (a two word 'title' is followed by 14 lines of 7 words each, centre margined), which hailed from noticing this structure in one of Adrian Clarke's word-count poems of the 1990s, and adapting it for my poems and sequences. Coincidentally, I have returned to this form, one dictated by a lack of punctuation and caesura and that develops a rhythmic celerity amid linguistic mix, in writing some poems that brood upon the disastrous vote of Britain to 'Brexit' the European Union. Indeed, this essay is in some senses a poetics for my on-going project of making sequences of innovative sonnet sequences, that mostly involve – though not exclusively – transformations of Petrarch's sonnets, beginning with *Petrarch 3* (the poet Richard Parker, who published *Petrarch 3*, declared this to be a 'corona of coronas' in conversation).

My predilection for the sonnet may be found even earlier. The opening poem of my first non-self-published booklet, *Dedicated to you but you weren't listening* (1979) is also a sonnet of sorts. Using titles from recordings by the seminal British band Soft Machine as the start of each line (the book's title is also one of their compositions) the poem claims, in its subtitle, to be 'influenced' by the sonnets of Raymond Queneau and Jacques Bens, two members of Oulipo. In fact, in 1978 when I wrote the poems, like most Britons, I knew little of the Oulipo, other than what I had picked up via the fortuitous possession of Simon Watson Taylor's *French Writing Today* of 1968, which anthologised both poets. Detailed knowledge of the Oulipo evaded me until the mid-1980s, but the construction of innovative sonnets is obviously rooted deep in my practice, and the memory of my first brush with three of Queneau's now well-known 'Thousand Billion Sonnets', for example, and Bens' much less well-known mathematical use of π as a determinant of rhyme-schemes in his 'irrational sonnets' – the 14 lines are arranged in stanzas dictated by the numerals of π to the third point: 3, 1, 4, 1 and 5 – must have lain dormant (Watson Taylor 1968: 205; [see also Sheppard 2021b: 32 for my later use of this constraint.]).

I embarked upon my recent critical volume *The Meaning of Form* (as I wanted to call it, though it now carries the search-engine-friendly *In Contemporary Innovative Poetry* after those emblematic words) under the sign of 'the turn to form'. The entire project is summed up in its opening statement: 'Poetry is the investigation of complex contemporary realities through the means (meanings) of form' (Sheppard 2016: 1). The central methodology is introduced via a reading of the formalist criticism of Derek Attridge, Susan Wolfson, Peter de Bola, Angela Leighton and others, though none of this criticism has addressed linguistically innovative poetry directly, which is strange, given its formally investigative strategies. These thinkers loosely share allegiance to a longer aestheticist tradition of regarding form as a *significant* force; Schiller is often read as the originator of the belief that 'the content should do nothing, the form everything' (Schiller 2004: 106). *Form* as a force and cognitive entity, particular *forms* as elements of poetic artifice, and *forming* as an event in active readerly engagement and transformation, are compared and differentiated, and all three italicised terms are used. Forms have to be formed in several ways, as Attridge puts it: 'The event of the literary work is a *formal* event, involving among other things, or rather among other happenings, shifts in register, allusions to other discourses, ... the patterning of rhythms, the linking of rhymes, the ordering of sections, the movement of syntax, the echoing of sounds: all operating in a temporal medium to surprise, lull, intrigue, satisfy' (Attridge 2015: 117). We need to apprehend 'the eventness of the literary work, which means that form needs to be understood verbally – as "taking form", of "forming", or even "losing form"' (Attridge 2004: 113). The two counters of my title, meaning and form, are related in an original and distinctive way by Attridge, when he reminds us: 'Meaning is ... not something that appears in defining opposition or complementary apposition to form ... but as something already taken up within form; forms are made out of meanings quite as much as they are made out of sound and shapes' (Attridge 2004: 114). Form is an active and mercurial process, not a fixed product of poesis; it is poesis.

Beyond this theoretical framework (which is expounded in Chapter One, the Introduction) two chapters are directly relevant to *Petrarch 3*, 'Convention and Constraint: Form in the Innovative Sonnet Sequence' and 'Translation as Transformation: Tim Atkins' and Peter Hughes' Petrarch'. The first of these analyses both the history of the sonnet and its transformation in contemporary innovative practice (as exemplified by the *Reality Street Book of Sonnets*): the works of Ted Berrigan, Jeff Hilson, Philip Terry, Geraldine Monk and Sophie Robinson are critiqued in detail. Questions of form (in terms of a consideration of the sonnet 'frame', as I rename what is commonly said to be sonnet 'form', its characteristic pattern or structure, its numbers of lines, its stanzas, its contrasting rhyme-schemes) are raised alongside issues of the historical form and its relation to politics and gender. The different 'frames' of the Petrarchan and Shakespearean patterns, for example, impose different structures of argument and rhetorical progress, and offer a simple example of the meaningfulness of form. The main business of the chapter is an examination of the breadth of experiment evinced in contemporary practice, in relation to the work of New York poetics, the Oulipo group, and quasi-concrete poetry experiments in a variety of visual 'sonnet' forms, and this prepares the ground for the chapter on Hughes and Atkins.

What could have been more fortuitous for my critical project, which hovers around notions of 'translation' as a formally investigative practice, than to discover, not one, but *two*, innovative 'translations' of Petrarch's *Canzoniere* appearing at around the same time by contemporary British writers? I put 'translation' in scare-quotes to alert the reader to the fact that neither project is a linguistic translation but each is a transposition of the original into contemporary modes. I have the two books on my desk now, two fat volumes (Atkins' slightly fatter because he tackles the complete *Canzoniere*, all 366 poems, while Hughes contents himself with the 317 sonnets), Atkins' *Collected Petrarch* (London: Crater Press, 2014) and Hughes' *Quite Frankly: After Petrarch's Sonnets* (Hastings: Reality Street Editions, 2015). The titles are indicative of two facts that both projects share: the 'after' of Hughes' title emphasises the fact of translation as transformation (with an emphasis, in my reading, on the presence of the word 'form' in that word), while Atkins' term 'Collected' alerts us to the fact that he had published selections and sections of his work as pamphlets with various small presses – as had Hughes – before these massive volumes appeared (Atkins' book is 544, Hughes' is 354, pages long). Crater and Reality Street are two of the most important independent presses that sustain linguistically innovative poetry in Britain.

This minor fact of publication is vitally important to the fortuity of my deliberately modest Petrarch project (which also appears from Crater). In general terms, and without repeating my analysis, I conclude that while Hughes (who reads Italian) emphasizes his *difference* from Petrarch's originals (by relocating the poems to the Norfolk coast and modernising their references, for example), Atkins (who does not read Italian) emphasises his *distance* from the originals (largely through the use of post-Oulipo techniques and constraints, which he outlines in his essay 'Seven Types of Translation' (Atkins 2020: 222-244 [the preceding pages to the original publication of this current piece]).

Hughes will eulogise his Norfolk love thus,

imagination had me hovering
with my lady in the Rings of Venus
one of Fakenham's premier nite-spots
she spoke although I couldn't hear a thing (Hughes 2015: 293)

while Atkins is often more mysteriously disconnected, though in ways that often bring us close to Petrarch as a poet and then back us away into paradox,

When you live 12 miles away from a lemon
Wyatt adapts Petrarch's lament into his own
Seeking shade from a shadow or a column
Until it splashes up against the back of the front teeth.
(Atkins 2014: 344)

Both writers manage to reflect Petrarch's elegiac mode (Hughes notes 'yet another windswept friend of the dead/ fixed petrol-station roses to the fence') (Hughes 2015: 323) while Atkins additionally injects a Buddhist negation of the things of the (contemporary) world that clutter his woeful lover's utterances: 'This is the Buddha life indeed/… I is empty inside it' (Atkins 2014: 537). One unintended consequence of the publishing history outlined above was the quotation of my critical evaluation of the sequences in Atkins' volume itself. The manner in which I managed to sustain myself through the writing of *The Meaning of Form in Contemporary Innovative Poetry* was to write blogposts on the developing project; one post (the most read, according to blogspot statistics) is about the two projects which I labelled 'The Petrarch Boys', rather cheekily it strikes me in retrospect. Jèssica Pujol i Duran's Introduction to *Collected Petrarch*, 'Multi-Atkins', picks up on my prefatory post and tells us:

Robert Sheppard worries; 'am I reading the poem, reading the tradition, or reading the *distance* between Atkins's poem and Petrarch' … We needn't really read *Petrarch* for the differences between Petrarch and Atkins, or indeed, their similarities – such concerns seem gleefully inessential for the British poet, in fact. The relationship between Italian 'original' and English 'version' forms a dialogue only at the point of our reception of the poems – not really during the creation of the works, when we would expect such a dialogue to develop. Thus we read Sheppard's *'distance'*, aware that the measure of that distance is hallucinatory; that most of the time Atkins seems to be having a conversation with a neighbour, with a Zen master, or with 'fucking-Jeffrey-fucking-Hilson,' rather than with the fourteenth century Petrarch (Pujol i Duran 2015: xii).

Whether or not the distance is a chimera for the ordinary reader, holding only Atkins' book in his or her hand (and I suspect Pujol i Duran is right about the point of reception and about Atkins' gleeful anarchy, which is partly what I was signifying as 'distance'), this disregard between original and version was not for me, and would not be for others, engaged in critical and formal comparison, with Atkins' project to weigh against Hughes', and with the need to contrast both with a 'straight' translation of Petrarch's poems; like Atkins, I do not have Italian. Robert Sheppard was more 'worried' than Pujol i Duran could have guessed. To establish my critical case about difference and distance, I needed to locate two poems for comparison; the methodology of reading for form required a lightly theorised close reading. If I were writing the chapter today, I would have 317 pairs of poems to choose from (which, with its dizzying possibilities, I am glad I did not have), but in 2013–14 when I was writing the chapter, I had a small gathering of Hughes' and Atkins' pamphlets and one of the only paired poems I could locate was Petrarch's third sonnet, particularly as this was also translated in Mark Musa's *Petrarch: Selections from the Canzoniere and Other Works* (1985). The scene was set. Actually, the scene was this: my little work room, whose floor space is nearly completely covered with piles of books and pamphlets (each relating to a particular chapter), was excessively untidy when I palmed my way through these pamphlets, and Musa's translation was unlocatable, lost as surely was Laura to Petrarch it seemed, buried in the wrong pile perhaps, but obdurately not turning up in time for the formal reading (critical writing, like poetry writing, is a kind of performance for me, as Attridge suggests, an action that is also an event).

The first refuge of the disorganised is the internet, and I located Petrarch's original poem 3 and several translations of it online in a trice, but they seemed cloggy neo-Victorian takes, and not usable; I think one was a prose gloss. But I thought I could see enough of the original (perhaps I was as 'gleeful' as Atkins at this point) to make my own version from these (now also mislaid) translations. (I had also realised I might mitigate the large sums in permissions fees that my methodological insistence upon extensive quotation had inflicted upon my pocket, so even if Musa had turned up, I might have preferred my illegitimate version.)

Attridge posits a range of possible translational responses to an original, from 'diligent reproduction of characteristic features... to inventive re-workings' (Attridge 2004: 75). Hughes and Atkins were undertaking the second of these options; at this stage, I was merely attempting the first. I took the frame as granted and draped the English through it, an amalgam derived from various translations operating like a trig point to confirm the target, to triangulate common denominators. Petrarch makes each stanza of the poem (as he may have thought of them) a complete sentence, and I reproduce this structure, though I was forced to make some amendments, either practical measures or egregious misrepresentations, depending on one's view.

> Era il giorno ch'al sol si scoloraro
> per la pietà del suo factore i rai,
> quando i' fui preso, et non me ne guardai,
> ché i be' vostr'occhi, donna, mi legaro.
>
> Tempo non mi parea da far riparo
> contra colpi d'Amor: però m'andai
> secur, senza sospetto; onde i miei guai
> nel commune dolor s'incominciaro.
>
> Trovommi Amor del tutto disarmato
> et aperta la via per gli occhi al core,
> che di lagrime son fatti uscio et varco:
>
> però al mio parer non li fu honore
> ferir me de saetta in quello stato,
> a voi armata non mostrar pur l'arco. (Petrarch: nd)

I rendered this poem thus:

Era il giorno ch'al sol si scoloraro

That pitiful morning when the light of Heaven
Was hidden for our mourning maker's sake,

I saw you first that day, My Lady, but
Was captured, disarmed, then bound to your stake.

It didn't seem the time for shields and armour
Against Love's arrows, his batters and blows;
So, unsuspecting, I wept with the world,
But that day my heartbreaks began, my woes.

Love stalked me, found me, unarmed and weak,
And opened my eyes, portals of tears, through which
Sorrow flowed from the passage of my heart.

But feeble was Love's triumph to triumph
With his arrow over one so enfeebled,
And to not even dare to flash you his dart.

(All future quotations from Sheppard 2017 and 2021a)

I use light rhyme, but on two occasions this distorts the sense. 'Bound to your stake' is an image of captivity that is loyal to the spirit of the poem but no 'stake' is mentioned. In the original poem Love shows his 'bow' but 'dart' was chosen to rhyme with 'heart' in my version (a decision that was to have consequences, as we will see), the possessor of both bows and arrows being Cupid. The 'pitiful morning' upon which the poem is set is Good Friday, the darkest day in the Christian year, and it was while the narrator 'wept with the world', participating in general mourning, that he was struck by Cupid's arrows: on Good Friday, April 6th 1327, Petrarch beheld the woman he called 'Laura' at mass in the church of Sainte-Claire d'Avignon. He was caught off-guard, like an ill-prepared soldier, but 'it didn't seem the time for shields and armour'. The result is extreme, and the tone at the *volta* is strident and emphatic: 'Love stalked me, found me, unarmed and weak'; these lines present the central emotive event of the poem. Only the composure of the final three lines recovers some dignity for the narrator. It was no victory at all to capture somebody so weak; I adopt wordplay to emphasise this sophistry: the repeated use of 'feeble' and 'triumph'. But the final line accuses Cupid of real cowardice: he smote the narrator but did not dare to show his bow and arrows to the beloved, who remains unsmitten. This account of my version is retrospective: I do not remember what I thought as I composed the text, though I was surprised that it came quickly. The poem is rhetorical, its argument follows the sonnet frame, its language colloquial but with heightened rhetoric at its climax, though, of course, such a capitulation to unrequited love is common to the tradition (and my previous encounters with hundreds of Petrarch-like English sonnets, whether Wyatt's close approximations or Shakespeare's innovations, lay behind my invention). The poem is addressed to the Lady (though Laura is not named in the poem) but she does not act in it. The only agency in the poem is invested in Love.

This version seemed workaday enough, segmented and analysed stanza by stanza, to use as an introduction to my comparison of the Hughes and Atkins sonnets. It is important to remember that *Petrarch 3* collects not so much my 14 variations on the Petrarch original, but upon this rough 'translation', which is why I have sketched it out in its own terms. Almost as soon as I finished the 'translation' I found myself playing with it. Initial toying with Google Translate produced a far-too coherent version (the technology nowadays is too smart; it 'learns' through repeated use to refine its choices according to contexts), although perhaps it was the transposition of 'dart' into the Italian 'darto' and then back into English to provide the comical last line, 'And to not even dare to flash you his dick', that suggested I should work creatively with my crib.

If I am asked to name my favourite poem I cite Harry Mathews' 'Trial Impressions' (1977). This consists of thirty 'variations' or 'versions' of a poem (song) by John Dowland, one with a pronounced rhetorical structure that can be mimicked and transformed, engendering recognition on the part of the reader: 'Deare, if you change, Ile never chuse again' (Mathews 1992: 63). It is a classic Oulipean work, in that each operates by constraint. Some use simple constraints (an 'up to date', beginning, 'If you break our breakfast date, I'll go begging in Bangkok' or a 'haikuization': 'change/love/no/next/choice') (Mathews 1992: 63/65). Some are procedurally elaborate ('Keep Talking' which is lengthy, or a poem of indeterminate duration formed by a multiple-choice narrative), through to the technically stunning (a palindrome, or the rendering of Dowland's 'doeful' song in the language of the King James Bible or as a sestina or traditional sonnet, the latter beginning, 'Who will in dearest love of Beauty change') (Mathews 1992: 68). There are several sections that I have not unravelled (they operate, at least for me, as the sequence's clinamen, that necessary procedural 'spanner in the works' that renders all Oulipean works inoperative, like a Jean Tinguely construction hammering itself to pieces), and I confess myself an enthusiast for this sequence rather than a critic of it. (The early exposure to Queneau may have heightened this enthusiasm.)

The same is true of Nicholas Moore's *Spleen* (1990), a collection of Moore's comic but disheartened pseudonymous multiple submissions to a competition to translate a single Baudelaire poem, 'Spleen', whose first line, 'Je suis comme le roi d'un pays pluvieux', can become 'I am the Pluto of a rainy hell' as well as 'I am like the T.S. Eliot of the new wastelands' (Moore 1990: 35/42). In Moore's case, the multiplicity was intended to 'illustrate my own thesis of the impossibility of translation', but in fact, he demonstrates the joys of making (and reading) serial versions (Moore 1990: 12). Both poets 'version' their original poem, to use a verb borrowed from dub reggae, and somehow I knew I wanted to attempt something analogous with my Petrarch poem. (I also avoided more mechanical Oulipo techniques like the S+7, which, in my practice at least, was losing its edge.) I knew even a failed attempt would be fun, though a residual guilt that realised my versions could not exist without Hughes and Atkins (even in the world of Kenneth Goldsmith's conceptual or 'uncreative writing') led me to acknowledge my debts, by dedicating the sequence to both poets, and to state that the work was 'in homage' to Mathews and Moore (Goldsmith 2011: 1-13). I also came up with the term 'derivative dérive' to describe the piece, by which I mean that the more derivative the pieces seem to become, of Petrarch, as well as of the works of the four cited poets, but not to them alone, as I shall show, the more wayward, off the beaten track, they become (and the more 'original' I hope readers will find them). Some became surprisingly and unexpectedly personal, as I gathered typical themes or returned to earlier works of my own to cohere around my Petrarch version.

In the first poem I turned to a familiar bête noire, Margaret Thatcher, and immediately twisted Petrarchan tropes, via medieval torture instruments and contemporary Sado-Masochist practices, to fit the image of 'The Iron Lady', who had died in 2013. (Postal workers were indeed observed in Liverpool pubs on the night of her funeral reprising their political chants from the 1980s.)

Iron Maiden

Latex skies. Low cloud obscuring celestial
domination. I clapped my fuck-eye on you,
which you then pierced on a glance, that day,
and dragged me naked to your torture chamber.

The funeral of Thatcher seemed the right time
for your whip and irons. Posties brushed up their
MaggieMaggieMaggie chants and I cried *onions-*
onions-onions, stinging eyes fixed on your heels.

You stalked me in your lace-up stockings, striding tight,
and took my tears for real pain, yet can't you see desire
burning under the dildo mask you've clamped on my kisser?

Easy prey for your domination, bitch! Slap!
I crumple to the floor. Would rubbery Love
through his pouch dare to flash you his horn?

This first version established a pattern that was repeated in some of the subsequent ones, as I realised I was probably approximating 'inventive reworkings' in Attridge's phrase (Attridge 2004: 75). The narrator is often a hapless 'lover', whether that is a pet dog (in the poem 'Pet'), a man watching soft pornography on TV, a losing poet at a prize-giving, or even myself on my first date with my future wife, to use four illustrative scenarios. Analogues to 'the pitiful morning', a particularised time for the poems' events, like Thatcher's funeral, recur across the sequence: the dog trots to Sefton Park, Liverpool, on 'Mad Friday' (it is also the Shortest Day of the year), defined as 'the Friday before Christmas, when Liverpool explodes in an orgy of drinking,' in the words of an abandoned note I find on a computer file. The idle TV watcher is seeking 'Relief from *Comic Relief*', an annual charity televisual ordeal for some, which was

found,
flipping past *Russia Today* onto the *ADULT Section*,
in fixing my eye upon *Babestation Academy*.

The poet on National Poetry Day cries out that Poet Laureate

Duffy's
droning on the radio (again) and you're on
at the Poetry Society, whither I am headed
to undress your double offbeats with my ears.

I return to the real events of the fortieth anniversary of Victory in Europe

Day 1985; however, the poem is signalled as 'after Wayne Pratt', a fictional poet I invented in the 1980s to parody the mainstream poetry of the time, and so the tone is distorted though the story is true, and both are of their time, as it were:

> At the VE Night piss up, the gloom of the Blitz, the chill
> Of V2s, Goering's capture, Berlin scorched, were recalled.
> Then forgotten, the old girls squawking along with Al Bowlly.
> On our first rendezvous we'd landed on this lot.

'It didn't seem the time for shields and armour,' in my translation authorizes a sense of inappropriateness registered in some of my versions; 'But this wasn't the time for cockney triumphalism', the VE Day poem continues, though the (genuine) martial details are indeed surprising: 'The cheeky young man in the SS glad-rags/ Tickled the dollies' flab.' The series of metaphors concerning the clash of *armour* and *amores* is extended differently in other poems. For the dog in the park, unrequited love for a bitch is literally held in bondage by his owner, who plays the part of an ironical Cupid:

> You lifted your tail like a poodle, fluffy tart,
> Tripping past my flailing mass of muscle and lust.
> He didn't even notice, phone in hand, boot in my nuts.

The bored pornographer rises to the occasion with a metaphorical climax:

> I'm tossed into the refrigerated hold of factory-line phone sex!
> Unflipping catch, desire slipping through the net,
> I dream of you divested of logo, mobile, and smut.
>
> There's only one way that one way communication ends: a flick
> of the switch. My weak song at your tight thong corpses,
> like a weathergirl cracking a dirty joke by mistake.

The hapless poet 'praises' the prize-winning poet, Laura, whom he secretly loves, while recognising, in similarly hyperbolic terms, the egotistical and stylistic awfulness of her National Poetry Day poem, 'your thumping Great I Am in clumping iambics' (a phrase I had been hoarding since the 1970s for this decisive moment). Phallicism is never far away. The poem ends with the lines:

You can't beat a posy conduit for poesy's soft con job;
yet neither can you beat off love's stiff competition.

Heads you win the laurels; tails I lose Laura;
my name is reduced to a rhyme-scheme you use:
the clapped-out alternative to you-know-whose.

This poem, the last of the sequence, is entitled 'You know' and the 'who' is, of course, Shakespeare, Petrarch's (assumed) rival in terms of sonnet frame invention (if only in the English sonnet tradition), and the final rhyming couplet is deliberately Shakespearean; but the palpable sense of unrequited love is mock-Petrarchan (and I ought to say I had no real-life model for this poet who has 'a voice like a spanked arse', but she is clearly a contemporary descendant of Wayne Pratt who narrates the 1985 poem; they are both voices of the detestable mainstreams of their times). Magically retranslated to 1985, 'I' may repeat the gloss of my 'translation', 'But it wasn't the time for cockney triumphalism', though all talk of triumph and cowardice is completely replaced at the end of the poem with a banal version of the recalled actuality: 'At dawn, we walked around the railings, Clissold Park./ Inside we could hear the parakeets sounding the all clear.' (Retrospectively, I detect the tone of Eliot's *Four Quartets* here among the Pratt tropes and the ambiguity on the medical and military uses of 'all clear'; the narrator's 'excuse' to not make love is his 'scabies'.) As though I am darting between the differential and distanciating practices of Hughes and Atkins, I am not afraid to non-systematically *dérive* from my presented derivations, when occasion suggests. 'Such concerns seem gleefully inessential for the British poet,' we might plagiarise Pujol i Duran; I seem 'to be having a conversation with "fucking-Wayne-fucking-Pratt",' 'rather than with the fourteenth century' poet (Pujol i Duran 2015: xii).

The poems also demonstrate something central to the poetics of Oulipo (and, in this local instance, in this project, to mine): that Petrarch's poem (or my pragmatic 'translation' of it) is but a potential realisation from myriad possible versions. It would be possible to read the Wayne Pratt poem as the original of the 'dog' poem, should one wish, in a Borgesian shuffling of the records of composition; they might create their own precursors. That is before we think of adding all the other existent versions of Petrarch's poem, Atkins' and Hughes' included, to the roster. My limit of fourteen variations stops potentiality turning towards eternality (Nicholas Moore perhaps has too many versions; Mathews stops at thirty). There were two versions I rejected, a 'Chinese' version, 'Li Po Suction', though the pun of the title was more effective than the story of the morbidly obese 'Laura'), and 'Good Morning Blues', which was a blues song (I was particularly fond of the line, 'Beatrice got a phonograph; Laura don't exist', which seems to compare the beloveds of Dante and Petrarch (and suggests that the *Canzoniere* are completely fictional), but is in fact an amalgam of Robert Johnson's classic 'Phonograph Blues' and Johnny Mercer's standard love song 'Laura', which I suspect is in any case knowingly inflected with Petrarchan tones. I occasionally perform this song at readings of the sequence with blues harmonica accompaniment. These poems are phantom limbs of potentiality; I can leave it to the reader to imagine more, which is the unspoken invitation of every Oulipean procedure.

To return to the main body of work, the sequence was influenced by two other studies in *The Meaning of Form*, to provoke a literary historical jest, and a return to an earlier homage. Working on Caroline Bergvall's sequence *Meddle English*, which involves numerous recastings of Chaucer's *The Canterbury Tales*, necessitated me reading and re-reading the Tales as background (Bergvall 2011). Then this appeared:

The morwe biganne when hevene its bemes
In routhe of our Lord hid al the lighte.
My Lady I espeyde, she rent al my dremes,
This wight bounden to wommens tendre myghte.

It was nat the tyme for speres sharp and stronge
Agan arwes of Love and his strook and smoot.
Withouten sheeldes or defence I wep ful longe
swich a love-longyne's desperaunce, as I woot.

Love cam russhyng to smerte my peynes sorwe
Fro the breething prisoun of my distempre hert,
To open myn eyen and resolven the flo.

Love's dominacion is yet deedly narwe
Yif I am so wrecche, wounden bi a dart
Whil you, unbuxomnesse Lady, escap his bow.

I was pleased with this 'Chaucerian' sonnet, a freak of literary history. My title 'Petrak: the first English sonnet, Good Friday 1401', suggests that somebody, not Chaucer, who knew Petrarch's work, adapted it, indeed 'introduced Petrarchan lyric into England over a century prior to the sonnets of Wyatt and Surrey,' but never adopted the sonnet frame, and who died a year before the poem's supposed date, got there before him (Rossiter 2010: 25). It is, course, a joke at the expense of Wyatt and Surrey too (though I had no presentiment that I might turn to their sonnets at this point)!

The second poem derives from my chapter 'Stefan Themerson: Iconopoeia and Thought-Experiments in the Theatre of Semantic Poetry', with my study of the literary form invented by the Polish-British writer Themerson in his 1944 novel, *Bayamus*: the Semantic Poetry Translation (Themerson 1965). In short, this proto-Oulipean procedure 'translated' a text word by word into its given dictionary definitions, and used lineation to orchestrate the results. When Themerson, whom I knew a little, and published recordings of, died in the 1980s, I attempted a Semantic Poetry Translation of one of my own poems, but it did not work (possibly because my original was asyntactic). The debt was finally paid by my deliberately prolix text that re-articulates, re-forms, Petrarch's poem; the last couple of lines of the poem become:

> But
> the exultation at the success
> of the deity of the devoted attachment
> to one of the opposite (or same) sex was
> > forceless
> > > vacillating
> > > > faint
> > in its celebration of victory with pomp
> > not even bold enough to venture
> > to make show in a blaze of brilliant sparkles
> > > of his pointed weapon
> > > or toy
> > > for throwing with the hand
> > or of a calcareous needle supposed to be used
> > > as a sexual stimulus
> > > > by snails

The (almost) literal sting in the tail here is the introduction of a concluding definition of 'dart' that is at once deliberately inaccurate but sexual in a semi-appropriate way.

The implications of each word of my translation are considered (as in Themerson's prototypes), for example: Cupid is 'the deity/ of the devoted attachment to one of the opposite (or same) sex'. However, my usually trusty 1970s Collins Dictionary omits references to same sex relationships so I augmented the definition. It is exactly this kind of slow motion pondering upon the ideological constructions of words that Themerson's technique was attempting to effect.

After such an excursion, it is perhaps not surprising that I contrasted this wallowing Behemoth with this fleet, tendrillar construction:

> dark morn
> sad god/sa
> w you/stak
> ed me/bad
>
> time for l
> ove's blow
> /wept woe/
> stalked my
>
> heart pou
> rs/weak Er
> os struck
>
> weak-me/no
> guts to s
> how a dart

Akin to an Oulipean haikuisation, this is in fact a 'twittersonnet' (it contains 140 characters and spaces, the social medium Twitter's then word limit), and is described as 'after René Van Valckenborch', a reference to another fictional poet, the bilingual Belgian who dominates my volume *A Translated Man* (2013), and who supposedly invented this form. Yet another intratextual reference to my work is woven into this 'derivative' structure. Somehow, in the writing of the translations (which came quickly between December 2013 and May the following year) I felt the need to link with other works of my own. 'Empty Diary 1327' goes further by adding an anomalous member to the series of 'Empty Diary' poems that runs through *Twentieth Century Blues*, 1901–2000 (though I have since extended it into the twenty-first century, and though there had long been a science fiction 2055 poem), a sequence dealing with sexual politics, generally narrated from the point of view of a woman. Here, Laura appears as an obscene vampiric vamp:

> His eye is pulled to the black hole
> at the centre of my white body. It's the reason
> I'm here this morning, snarling under my wimple…

This Laura wants nothing to do with the tradition within which she finds herself inserted, and she exposes the sexuality at the heart of her narrator's fawning religiosity. She rejects Petrarch and his Saviour: 'Trust a Florentine not to have seen where the fault lay:/ the strung-up Megalomaniac rapping in riddles.'

This poem could be thought of (in Oulipean terms) as the sequence's clinamen, but I would nominate instead the poem I call 'the Jimmy Savile' poem. It is actually entitled 'Now then now then then and now', playing on one of the dead, disgraced celebrity's insidious media catchphrases; he is open about his paedophilic operations and his inner psyche, as perversions of the love that sustains Petrarch:

> In my time I spun the grooves and groped the grubs
> from the milk bars of Leeds to the morgue at Broadmoor,
> consummate in the toilets of Broadcasting House. Now
> then: hate is when you're feeling Top of the Pops.

One of the covers of this man, probably Britain's most predatory paedophile, was his seduction of the establishment, and its catastrophic handing over of responsibility to this criminal; his threat to children, *'I'm the rock-hard tart who's pecked his way up Thatcher's snatch!'* is an imaginative recasting of a classic silencing device, the boasting of power by paedophiles: Savile was originally a disc jockey, and the closing, 'Yours is a request that will never be played', refers to his 'escape' from justice in death. Although I generally eschew self-interpretation, I wish to be explicit about this poem's criticism of Savile to avoid any misunderstanding of my treatment of its controversial theme. Whenever I read this poem in public, I notice the audience is ill at ease, goes silent. Despite the sequence carrying the jocularity of a talking dog and a post-Chaucerian sonneteer, I want to show that 'versioning' can involve abrupt changes of tone, ones which are capable of considerations of the most serious subject matter of our time.

At this point I have been forced to renounce my writerly distance from the material, and – in contrast, and in respect to readers – I want to give a flavour of the rest of the sequence without too much comment. Running through the sequence are four poems which align Petrarch's sonnet with French symbolist poets (and sonnets). I think of them as impossibly 'half Petrarchan, half symbolist, and half me,' to quote my characteristic introduction to them in performance. These poems again came about during the writing of *The Meaning of Form*. Critiquing Sean Bonney's political book *Happiness,* I referred repeatedly to Rimbaud's famous 'vowel' poem, which Bonney re-functions in various ways throughout his book, which is sub-titled 'Poems After Rimbaud', although he warns: 'If you think they're translations you're an idiot' (Bonney 2012: cover). Rimbaud's 'Voyelles' begins with a statement of his famous and baffling alphabetic equation: 'A noir, E blanc, I rouge, U vert, O bleu, voyelles,' and I realised I needed to concoct a partial translation to quote in the essay. (I do have *some* French.) (Rimbaud 2008: 19):

A black, E white, I red, U green, O blue, vowels,
One day I'll tell of your latent spawnings;
A: black velveteen belt of flies
Blusters and clusters over the cruel stench,

The shadowy gulf.

In making my 'version', I could not resist injecting 'U LAUrA,' impersonating the letter-play one finds in some of Petrarch's sonnets, and 'I another,' a phrase that echoes (or parodies) Rimbaud's famous disavowal of self, or submergence into political community, in Bonney's fresh reading, which argues that 'For *I* is an *other*' (Rimbaud 2008: 115) is a prediction of 'the destruction of bourgeois subjectivity, yeh!' into collective consciousness (Bonney 2012: 64).

I offer, in this 'Symbolist Quartet', as I think of it, a vampire Baudelaire poem, derived from his famous 'A Une Passante', but which contains quotations from Robert Herrick and Bob Dylan (Baudelaire 1971: 78-9); a Mallarmé poem that owes to Peter Manson's version of 'Angoisse' (Manson 2012: 36-7); my version of Rimbaud's 'Voyelles' (Rimbaud 2008: 139), which additionally has a reference to Barry MacSweeney's book title *Our Mutual Scarlet Boulevard*; and Verlaine's 'Luxures' (Verlaine 1999: 128-9). [These poems, indeed all the poems constituting 'Petrarch 3', including my

'Symbolist Quartet', may be read in *Petrarch 3* (Sheppard 2017) and *The English Strain* (Sheppard 2021a).]

This tracking of the processes of writing *Petrarch 3* – which I perceive to be a peculiar species of poetics, a progress report for others – has convinced me that the subtitle, a 'derivative dérive', is in some senses accurate: the further I investigated my single poem with techniques borrowed from others (though with situations I devised myself, but sometimes suggested by those techniques, in endless interplay), the more I lost myself in the exploration of the suburbs of the poem, and the more I kept meeting myself, or rather, my aesthetic concerns, as I encountered Wayne Pratt, René Van Valckenborch or the voice of the 'Empty Diaries' sequence, which were unforeseen and could only have emerged from the formally investigative processes undertaken. The four poets named in its dedications inspired by example, Hughes and Atkins in their breathtaking breadth in taking on all of Petrarch (which I had to turn away from, a swerve from influence), and Mathews and Moore, by example of their consistent re-functioning of the same material, gnawing like dogs at a bone perhaps, or more like the performances of Thelonious Monk returning again and again to 'Monk's Mood' to mine fresh ore, rather than to mime with awe, from the same melody. I am also convinced that this has less to do with Petrarch than I had thought hitherto, although it has a great deal to do with the sonnet as a (continuing) obsession of mine, and in this piece I found new tones and voices *for me* (though I will not make claim to my nevertheless *hoped for* originality). Frankly, it allowed me to play with elements of poetic artifice that I usually eschew (rhyme and metre in particular), safe in my parodic frame. How does this meld with my formalist turn in my criticism? Strictly speaking, this is not for me to say, but Attridge argues

> The inventive artist is one who is fully in command of the materials and conventions of his art-form, or *techne*, but rather than simply producing a rearrangement of that material finds a way of making a space for the new, the other, the hitherto unthinkable or unperceivable. The scenario is exactly that of the hospitality of visitation: rather than inviting some already known idea or formal arrangement or quality of feeling into the work in progress, the successful artist finds a way of destabilizing the fixed structures of knowledge, habit, and affect, so as to make a *visitation* possible, and seeks to welcome the other, the *arrivant*, in a work that does justice to its singularity (Attridge 2015: 304).

I make no claims to invention in this specialised sense (neither do I refute it), but I wonder whether the gimp-masked submissive, Petrarch, the Scouse dog, Laura, even Jimmy Savile in his unmarked grave, are not arrivants in this hospitable sense? I believe I may have destabilised at least my own formal habits of writing and created something which is both a 'rearrangement' of the derivatively known and the making of a new space for dérive.

No wonder my next set of sonnets were 'overdubs' of Milton's. Although I have written a number of other sonnet sequences since, Petrarch was not absent for long, even if the next arrivant was Sir Thomas Wyatt. *Hap: Understudies of Thomas Wyatt's Petrarch* (2018) weaves Wyatt's versions of Petrarch, Wyatt's life as an endangered servant of that first Brexiteer, Henry VIII, and a modern day civil servant of the Brexit-obsessed administration of Theresa May, together into a satirical narrative. History almost dictates that Henry Howard, the Earl of Surrey, should be submitted to a similar fate, and 'Surrey with the Fringe on Top', whose title suggests the growing irreverence of the enterprise, forages further into the dark undergrowth of Brexitland Britain, both in my versions of Surrey's versions of Petrarch (the seven poems of 'The Unfortunate Fellow-Traveller') and in my responses to seven of his occasional poems, 'Direct Rule', in which I operate a controlling meta-narrative over the poems, and its narrative of Surrey's hubristic behaviour in the face of the Henrician Terror that finally destroyed him, while presenting a comic post-Brexit Britain peppered with rural dogging sites and self-serving Brexiteers. I freely admit this process, begun in *Petrarch 3*, is addictive. Latterly, I have adapted female sonneteers, and taken the works of Charlotte Smith as transformational models: four of *her* versions of Petrarch preface responses to some of her 'Elegaic Sonnets' that evoke the Sussex countryside (where I was also born). At the time of writing, I am adapting some of Elizabeth Barrett Browning's 'Sonnets from the Portuguese' to the voice of a mistress of a Conservative MP. [The sequences I describe here developed into *The English Strain*, book one of the 'English Strain Project', Sheppard 2021a. Books two and three are accounted for in previous chapters.]

If poetics is the speculative discourse about future possibilities for writing, then these sonnets, and this piece about them, suggest formal investigation of the sonnet frame in my work has not reached its limits. Poetics is, as Rachel Blau DuPlessis states, a 'permission to continue' (DuPlessis 1990: 156). What is unusual is that literary critical enquiries *suggested* the work, *informed* the work, but did not dictate (nor could it explain) the work.

BIBLIOGRAPHY

Atkins, Tim. *Collected Petrarch*. London: Crater, 2014.

Atkins, Tim. 'Seven Types of Translation' in eds. Carole Birkan-Berz, with Guillaume Coatalen and Thomas Vuong, *Translating Petrarch's Poetry: L'Aura del Petrarca from the Quattrocento to the 21st Century*, Oxford: Legenda, 2020: 222-244.

Attridge, Derek. *The Singularity of Literature*. London and New York, NY: Routledge, 2004.

Attridge. Derek. *The Work of Literature*. Oxford: Oxford University Press, 2015.

Baudelaire, Charles. trans . Wagner, Jeffrey. *Selected Poems*. London: Panther, 1971.

Bergvall, Caroline. *Meddle English*. Callicoon, NY: Nightboat Books, 2011.

Bonney, Sean. *Happiness: Poems After Rimbaud*. London: Ukant Publications, 2012.

Brigden, Susan. *Thomas Wyatt: The Heart's Forest*. London: Faber and Faber, 2012.

DuPlessis, Rachel Blau. *The Pink Guitar, Writing as Feminist Practice,* New York and London: Routledge, 1990.

Goldsmith, Kenneth. *Uncreative Writing: Managing Language in the Digital Age*. New York: Columbia University Press, 2011.

Hilson, Jeff. ed. *The Reality Street Book of Sonnets*. Hastings: Reality Street, 2008.

Hughes, Peter. *Quite Frankly: After Petrarch's Sonnets*. Hastings: Reality Street, 2015.

MacSweeney, Barry. *Our Mutual Scarlet Boulevard*. London: Fulcrum, 1971.

Manson, Peter. *Stéphane Mallarmé; The Poems in Verse*. Oxford, Ohio: Miami University Press, 2012.

Mathews, Harry. *A Mid-Season Sky: Poems 1954-1991*. Manchester: Carcanet, 1992.

Moore, Nicholas. *Spleen*. London: Menard Press, 1990.

Petrarch, Francesco. trans. Musa, Mark. *Selections from the Canzoniere and Other Works*. Oxford and New York: Oxford University Press, 1985.

Petrarch, Francesco, *Canzoniere,* poem 3, at http://petrarch.petersadlon.com/canzoniere.html?poem=3 (accessed 7 May 2014)

Pujol i Duran, Jèssica, 'Multi-Atkins', Introduction to Tim Atkins, *Collected Petrarch*. London: Crater, 2014: i-iv.

Rimbaud, Arthur. trans. Schmidt, Paul. *Complete Works*. New York, London, etc: Harper Perennial, 2008.

Rossiter, William. *Chaucer and Petrarch*. Chaucer Studies. Cambridge: Boydell & Brewer, 2010.

Schiller, Friedrich. *On the Aesthetic Education of Man*. trans. Reginald Snell. Mineola: Dover Publications, 2004.

Sheppard, Robert. *The Poetry of Saying: British Poetry and Its Discontents, 1950-2000*. Liverpool: Liverpool University Press, 2005.

Sheppard, Robert. *Complete Twentieth Century Blues*. Cambridge: Salt Publications, 2008.

Sheppard, Robert. 'Poetics as Conjecture and Provocation: an inaugural lecture delivered on 13 March 2007 at Edge Hill University', *New Writing: The International Journal for the Theory and Practice of Creative Writing*, Vol 5: 1, 2008: 3-26.

Sheppard, Robert. 'Robert Sheppard on the Petrarch Boys', (December 2013) at www.robertsheppard.blogspot.co.uk/2013/12/robert-sheppard-on-petrarch-boys-peter.html (accessed 29 June 2014)

Sheppard, Robert. *A Translated Man*. Bristol: Shearsman Books, 2013.

Sheppard, Robert. *The Meaning of Form in Contemporary Innovative Poetry*, Cham: Palgrave Macmillan, 2016

Sheppard, Robert. *Petrarch 3: a derivative derive*. Izmir/Minneapolis: Crater 36, 2017, reprinted in Sheppard 2021a.

Sheppard, Robert. *Hap: Understudies of Thomas Wyatt's Petrarch*. Newton-le-Willows: Knives Forks and Spoons, 2018, reprinted in Sheppard 2021a.

Sheppard, Robert. *The English Strain*. Swindon: Shearsman Books, 2021a.

Sheppard, Robert. *Bad Idea*. Newton-le-Willows: Knives Forks and Spoons, 2021b.

Taylor, Simon Watson. ed. *French Writing Today*. Harmondsworth: Penguin Books, 1968.

Themerson, Stefan. *Bayamus and the Theatre of Semantic Poetry*. London: Gaberbocchus Press, 1965.

Verlaine, Paul. trans. Sorrell, Martin. *Selected Poems*. Oxford and New York, NY: Oxford University Press, 1999.

Two

The Necessity of Poetics

Despite the present prominence of the critic, it is to the poet we must turn for poetics. With few exceptions, those qualified to theorise about poetry are those who write it. And the most effective poetics take the form of an *apologia* for one particular style of writing – usually the poet's own. The nature of the *apologia* can vary enormously – from the brusque practicality of Pound's *Don'ts* to the introspective pondering of Valéry – but they are all stratagems of defence, and usually gain in polemical edge for being so. In addition to these qualities we find, in the finest poetics, a profound reserve before the fact of poetry, and a refusal to be dogmatic; after all, the great poems have usually broken laws (Romer 1982: 63).

Thus opens Stephen Romer's review of Jean-Claude Renard's poetics with a matter-of-factness that perhaps does not allow for the force of resistance towards poetics (in this country anyway) and perhaps lacks a sense of the speculative nature of poetics itself, but it does acknowledge the kinds of irony and ambiguity that colour relations between poetics and poetry (and writing more generally).

I present next a proliferation of definitions, deliberately miming poetics' own refusal of laws and templates, a mode which I believe best captures the spirit and meaning of the enterprise, its excitements, incitements and its spirit of exploration and innovation (and its occasional excessiveness).

Metapoetics: Definitions of Poetics

Poetics is the product of the process of reflection upon writings, and upon the act of writing, gathering from the past and from others, speculatively casting into the future.

Poetics is a discipline, though a flexible one.

Poetics is a discourse, though an intermittent mercurial one. Poetics is a writer-centred, self-organising activity.

Poetics is a way of letting writers question what they think they know.

Poetics is a way of allowing creative writing dialogue with itself, beyond the monologic of commentary or reflection.

Poetics exists for oneself and for others, to produce, to quote Rachel Blau DuPlessis, 'a permission to continue' (DuPlessis 1990: 156).

Poetics is not theory in the ordinary rationalistic sense.

'Poetics don't explain; they redress and address' (Bernstein 1992: 160).

Poetics is not practice in the ordinary empirical sense.

Poetics could be a test of practice; but practice will test poetics.

To talk of theoretical poetics is not accurate; to talk of practical poetics is no less accurate.

Poetics involves a theory of practice, a practice of theory.

Poetics, to take it back to Aristotle, where the category began, is distinguished from *theoria* or *praxis*, theory or practice, in the primacy of its activity of *making, poesis*. Poetics is the active questioning about how does, how should, how could, art be made.

Poetics is also to be distinguished from aesthetics and rhetoric.[1]

Poetics and poetry are only etymologically linked, dually from the Greek root *poiein*: to make.[2]

---

[1] 'Poiesis', writes Gerald F. Else, of Aristotle's *Poetics,* 'is the actual process of composition … is the activation, the putting to work of poietike' (Aristotle 1970: 79).

Poetics is not Aesthetics. Aesthetics is a contemplative analytic of art: what is art? what is beauty? what is the sublime?

Poetics is not Rhetoric. Rhetoric is to do with the laws of composition, not with the lore (or lure) of writing.

[2] Poetics within literary studies is used by structuralists like Todorov, *(Introduction to Poetics)* or by Bakhtin (*The Problem of Dostoyevsky's Poetics*) or even Harold Bloom, to speak of a theory of making that properly belongs to literary criticism. (It is common to read of the poetics of the novel, or of feminist biography, in this

Poetics only makes sense if your sense of art, artifice, artificer, is concentrated on the act of making, rather than self-expression.

Poetics is a secondary discourse, but is not 'after the event'; it does not simply react to making. The making can change the poetics; the poetics can change the making.

The aim of literary criticism, to parody Marx, is to describe writing; the purpose of poetics is to change it.

Poetics is born of a crisis – the need to change.

Poetics has a history as long as writing, because writing has always changed.

Poetics may be textually specific; or it might not be so focussed, not least of all if the 'examples' of which it speaks do not yet (and may never) exist.

'Poetics needn't be understood as explanations of some prior body of work' (Bernstein 1992: 154).

Poetics is a prospectus of work to be done, that might involve a summary of work already done.

Poetics is a speculative discourse, not a descriptive one.

Poetics says: look back, look forward, look straight ahead, and cross the page.

'One of the pleasures of poetics is to try on a paradigm … and see where *it* leads you' (Bernstein 1992: 161).

Poetics could be a *running* commentary, but it might overtake, or equally lag behind.

---

sense.) Poetics has also found many uses to describe various non-literary or even non-artistic kinds of making: in psychiatry to describe the making of self (auto-poesis); in musicology to describe the compositional (poietic) dimension of music. Titles like Bachelard's *The Poetics of Fire* adorn philosophy shelves.

Poetics' 'answers' are provisional, its trajectory nomadic, its positions temporary and strategic.

Poetics offers generative schema.

Poetics is more concerned with form than with content, but will not respect that boundary.

Micropoetics: whose domain is the text and its techniques; everything below the level of the text.

Macropoetics: whose domain is the text and the world: everything above the level of the text.[3]

One reason to make your poetics public is to test it, to build a community of writers, or of risk. The manifesto may be its gateway or its trap.

Poetics is contained in, and by, the great art manifestoes, both in the sense of being locatable there, and in the sense of being restricted. A manifesto colonizes the field of literary production, rather than opens it up.

Poetics can be located in Poe's term 'Philosophy of Composition' so long as it composes, decomposes, re-composes that 'philosophy'.

Poetics involves 'how to' (as in 'How To Write a Melodrama') as long as knack plays second fiddle to knowledge, as long as craft stays crafty.

A danger of poetics is that it might operate as self-justification, but when it does it will be settling into argument like someone embedding him or herself into an armchair to bore you with his or her monologue, reflections. It has ceased dialogue with the activity of making.

When poetics stops it becomes theory, retrospective rather than speculative, definitive rather than open to infinitude.

Poetics provides strategy for the writer. To look for truth value in its

---

[3] Bernstein writes: 'Equally at play in the context of poetics is the political and social situation, including the social configuration of poetry [writing] in terms of distribution, publishing, capitalization, jobs, awards, reviews' (Bernstein 1992: 157).

propositions may be beside the point for the writer, though it might not be for you, particularly if you are another writer. It speaks to a working practice as much as it speaks to you.

Poetics is not about creating equilibrium, but about causing a structured disequilibrium.

'Poetics becomes an activity that is ongoing, that moves in different directions at the same time, and that tries to disrupt or problematize any formulation that seems too final or preemptively restrictive' (Bernstein 1992: 150).

Poetics may involve strategic self-deception.

Poetics may mismatch the writing that results. It is not necessarily a ground plan. Poetics as snapshots, thumbnails.

Some poetics contains a goodly portion of gobbledegook; it may be a strategy to get texts moving, to get the writer creatively into spaces that otherwise might not be accessed, or to divert attention away from the creative act.

Poetics may not judge the *use* of its findings well.

'The test of a poetics,' to adapt Charles Bernstein, 'is the [writing] and the [writerly] thinking that results' (Bernstein 1992: 166).

Poetics steals from anywhere.

Poetics finds things by accident, by mistake.[4]

Poetics takes structural homologies from science and philosophy, but also from gardening and pinball, if it needs to.

---

[4] Looking for a book to put the slips of paper containing the above 'definitions' of poetics safely in, I took down one containing some uncollected essays by Robert Duncan. One, entitled 'The Poetics of Music: Stravinsky' (1948) begins with a slightly overpassive definition but one which reminds us of the term's use in the other arts: 'Poetics is the contemplation of the meaning of form: it is what is common to painting, music, sculpture and poetry. *Poiein*, Stravinsky reminds us, means *to make*. We might keep in mind that in the days of William Dunbar the poets were the Makaris' (Faas 1983: 335).

Poetics breathes creative potential into uncreative material.

Poetics is not *just* a discourse, a way of thinking, saying or writing about making, but a discursive practice with rules of its own.

Poetics can never offer readings of the writer's literary works. He or she cannot read his or her own work as a critic.

Poetics, of necessity, makes its practitioners creative readers as well as writers.

Poetics is a way of reading or misreading texts (in the widest sense) not normally thought of as poetics: to refunction their discourses as part of its own. The infuriating magpie descends upon science or aesthetics, theory or history, rhetoric or popular culture, even the author's own earlier work. All the discourses that are poetics' Others.[5]

'Poetics as an invasion of the poetic into other realms: overflowing the bounds of genres, spilling into talk, essays, politics, philosophy...' (Bernstein 1992: 151).

Poetics doesn't always call itself poetics.

Poetics is mercurial enough for writers to not know that they are producing it, to think that they are constructing something else: a letter, a preface, an apology, a defence, an essay, a memo, a diary or journal entry, even an art work, a manifesto, a job application, a lecture, a description of somebody else's poetics, a conference paper, a witty aphorism, an anthology, an editorial,

---

[5] Poetics at one limit is apoetics, formulations that deconstruct poetics, as the continuous lower case typography on the extra title page of Bernstein's *A Poetics* suggests: 'a p o e t i c s'. (Bernstein 1992: vii). In this sense, poetics must eat itself! At another limit is anti-poetics, a discourse that accompanies the practice of not, or no longer, writing, as in the pronouncements of Laura Riding (see Seymour Smith 1970) or John Hall's 'Writing and Not Writing' (in Riley 1992:41-49). See my essay on the latter in Sheppard 2011, 'The Price of Houses the Cost of Food: The Poetics of Not Writing': 55-67. Other essays in this volume treat the poetics of Ken Edwards and Maggie O'Sullivan, as well as the communal poetics of the Poetry Society 1976 and the cultural poetics of Iain Sinclair. Also of note is Sheppard 2008: 'Poetics as Conjecture and Provocation: an inaugural lecture delivered on 13 March 2007 at Edge Hill University', included in this volume.

a biography of the mind, a questionnaire, being tape interviewed, having a drink, making comments between reading texts to a creative writing group, dreaming, reading a book, summarising Western metaphysics on the back of an envelope, pillow talk…

Poetics could be a commonplace book full of favoured quotations.

Poetics could be a sentence from a novel you use as an epigraph to a half-written project, which you remove once the project is completed.

Poetics often appears as, results in, hybrid texts.

Poetics can appear in the creative work itself, as content, as theme or aside.

Every literary work *is* a statement of poetics itself, as a formal statement about its own form, a model for itself, as it were.

When poetics absorbs a writer's politics, cosmology, philosophy, religion, it becomes most luminous and individual, but less communal, less of use, perhaps even to the writer him or herself.

Writers who say they have *no poetics* should logically find no continuity between any of their texts, but also no change. That they do is the inauguration of their discursive practice of poetics.

Poetics disappears at moments of intense creative fruition, until the next moment of critical reflection and change.

A test to see if you've produced explicit poetics is to ask of your discourse about writing: is this literary theory or literary criticism? If the answer is 'Neither of these,' then it *might* be poetics. (If the answer is yes, it *might* still 'contain' poetics.)

Poetics is an intermittent discourse, and when it is found in literary criticism, it is *revealed* there rather than contained.

Poetics could re-read the literary canon (or any literature) as it re-reads everything else.

Poetics could be a bridge back to literary criticism, built upon the making of texts rather than upon its rhetoric or effects.

'Resisting the institutionalization of interpretation', says Charles Bernstein, 'is a motivation for poetics' (Bernstein 1992: 157).

Poetics could shape the way we read work.

Another danger of poetics is that it could present the 'ideological imaginary' to prejudge reading, to offer preferred reading strategies of literary works to readers, as Jerome J. McGann says of Romantic Ideology[6] (McGann 1983: 1). This can be countered by keeping poetics speculative, to avoid the armchair monologue. Or in formal terms, by keeping the documents open to future readings, by use of hybrid or discontinuous forms, to internalise gestural poetics into their presentation.

Poetics should be written (and read) with an awareness of its function in the creative process.

Poetics should be studied as such.

Poetics can stop being absorbed by the metalanguage of literary theory or criticism by asserting its own claims as a discourse, a language game with its own players, rules and purposes.

Poetics in hybrid, fragmentary, collage, playful, jokey, patapoetical, forms, avoids co-option into the explication of the writing that results.

Poetics' function is both oriented towards, and in, new form.

---

[6] McGann argues that 'Literary criticism too often likes to transform the critical illusions of poetry into the worshipped truths of culture' (McGann 1983: 135). In poetry 'we can to a degree, observe as well our own ways of thinking and feeling from an alien point of view. That alienated vantage, which is poetry's critical gift to every future age, permits us a brief glimpse at our world and our selves' (McGann 1983: 66). Perhaps a similar critical function for the writer of contemporary poetics might reside in the poetics of past ages.

> But the world we share, & our interplay with it, calls again & again
> for *discourse*: in the case of Poets, the setting forth of a poetics.
> *Jerome Rothenberg* (Rothenberg, 1981: 3)

In the preceding definitions, I have adopted an unacknowledged Foucauldian vocabulary in describing poetics as a 'discourse', which requires further exposition. Whereas followers of Michel Foucault conceive of discourse as 'a type of language associated with an institution, and which includes the ideas and statements that express an institution's values', I argue that the *ordering* and *categorising* of poetics is something that has barely begun, and that its elements have been located in different categories rather than in any single institution (Danaher 2000: x). It ranges historically from treatises for gentlemen on the composition of verses, through literary criticism (even as it developed as an autonomous discourse); or even in bland bibliographical designations such as 'authors' miscellaneous prose' or the 'literary interview'. Poetics is not necessarily a shared form of writing; it has an ambivalent social location. 'Poetics' is not (yet) a unifying principle to structure and arrange a discourse; although an often-used term, it has seldom been defined. (In the volume entitled *The Poetics of the New American Poetry*, for example, the meaning of poetics is taken for granted by the editors.) I use poetics as a central principle in a method to *constellate* various writings that only constitute a discourse if viewed perspectivally, and retrospectively.

The effect of this indetermination is that there has been little historical consciousness in both the writing and the reading of the discourse to date, little evidence of a 'tradition' of poetics in the traditional sense, even though one can trace a loose history of its proto-forms and development, as I shall show. One has to admit there is also a refreshing lack of a need for discursive legitimation. Unlike the body of knowledge built up in the social sciences, for example, where references to the theories of Weber or Kuhn (or Foucault, of course) are almost obligatory if the discourse is to be *legitimate*, it is not thought necessary to refer (back) to the poetics of Alexander Pope or Ezra Pound, S.T. Coleridge or Clark Coolidge as 'authorities' in quite the same way, in order to demonstrate that the discourse *is* legitimate – part of the discourse rather than outside of it, professional rather than amateur – amongst the fraternity of its users. This is not to say that, in specific local circumstances, in focussed works of poetics, amongst groups of poets, these figures do not carry authority as writers of previous poetics; think of

Pound's position as a provider of poetic strategies and categories amongst the North American avant-garde. But in other groups, say, among the Movement Orthodoxy in Great Britain, his influence is less and his name often a by-word for incoherent thinking. In other words, these names – and many others – do not operate as what Foucault dubs 'founders of discursivity' for poetics – in the same way that he says Marx dominates the 'ism' to which he gave his name, or Freud, who spread his foundation-ness over an entire discipline: those 'figures who provide a paradigmatic set of terms, images, and concepts which organize thinking' across an entire field of cultural production (Rabinow 1986: 25). Not even Aristotle, who wrote the first 'Poetics', operates in quite this way now, although he did, as part of the general reverence in Western thinking towards classical models in the proto-poetics of the past; in the works of Horace, Dante and Ben Jonson, he is quoted as an authority, but as the founder of categorising philosophy as a whole rather than as a founder of the specific discourse of poetics (which he never practised if we strictly refer to 'writerly' poetics). The mercurial nature of poetics since modernism at least – the magpie nature of its inspiration, the piebald gathering of its writings, its discontinuous discursivity – make this foundation-ness difficult to maintain. When all this is combined with more individualised aspects of its practice, such as the necessary distance a writer might want to preserve between creativity and conceptualisation, for fear of fixing his or her own image as a writer through an authoritative poetics which he or she cannot escape with ease, we can imagine that few writers would care to identify so completely with the activity of poetics that their own 'creative' work would become eclipsed. It would be as though Pound were willing to become known solely as the theorist and master of ceremonies of Imagism and not as the author of *The Cantos*. More practically speaking, writing poetics cannot be a full-time occupation since it implies another occupation, or is best thought of as an integral part of literary authorship as that has developed into the modern era. Perhaps most writers also know that they can seldom provide, or would want to provide, 'paradigmatic' terms and concepts through their poetics, and that poetics tends to be paradigm-breaking rather than paradigm-shifting, permissive rather than dismissive, locally organising rather than globally organising (either for a group or individually).

Whether or not poetics can (or would want to) claim founders for its discursivity, Foucault writes that

> To expand a type of discursivity, such as psychoanalysis as founded
> by Freud, is not to give it a formal generality that it would not

have permitted at the outset, but rather to open it to a certain number of applications … In addition, one does not declare certain propositions in the work of these founders to be false: instead … one sets aside those statements that are not pertinent … Reexamining Freud's texts modifies psychoanalysis itself (Rabinow 1986: 25).

'Opening up' parts of poetics may be thought of as an exemplary strategy for those wishing to build a new poetics using elements of older thinking, but such an activity lacks the emphasis in Foucault's last clause on whether the discourse and its practices will be 'modified' in any definitive sense.

Of course, apprehension of that 'modification' *may* become visible if poetics is seen through time, via something like a Foucauldian framework. It would seem more a discursive practice, at least in its thinking *about* poetics – metapoetics as I define it – if not in the writing of the discourse itself, which, I suspect, may of necessity remain too intermittent and wild for such discursive decorum. On the other hand, Foucault's rejection of 'proving' the falsity of earlier statements of a discourse is in accord with my thinking here about how poetics develops. Re-examination of Coleridge or Coolidge can further poetics itself, modifying without permanently re-modelling, 'trying on a paradigm' as Bernstein experimentally and experientially puts it, rather than providing paradigmatic sets of organising principles (Bernstein 1992: 161). Previous poetics usefully can be 'set aside' if they do not provoke writing or thinking that results in creative writing.

If we follow Foucault in declaring that 'such discourses as economics, medicine, grammar, the science of living beings give rise to certain organizations of concepts, certain regroupings of objects, certain types of enunciation, which form, according to their degree of coherence, rigour, and stability, themes or theories,' may we effortlessly add 'poetics' to his list? (Foucault 2002: 71). While my task is not Foucault's – 'to discover how such' themes and theories 'are distributed in history' – it is not impossible to discern the presence and persistence of concepts, objects and so on in poetics (Foucault 2002: 71). Certain weak themes can be detected, for example, in the theories of rhythm during the age of free verse – Pound, Loy, Lawrence, Zukofsky and Mayakovsky can be found testing their theories – but they offer conjecture rather than definition. Even Pound with his 'brusque practicality' cannot claim to adjudicate the whole field of poetic production, although it is important to remember the level of factional antagonism inherent in avant-garde formations, particularly where poetics finds its functions compromised by the more territorial claims of the 'manifesto'. Indeed, Foucault's conception of discourse is not monolithic: he writes of finding a paradoxical 'system of dispersion', in accord with both my sense of situated constellations and the position-taking of avant-gardes.

> Whenever one can describe, between a number of statements, such a system of dispersion, whenever, between objects, types of statement, concepts, or thematic choices, one can define a regularity (an order, correlations, positions and functionings, transformations), we will say, for the sake of convenience, that we are dealing with a *discursive formation*.... (Foucault 2002: 41).

He argues that it is 'a space of multiple dissensions' and his analysis must 'maintain discourse in all its many irregularities', a formulation that looks not unlike poetics as I have defined it with a care I hope is commensurate with its possible *forms* (Foucault 2002: 173).

Another of the components of Foucault's theory of discourse, touched on but not commented on above, complicates this dispersion: that is, a discourse's reliance upon institutions to mediate and propagate it. 'In every society the production of discourse is at once controlled, selected, organized and redistributed according to a certain number of procedures, whose role is to avert its powers and its dangers,' Foucault says, procedures that rely on 'institutional support: it is both reinforced and accomplished by whole strata of practices such as pedagogy – naturally – the book system, publishing, libraries' (quoted in Golding 2006: 24). While the discourses Foucault analyses are more universal in their impact than poetics as I have defined it, it is true that its procedures are not institutionalised in this way (as a recognisable discourse), and indeed in the areas of contemporary poetry they often barely exist, limited to what Charles Bernstein calls the 'provisional institutions' of marginalized poetries (Bernstein 1999: 145), such as fugitive publishing of magazines and books, readings and – importantly for poetics – *talks* series; indeed, non- or anti-institutionalization might be part of its strategy, as Bernstein suggests (in a passage quoted in one of the preceding definitions). The antagonistic landscape of recent poetries (on both sides of the Atlantic) affects poetics, in that energy is spent (wasted, even) on defining poetic activity against another group (or individual) but it is also true that the lack of institutional reinforcement keeps poetics relatively free of forces that might avert its powers and danger, and precisely *institutionalise* it. (However, the poetics of any 'mainstream' poetry can be said to have one identifiable institution, in Britain at least, the school and higher education syllabus, but that is a subject beyond the scope of this essay.)

Poetics, as I have defined it, at this stage of its development, is a weak case of a Foucauldian discursive formation, but one still deserving of the name. The lesson remains: poetics must be read differentially, not deferentially.

FROM ARISTOTLE TO NOMADIC POETICS: SOME EXAMPLES

Poetics has a long history: from Aristotle, through Horace, into (in English anyway) Sidney, Puttenham, Campion, Dryden and Pope (both in verse), Mary Robinson's essay on her 'Sappho and Phaon', onto Wordsworth's 'Preface', Coleridge's *Biographia*, the assertions of Shelley's *Defence*, some of Keats' letters. Onto: Henry James' essays and *Prefaces*, and DH Lawrence's spirited defences of both free verse poetry and the modern novel – to summarise the contents page of a possible volume of historical poetics. (My rough chronology of these and other (later) documents may be found online).[7]

In the twentieth century the discourse of poetics proliferated. The intense artistic innovation of the era demanded such a discourse, not least in the manifestoes and documents of the great modernist and post-modernist movements from Dada to Situationism, from Negritude to Neo-HooDoo, from Stein's 'Lectures' to DuPlessis' feminist poetics, to take a few examples from the two volumes of *Poems for the Millennium*, edited by Jerome Rothenberg and Pierre Joris (Rothenberg and Joris 1995 and 1998).

A well-known collection such as Allen and Tallman's *The Poetics of The New American Poetry* (1973) collected documents ranging from Pound's group manifestoes to Frank O'Hara's patapoetical one man movement statement 'Personism', from Lorca's essay on 'duende' to Olson's influential 'Projectivist Verse' essay. America, as if asserting its cultural autonomy, seems particularly attracted to the discourse, from the Imagists to the

---

[7] My blogzine *Pages* (robertsheppard.blogspot.com) carries a serial catalogue of hundreds of examples of historical and contemporary poetics under the title 'The History of Poetics', in four parts, beginning here: robertsheppard.blogspot.com/2009/06/robert-sheppard-poetics-1-poetics-and.html.

Language Poets. In Britain this has not been the case, certainly since the Apocalyptic Manifestoes of the war years. To think of Basil Bunting's dust jacket disavowal of meaning in poetry alongside the critical corpus of his mentor, Ezra Pound, is emblematic.

However, one of the most prolific examples of twentieth century poetics comes from the British Isles. In 1944, Scottish poet Hugh MacDiarmid published parts of a long associative list poem – he called it a 'testament' (MacDiarmid 1985: 1030) – written in the late 1930s, entitled 'The Kind of Poetry I Want' as the backbone of a chapter of his intellectual autobiography *Lucky Poet*, in order to argue for a poetry of fact and wonder, 'a poetry full of erudition, expertise, and ecstasy', as he put it (MacDiarmid 1985: 1019). Politically it is 'a poetry that stands for production, use, and life,/ As opposed to property, profits and death' (MacDiarmid 1985: 1023), and for the development of a modern consciousness of 'super-individuality … to assimilate, utilize, override, and fuse/ All our individual divergences', a fusion that would represent a technological, artistic, scientific, and political synthesis of World Thought – Eastern as well as Western, folk and popular as well as high cultural, with MacDiarmid's international Communism perfectly counterpointing his Scottish Nationalism (MacDiarmid 1985: 1004-5).

This example makes me wonder whether there is something essentially 'English' about a refusal to *theorize* in poetics, as in other areas? Does philosophical empiricism rule the day (which matches the continuing lyric empiricism of the dominant post-Movement orthodoxy itself) – or is it the geopolitical centrality of the English imagination, and its refusals of the necessity of poetics, the defensive and normative restrictive practices of the colonial centre? It may well be that a declaration of independence (cultural or poetic) generates more necessity than an act of union!

One exception (and to remember that poetics pertains to all genres) is a collection by Malcolm Bradbury, a pioneer of creative writing teaching at the University of East Anglia, who saw the value of poetics, though I do not remember him using the word when I was a student of his. His anthology *The Novel Today* (1977) still constitutes an important sourcebook for the poetics of fiction: from Doris Lessing's influential Preface to *The Golden Notebook*, to the in-the-thick-of-it 'Notes on an Unfinished Novel' by John Fowles, which are preliminary studies for *The French Lieutenant's Woman*, along with some American and continental poetics, such as pieces by John Barth and Robbe-Grillet.

With respect to the more adventurous British poetry, Eric Mottram, in his still-uncollected essays, delineated a poetics deriving from the American modernist inheritance, although his polemics often obscured its positive aspects. However, he did coax poetics out of dozens of recalcitrant poets in his interviews, chiefly in the context of 'Poetry Information' evenings at the ICA during the 1960s and at the Poetry Society during the 1970s, which, transcribed, were mostly published in the important magazine *Poetry Information*. One such interview, with Roy Fisher, also forms part of one of the few British Poetry Revival publications to rival the American collections of interviews with single poets. Roy Fisher's *Interviews Through Time and Selected Prose* (2000) includes 90 pages of various interviews garnered at various times, by various methods ranging from face to face to email exchange. There have also been valuable interviews spread among the pages of little magazines, and some of these are collected, and augmented by especially commissioned interviews, in Tim Allen and Andrew Duncan's *Don't Start Me Talking: Interviews with Contemporary Poets* (2006) with British and Irish poets, ranging from so-called Cambridge poets Andrew Crozier and David Chaloner to younger poets such as Sean Bonney and Peter Manson, as well as independent voices such as R.F. Langley and Elisabeth Bletsoe.

One pioneering example of British poetics is Denise Riley's edited volume *Poets on Writing* (1992), which contains a rare number of essays of poetics as well as a selection from Veronica-Forrest Thomson's important *Poetic Artifice*. But tellingly, Tom Raworth provides a selection of (presumably) his most recent poems from *Eternal Sections* under the inviting banner: 'The State of Poetry Today' in a typically British refusal to tackle that very theme in a discursive way! The seventeen-year gap between this volume and Rupert Loydell's poetics anthology *Troubles Swapped for Something Fresh: Manifestos and Unmanifestos* (2009) is telling, but the latter volume demonstrates the full range of poetics as a discourse.

[*Atlantic Drift*, which I co-edited with James Byrne (2017), presents a selection of transatlantic poetry and poetics, the pieces often written especially for our volume, and features many women and women of colour: Andrea Brady, Sophie Collins, Lyn Hejinian, Bhanu Kapil, Geraldine Monk, Valzhyna Mort, Érin Moure, M. NourbeSe Phillip, Claudia Rankine, Zoë Skoulding and Rosmarie Waldrop, a deliberate rejoinder to the male-dominated taxonomies of poetics.]

The only reason to make a poetics public is to share with others, either collectively as a manifesto, or agonistically as position statement – in both cases it is a social fact, and implies at least community of exchange or risk. These have not been the favoured British options; there is little explicit work (although it doubtless exists, implicitly, as private meditation and notebook jottings, etc…). This is one reason why the pedagogy of creative writing seems central to me, particularly as the advocate of a particular poetics myself (and again the evidence of creative writing is seen in Loydell's collection).[8]

The Flavour of Poetics

I want to focus on three well-known texts to give a flavour of poetics and to suggest that it is not the preserve of the avant-garde (although I will add some flavours from that area too). The first is an example of the revelation of poetics in literary criticism. T.S. Eliot's essay 'The Metaphysical Poets' (1921) contains this memorable passage that describes the multifaceted complexity he located in John Donne, but in terms which are obviously constructing the poetics of *The Waste Land*, which he was then composing. The slippage from Donne to typewriter is a giveaway.

> A thought to Donne was an experience; it modified his sensibility. When a poet's mind is perfectly equipped for its work, it is constantly amalgamating disparate experience; the ordinary man's experience is chaotic, irregular, fragmentary. The latter falls in love, or reads Spinoza, and these two experiences have nothing to do with each other, or with the noise of the typewriter or the smell of cooking; in the mind of the poet these experiences are always forming new wholes (Eliot 1975: 64).

This is only one revealing example in Eliot's work, as JCC Mays has pointed out: 'When he writes about tradition and the individual talent, he described how his allusive method works; when he wrote about a dissociation of

---

[8] Loydell (2009) contains a number of pieces that derive from creative writing research at Edge Hill University. Cliff Yates' piece 'Flying: A Poetics' (28-38) and Andrew Taylor's piece 'The Poetry of Absence' (4-17) – both fragmentary aphorisms and quotations – come directly from PhDs written there. Scott Thurston's piece 'Acrreted Statement (Notes)' (123-131) was written after such study. My own 'A Voice Without', 'Not Another Poem' are reprinted in *Berlin Bursts*, Exeter: Shearsman Books (2011), which also contains the poetics piece 'Rattling the Bones (for Adrian Clarke)'. See my 'Experiment in Practice and Speculation in Poetics' in *Teaching Modernist Poetry*, ed. by Peter Middleton and Nicky Marsh (Basingstoke: Palgrave Macmillan, 2010: 158-69) for statements about how pedagogy, practice and poetics relate to one another.

sensibility taking place in the seventeenth-century mind he described the subject of his own poetry; when he wrote of the objective correlative in *Hamlet,* he defined its method' (Mays 1994: 115).

While my critical and writerly focus is upon the poetics of poetry, the existence of poetics for other genres may be exemplified by my next two examples. Samuel Beckett's 'Three Dialogues' (1949) looks like a carefully orchestrated Socratic exchange on aesthetics, apparently on visual art, but it contains what looks more like a credo for the rest of Beckett's novelistic, dramatic and poetic career – he was already writing the trilogy – a new art premised upon 'the expression that there is nothing to express, nothing with which to express, nothing from which to express, no power to express, no desire to express, together with the obligation to express' (Esslin 1965: 17).

Salman Rushdie's speech (originally delivered ventriloquially by Pinter) 'Is Nothing Sacred?' (1990) carves out a space for the novel in terms reminiscent of Henry James' poetics of the house of fiction, as well as Bakhtin's sense of polyphony, whilst integrating Lyotard, Foucault and Rorty into his poetics, all delivered with the *brio* of Lawrence: 'Literature is the one place in any society where, within the secrecy of our own heads, we can *hear voices talking about everything in every possible way*' (Rushdie 1991: 429).

Two prominent examples of poetics in my own research area of American language poetry and British linguistically innovative poetry are Allen Fisher's *Necessary Business* (1985) and Charles Bernstein's 'The Artifice of Absorption' (1986) (Bernstein 1992: 9-89). Without repeating a comparative analysis available elsewhere (Sheppard 1999b), these two formally hybrid texts constitute exemplary poetics. Fisher's text is an essay collaged into interviews with poets. In it, or rather, through it, he manufactures a poetics for himself, one that others may use and develop. (See Sheppard 1999a and the long account in Thurston 2002). Similarly, Bernstein, who presents a verse-essay, plays off the conventions of the essay (footnotes and quotations) against the conventions of poetry (chiefly line breaks) to produce an oddly associational and playful 'patapoetics'. It refuses to settle the arguments it presents, chiefly through a monstrous proliferation of new critical terms and manifold examples. It is also comic! Both documents keep the arguments open by their dispositions in form. They refuse the essay discourse they approximate and, most importantly, they demonstrate and *embody* their two authors' poetic practices, the collage of Fisher and the playful mixture of discourses found in most poems by Bernstein.

Bernstein himself provides a further model that it is worth acknowledging. After two decades of consciously producing poetics outside of the academy he fronted the Poetics Program at the State University of New York at Buffalo for a number of years, which favours an 'interdisciplinary approach to literary, cultural and textual studies' ('Poetics' 1999: 1). It focuses upon poetics as 'an unruly, multisubjective activity' ('Poetics' 1999: 3). Reference to the massive Electronic Poetry Center website the program administers (wings.buffalo.edu/epc) reveals it as a model institution, for its many poetics documents. This site inevitably includes links with what has been called *Cyberpoetics*: how the now not so new technologies may be used in literary creation. Documents relating to cyberpoetics may also be found in the two volume *Poems for the Millennium* which Jerome Rothenberg and Pierre Joris edited (Rothenberg and Joris 1998: 817-829). That the experience of compiling these volumes was itself an act of poetics is evidenced by Pierre Joris' *Towards a Nomadic Poetics* which, like *Necessary Business,* was first published by Allen Fisher's own Spanner press. Its millennial appeal to a nomadic sense of 'moving & connecting all contents, languages, bodies, machines' (Joris 1999: 29) has provoked comment, both for and against. Whatever the arguments for a nomadic poetics, it is clear that poetics, as I have defined it, has always been nomadic.

Don't Explain

None of the above poetics *explain* works of art. They permit. Explanation is not to the point of poetics. But why do I think that poetics cannot, or better not, describe? Part of the story, as I've hinted above, derives from the usefulness of poetics; but there is another, perhaps deeper, reason, that we should consider. As C.G. Jung stated:

> Being essentially the instrument for his work he (the artist) is subordinate to it and we have no reason for expecting him to interpret it for us. He has done the best that is in him by giving it form and he must leave interpretation to others and to the future (Jung 1967: 9).

Being *the* self and in his or her tightly scheduled now, how can the writer provide this kind of discourse, or be the work's reader? As I read, as I do, poetry magazines from cover to cover, I occasionally come upon my own work. Try as I may, I cannot get it to inhabit the same space as the poems that surround it. I cannot read it, partly because as I read I read every design decision I made to complete it. There are palimpsest versions beneath the text. It is like trying to look at the back of my head; I cannot map it with a freshness reading requires.

Writers, in any case, are notoriously bad at reading their own work; indeed, that they deliberately misread it in the service of speculating about future works is a constituent of poetics. This can be very productive, but is baffling for critics and for readers, who expect the kind of match they themselves might provide.

There have been a few examples where artists have been compelled to become their own works' explainers. I would like to mention one of the most notorious of these. In 1946 Malcolm Lowry, faced with a hostile reader's report and the threat of non-publication, was forced to write Jonathan Cape a thirty page letter, explaining, chapter-by-chapter, the meaning of his novel *Under the Volcano*, and was forced to evaluate it, and write about it like this: 'The chapter is a sort of bridge, it was written with extreme care… It is an entity, a unity in itself, as are all the other chapters; it is, I claim, dramatic, amusing, and within its limits I think is entirely successful' (Lowry 1967: 72). This strikes the false note of impossibility. Indeed, the letter and the novel together might constitute an anti-model for the creative writing PhD as I envisage it: a text and commentary by an exegete who is also the writer. Put thus, and admittedly as rhetorical as any story, does it not sound narcissistic? And if not that, then possibly harmful? Especially when it is recalled that, unmentioned in the letter, which is discursive and explicatory, Lowry attempted suicide at the anguish of this epistolary nightmare.

The letter ends, though, with a piece of writerly poetics, one which actually shows the futility of the exercise itself (and indeed it deconstructs the notion of the monologic reading implied by reading one's own work): 'For the book was so designed, counterdesigned and interwelded that it could be read an indefinite number of times and still not have yielded all its meanings or its drama or its poetry' (Lowry 1967: 88). And not all of those meanings are accessible to one reader, let alone the writer, with his or her unique memories of the experience of having conceived and written it (and in Lowry's case, re-written it).

1999/2000/2002/2011

WORKS CITED

Allen, D., and Tallman, W., (eds.), 1973, *Poetics of the New American Poetry*, New York: Grove Books.

Allen, T. and Duncan, A., (eds.), 2006, *Don't Start Me Talking: Interviews with Contemporary Poets*. Cambridge: Salt.

Aristotle, (trans. Else, G.F.), 1970, *Poetics*, Ann Arbor, MI: The University of Michigan.

Bernstein, C. 1992, *A Poetics*, Cambridge, MA: Harvard University Press.

Bradbury, M. 1977, *The Novel Today*, Glasgow: Collins/Fontana.

Byrne, J. and R. Sheppard, 2017, *Atlantic Drift: an Anthology of Poetry and Poetics*. Todmorden: Arc and EHUP.

Danaher, G., Schirato, T., and Webb, J. 2000, *Understanding Foucault*. London, Thousand Oaks; Delhi: Sage.

DuPlessis, R.B., 1990, *The Pink Guitar, Writing as Feminist Practice*, New York and London: Routledge.

Eliot, T.S., 1975, *Selected Prose*, London: Faber and Faber.

Esslin, M. (ed.), 1965, *Samuel Beckett*, New Jersey: Prentice-Hall.

Faas, E.,1983, *Young Robert Duncan*, Santa Barbara, CA: Black Sparrow Press.

Foucault, M. 2002, *The Archaeology of Knowledge*, London and New York: Routledge Classics.

Fisher, A. 1985, *Necessary Business*, London: Spanner.

Fisher, R. 2000, *Interviews Through Time and Selected Prose*. Kentisbeare: Shearsman Books.

Golding, A. 2006, 'Experimental Poetics and/as Pedagogy', in eds. Retallack, J. and Spahr, J. *Poetry and Pedagogy*. New York and Basingstoke: Palgrave Macmillan.

Joris, P., 1999, *Notes Towards a Nomadic Poetics*, Spanner 38.

Jung, C.J., quoted by Ezra Pound in Foreword to Pound., E. 1967, *Selected Cantos of Ezra Pound*, London: Faber and Faber.

Lowry, M. 1967, *Selected Letters of Malcolm Lowry*, New York: Capricorn Books.

Loydell, R. (ed.), 2009, *Troubles Swapped for Something Fresh: Manifestos and Unmanifestos*, Cambridge: Salt.

MacDiarmid, H. 1985. *The Complete Poems (Volumes 1 and 2)*, Harmondsworth: Penguin.

MacGann, J. 1983, *The Romantic Ideology*, Chicago: University of Chicago Press.

Mays, J.C.C., 'The Early Poems' in Moody, A.D. 1994, *The Cambridge Companion to T.S. Eliot*, Cambridge: Cambridge University Press.

'Poetics': 'Poetics at Buffalo', at wings. buffalo.edu/epc/poetics/prog.html: accessed 1 March 1999.

Riley, D. (ed.), 1992, *Poets on Writing*, Basingstoke and London: Macmillan.

Rabinow, P. (ed.), 1984, *The Foucault Reader*, London: Penguin.

Romer, S. 1982, 'Correctives', *PN Review* 27: pp. 63-64

Rothenberg, J. 1981, *Pre-Faces and Other Writings*. New York: New Directions.

Rothenberg, J., and Joris, P. (eds.), 1995, *Poems for the Millennium, Volume One from Fin-de-Siècle to Negritude*, Berkeley and Los Angeles: University of California Press.

Rothenberg, J., and Joris, P. (eds.), 1998, *Poems for the Millennium, Volume Two from Postwar to Millennium*, Berkeley and Los Angeles: University of California Press.

Rushdie, S. 1990. *Is Nothing Sacred: The Herbert Read Memorial Lecture: 6 February 1990*. Granta: First American Edition. No place of publication.

Seymour Smith, M.,1970, 'Laura Riding's "Rejection of Poetry"', *The Review*, no. 23.

Sheppard, R. 1999a. *Far Language, poetics and linguistically innovative poetry 1978–1997*, Exeter: Stride Research Documents.

Sheppard, R. 1999b. 'The Poetics of Poetics: Charles Bernstein, Allen Fisher and the poetic thinking that results', *Symbiosis*, 3:4.

Sheppard, R. 2002, *The End of the Twentieth Century: Twentieth Century Blues 63*, Liverpool: Ship of Fools, re-published in *Complete Twentieth Century Blues*. Cambridge: Salt Publishing, 2007.

Sheppard, R. 'Poetics as Conjecture and Provocation: an inaugural lecture delivered on 13 March 2007 at Edge Hill University', *New Writing*. Vol 5: 1 (2008): pp. 3-26.

Sheppard, R. 2011, *When Bad Times Made for Good Poetry*, Exeter: Shearsman.

Thurston, S. 2002, *Rescale: Method and Technique in Contemporary Poetry*, University of Lancaster (Edge Hill): PhD thesis.

Speaking Differently:
Poetics in the Twenty-first Century:
Pierre Joris and Adrian Clarke
(with reference to the poetics of Maggie O'Sullivan)

The writings writers write about writing have been curiously misread.

Battling with the impossibility of being their own readers, writers are drawn to fuzzy logic when it comes to thinking and externalising their thinking about the purpose, activity, outcomes, and future of writing that results in text that can be unstable in a variety of ways, and is sometimes difficult to read.

My first principle is that there is enough commonality about these writings to group them as members of a discourse, one called 'poetics'. A prospective study of poetics – 'metapoetics' – is best conducted using examples which orient themselves in form, towards form, and reveal themselves as hybrid and playful, fragmented or highly formal, or that reflect the writing practice which is reviewed or projected. Patapoetics, embedded poetics in literary works, hybrid-essays – all these limit cases offer fuller scope for investigation than the pure essay, though, of course, there is still room for the apparently straightforward, and often brief, 'statement' (which, statistically, I would judge, is the dominant form of poetics).[1]

It is important to focus upon generic questions about the discourse as well as the particulars of various poetics. The former focus conforms to metapoetics; the latter tends to become a kind of poetics itself or a species of literary criticism, in which case one is drawn into the ideas rather than standing apart to test the forms of ideation.

First, I want to draw a distinction between poetics and manifestoes, to crystallise the nature of each. Manifestoes may contain poetics (sometimes) but poetics itself is a more mercurial discourse, speculative, conjectural and provocative, suggestive of formal possibilities for the art practice concerned. Mary Ann Caws helps to clarify this discrimination: 'As if defining a moment of crisis, the manifesto generally proclaims what it wants to oppose, to leave, to defend, to change. Its oppositional tone is constructed of *againstness*' (Caws 2001: xxiii). This 'tone' is absent from

---

[1] See my inventory of poetics, in four parts, beginning here: robertsheppard.blogspot.com/2009/06/robert-sheppard-poetics-1-poetics-and.html.

poetics in its purer forms, as Stephen Romer reminds us: 'We find in the finest poetics, a profound reserve before the fact of poetry, and a refusal to be dogmatic' (Romer 1982: 63). Although there may be provocation in its exhortations, poetics will be provocative of artistic innovation or change.

Apparently contrary to this distinction, literary critic Donald Wesling asserts that 'poetics resides largely in the more strident form of the manifesto' (Wesling 1980: 104). However, his characterisation of manifesto poetics since modernism is illustrative in that he balances what I call the conjectural and speculative nature of poetics against what Caws particularises at the combative tone of the manifesto:

> The manifestos are histrionic and heuristic. They dare and supplicate the reader as they project into the future a schedule and strategy for personal work. And if, for the writer, they define a field of action, for the reader they afford a gesture of solidarity, suggesting what lenses are necessary for appreciation of the work. Thus to read these productions in a univocal way, to be insulted by them, or to disregard them completely as oversimplifications, is to misunderstand their nature (Wesling 1980: 104).

Misreading poetics as a unified or simple discourse (as underdeveloped literary criticism, for example) is to mis-comprehend the complexity and doubleness of the discourse, its incompleteness, its mercurial nature, its often teasing relationship to the originating writer's (or writers') literary productions. But Wesling strikes a false note, despite his nuanced description, when he considers the role of the reader. Manifestoes, he says, 'are in fact clues, historical and methodological study guides to aid us in our task of reading' (Wesling 1980: 104). This attitude colludes with what Jerome J. McGann calls the 'ideological imaginary', the process by which 'literary criticism too often likes to transform the critical illusions of poetry into the worshipped truths of culture' (McGann 1983: 135). By analogy or extension, the speculations of poetics are prey to a similar petrifying assimilation in Wesling's description: it is utilised as a 'lens' to 'appreciate' the resultant work, even seen as a 'study guide', not as cultural work in its own right.

I will proceed with the premise that the only good reasons to show and share a poetics is if it assists in the definition of literariness or if it is of any practico-theoretical use as a poetics for other practitioners. Readers will perhaps one day read poetics in its own right as a performative discourse but poetics must never become simply a 'study guide'. I am not denying the value in, say, reading Coleridge's *Biographia Literaria* alongside his poems, so long as the former is read in its precise textual specificity, as poetics. An indecisiveness that haunts my essay on Maggie O'Sullivan's poetics in *When Bad Times Made for Good Poetry* is not willed away by my enduring sense that a 'useable *metapoetics* has yet to develop as a critical tool', for I end that episode, 'Talk', with a string of unanswered questions, prefaced with a corrective on how to read O'Sullivan's poetics piece 'riverrunning (realisations' as a specific discourse, and how the poetics of form can only be fully apprehended if we take on board the form of poetics: [2]

> We can, if we choose, treat poetics as a secondary discourse that informs the author's writing, and the critic's reading, of the primary texts, though we would be wise to observe the mismatch there nearly always will be between poetics and creative writing. Much wiser is to read the poetics as an *act* of poetics, respecting its general nature, tracing not just the ideas contained in the piece, but the energy that runs through it, its provocation to creative writing and creative reading (for herself and for other writers). I have not, I hope, treated it simply as an essay. Its formal construction deliberately obviates this option; poetics will often *embody* the creative design decisions it suggests. Yet neither have I treated it as a poem, in that it announces at moments claims to provisional truths of an intellectual kind that belong to, or at least allude to, expository prose. These include authorial filiations to other artists who share her sense of linguistic materiality *and* transformation, and to those who share her belief in the apposite nature of the shamanistic metaphor, which she uses to express both her growing sense of (lost?) Irishness and the sense of her kinship with nature. Her sense of shamanism as a model for a developed and skilful social and cultural function for poetry today is paramount.
>
> One question remains. May one *contest* a poetics? Crudely put, can we say a poetics is *wrong*? We may say Pound was wrong about the Chinese written character but wonderfully right in his development of the ideogrammic method, which he

---

[2] The book also contains readings of the individual poetics of Allen Fisher, John Hall, Ken Edwards, as well as the communal poetics of the Poetry Society (1976) and the cultural poetics of Iain Sinclair.

derived from it (although these are differing uses of *wrong* and *right*, one being factual, the other an aesthetic judgement). We are more concerned that Pound was wrong in his politics – an ethical judgement – than his poetics (which is not to deny a connection between the two). What would it mean to challenge O'Sullivan's shamanistic borrowings as essentialist or partial? Would it matter that her 'sources' date from the 1940s? Or that her sense of Irishness might be thought by some to be selective and romantic? Put another way, if, as Charles Bernstein says, 'The test of a poetics is the poetry and the poetic thinking that results,' are these questions pertinent at all? (Bernstein 1992: 166; Sheppard 2011: 177).

I wish to begin to answer these questions – and others – by looking at Pierre Joris' 'Notes towards a Nomadic Poetics' before turning to Adrian Clarke's angry reaction to it. I will be citing chiefly the text mysteriously numbered 'version 2.0b', which was first published as an issue of Allen Fisher's *Spanner* magazine in 1999. Version 4.00 is found in Joris' collection of essays *A Nomad Poetics* published in 2003, which largely differs by including interpolations by the critic Brian Massumi. A mutating document is fully congruent with its theme, of course, but I wish to remain largely with the earlier version (partly because this was the one contested by Clarke) (Joris 2003: 25-55). *A Nomad Poetics* as a whole might be seen as an extension of this text as poetic thinking that results from the poetics.[3]

Pierre Joris, who hails from Luxembourg, spent several years in London from 1971, where he formed friendships with poets such as Lee Harwood and Allen Fisher. He edited the ambitious journal *Sixpack* and continued to write original poems and translations, between his four languages, Lëtzebuergesch, French, German and English. He lived in Algeria for three years before a long-term return to the USA (where he had already lived in 1967) and where he is currently domiciled. When he co-edited the two-volume *Poems for the Millennium* anthologies in the late 1990s with Jerome Rothenberg, he was jointly responsible for the fact that at least J.H. Prynne, Bob Cobbing, Allen Fisher, John Cayley and Maggie O'Sullivan from the work of the British Poetry Revival and Linguistically Innovative Poetry appear in the second volume of this transnational anthology. I have praised this anthology in a poetics-essay of my own, 'The End of the

---

[3] In addition to published sources by Joris, see his ongoing Nomadic Poetics blog at: www.pjoris.blogspot.com.

Twentieth Century', as 'a loose-leaf anti-canon of World Wide investigative poetries' (Sheppard 2008: 346); I also comment 'Anthologising is poetics' (Sheppard 2008: 345). This document will re-surface in connection with Clarke's contention with Joris' poetics.

Joris' own remarks in 'Notes towards a Nomadic Poetics' on the editorial process with the veteran anthologist Rothenberg make it clear that the anthology is at the heart of a nomadic poetics and should be seen as 'a nomadology in action, an event authored by us, which means the two multitudes that Jerry & I are, plus the multiplicities the poets in the book make' (Joris 1999: 17). He quotes Deleuze and Guattari's remark in *A Thousand Plateaus* that those two authors were, like Rothenberg and Joris, 'Each of us … several, there was already quite a crowd' (Joris 1999: 17; Deleuze and Guattari 1988: 3). The famous 'treatise' on Nomadology in that book is the source for Joris' assertion that 'A nomadic poetics is a war machine, always on the move, always changing, morphing, moving through languages, cultures, terrains, times without stopping' (Joris 1999: 17). (That this sounds a little like Joris' life-story is not coincidental.) Deleuze and Guattari argue that, unlike the migrant, the figure of the nomad (who operates at both a literal and metaphorical level in their argument) deterritorialises, holds to a purely relational sense of the earth as ground, as passage. As opposed to the static military bodies of the State, the nomad (and his mobile war machine) is 'itinerant, ambulant' following (rather than representing) 'a flow in a vectoral field' (Deleuze and Guattari 1988: 372); nomads 'are vectors of deterritorialisation' that refuse to re-territorialise, unlike the migrant who simply settles elsewhere (Deleuze and Guattari 1988: 382). The spaces they traverse are therefore 'smooth' while the geopolitical divisions of the state result in borders, striations. Deleuze had earlier written of nomadology: 'There is no longer a division of that which is distributed but rather a division among those who distribute *themselves* in an open space – a space that is unlimited, or at least without precise limits' (Deleuze 1994: 36). Many of the U.S. and British poets in the Millennium anthology – and perhaps some of those from elsewhere – have often indeed had to organise themselves, operating with a self-distributive sense of literary function – organising their own networks of publication, for example – against the readymade distributed literary tradition or canon. They perhaps are the 'nomads-by-choice' mentioned in the notes' epigraph from Allen Fisher (Joris 1999: 2). To these notions, where Joris freely adapts Deleuzoguattarian concepts, he adds qualities of mutability that extend into one of his own poetic concerns: translation.

There is no doubting the stridency of Joris' ambitions for his twenty-nine page 'Notes Towards a Nomadic Poetics'. It takes on many of the characteristics of the manifesto and, as I shall show later, even echoes one of the major art manifestoes of modernism. Mary Ann Caws tells us that 'The manifesto is by nature a loud genre' (Caws 2001: xx), 'immodest and forceful, exuberant and vivid, attention-grabbing. Immediate and urgent, it never mumbles, is always in overdose and overdrive' (Caws 2001: xxi). But Joris also assimilates quieter de-territorialised modes of contemporary poetics, ones that often mime or merge into the poetry that is envisaged. Indeed, Joris has invented the hybrid category of the 'manifessay' to describe his text, to reflect his deflection of the manifestic impulse into the poetics essay form (Joris 2003: 128). It is indeed made up of 'notes', a form which suggests provisionality, and the 'towards' of the title suggests nomadic preference for events of becoming over states of being. Often aphoristic and elliptically allusive, with quotations from poems and other documents, its final pages present a translation from a pre-Islamic ode by Tarafah, 'the most modern, rebel of the nomad poets, an early Rimbaud', according to his admiring translator (Joris 2003: 23). Joris' interest in Arabic and Maghrebian poetry concretises the metaphor of nomadism, and in some cases makes it literal as well a theoretical. Like much poetics, his hybrid text borrows, steals and distorts his influences in the service of his picture of a twenty-first century poetics. At times this can be vertiginous, even confusing, as when he grafts onto this nomadism the Situationist concept of drift, the willed pointlessness of the *dérive*, so beloved of the psychogeographer, although the point he is making – the 'ever more displaced drifting' of language itself – is a pertinent one (Joris 1999: 3). There is a world of difference between the lines of flight of actual nomads — say, the purposeful, economical tracking between oases — and the deliberate and often delirious abandon of the psychogeographer.

The proliferation of concepts is a Deleuzoguattarian technique – indeed, is their definition of philosophy – and the development of novel borrowings and neologisms can be observed in many poetics documents and Joris' 'manifessay' does not disappoint, indeed may be largely read through them. To call the Nomadic Poet a 'Noet' is not just a neologistic contraction for Joris. It implies, at once a rejection of place-bound poetics in favour of a space-determined sense of nomadic movement. 'There is no difference between inside & outside at the poem's warp speed,' he promises, though it is difficult to relate this to specific textual practices (Joris 1999: 6). However, this is generally congruent with the views of one contemporary geographer, Doreen Massey, who sees space not place as the determining factor of contemporary existence, 'space' conceived narratively as 'a simultaneity of stories-so-far' (Massey 2005: 9), or as communal Deleuzoguattarian 'co-eval becomings', as she puts it, although Joris does not refer to her work (Massey 2005: 189). In fact, he prefers to develop the associative implications of his neologism. 'NOET: NO stands for play, for no-saying & guerrilla war techniques', in a grand refusal, eliding the Deleuzoguattarian war machine with a distantly romanticised sense of guerrilla warfare (Joris 1999: 7). But ancient knowledges are hinted at in 'gNOsis' and modern ones in 'Noetics', but again, the collocations are vitiated by lack of detail ('noetic' operates also as an adjective from the Greek, *nous*).

However, there is one citable example: John Cayley's *Indra's Net*. 'The nomad poet, the NOET, gives allegiance to INDRA the warrior god,' Joris states, quoting Deleuze and Guattari on Hindu deity Indra as a 'pure and immeasurable multiplicity', before he quotes Cayley's description of his cyberpoem which is mediated through an ever-changing screen of words morphing between languages (Joris 1999: 13). (Rothenberg and Joris excerpt this text in a section of *Poems for the Millennium* called 'Towards a Cyberpoetics' (Rothenberg and Joris 1998: 827-8).) In essence, the technological advances in cybernetics are applauded by Joris and embraced by Cayley, because of programmable media's ability to generate a mutating textual entity that the reader may operate and – more radically – enter in order to change, so that one copy of the text eventually will be quite different from any other, a true 'plastic literary object' in Cayley's words (Joris 1999: 14). Here we have a literal example of 'the nomadic poem as ongoing & open-ended chart of the turbulent fluxes the dispersive nature of our realities make inevitable', though it is worth questioning whether this does not simply amount to a close representation of chaotic and fractal reality rather than an intervention in it.[4]

---

[4] My *The Poetry of Saying* (Liverpool: Liverpool University Press, 2005) concludes with a consideration of Cayley's work, and – judged from my Levinasian distinction between the poetry of saying and the poetry of the said that I carried through that study – the continuous 'saying' of this technological eternality unsettled me:

It is clear that *Indra's Net* allows for an openness of eternal saying, with never more than a screen's space of temporary saidness and thematization for a few moments. However, Levinas' insistence upon the inevitability of the saying being materialized in the said may give pause for thought. Whether the cyberpoetics of the future can accommodate the ethical poetics that underpins this study is an open question (Sheppard 2005: 247).

Joris, of course, is not offering cyberpoetics as the only mode for the noet. Elsewhere, he becomes relatively specific about the process of becoming a noet: 'The NOET learns & then writes in foreign languages (real or made-up ones) in order to come to the realization that all languages are foreign' (Joris 1999: 16). As 'mother tongue' morphs into 'other tongue', through yet more wordplay, language becomes a drifting substance, 'consonants' like 'continents', he says (Joris 1999: 16). Everything is flux, it seems.

However, Joris does develop a principle of rest and pause, 'poasis'. Collocated from the words poem and oasis, and hinting at the poesis from which we name poetics itself, poases are the 'refuelling halts' that are necessary for the paths of flight of nomadic writing to be achieved: 'They last a night or a day, the time of the poem, & then move on' (Joris 1999: 3). Joris has ancient authority for this neologism. The tenth century Sufi term 'mawqif', as modulated through the poetics of the contemporary Tunisian poet Abdelwahab Meddeb, who Joris has translated, refunctions the term in 'his poetics in order to define what the poem is: The mawqif is the pause, the stop-over, the rest, the stay of the wanderer between two moments of movement, two runs, two sites, two places, two states' (Joris 1999: 17). Thus formulated, the term implies 'between-ness as essential nomadic condition', a condition of not digging down into the territory, but of being strung above it between two points, paradoxically at rest and in transit (Joris 1999: 6). Thus the poem is not written at rest, but is itself that restless rest, as Olson realised decades before when he asked: 'How to dance/ sitting down' (and which Joris quotes approvingly) (Joris 1999: 18). Meddeb himself says: the poem 'enjoys a rest, raises itself upright; between two durations it scrutinizes briefly the instant when from its height it confronts the vision or the word exteriorising itself' (Joris 1999: 17-8). It is thus a moment of simultaneous recreation and creation, an exfoliation of poetic potentiality without having roots or taking root. It is 'en route'. It is a 'moving placement on a smooth space' to quote Joris in Deleuzoguattarian mode; 'it is a (momentary) stance in relation to & with space', precisely part of the rhizomatic potential of lines of nomadic flight, which, as always, hovers between the literal and the metaphorical (Joris 1999: 18). Elsewhere Joris reminds us about ancient forms of flight:

Perhaps Joris' attractive concept of the 'poasis', which I entertain in the following paragraph, is broadly akin to my sense that the saying of poetry has to acknowledge relationship with the condition of the said, which will (temporarily) fix it, before the movement of the saying – the mobility of text that Joris typifies as drift – resumes in the restlessness of reading and interpretation.

'This *hajara* is an exile, but not an exodus, that is to say it is not a flight in search of a goal, a promised land, a *telos* that would reinscribe all the more forcefully all the lost identities, the unities of the individual, group or state' (Joris 2003: 129). As Joris makes clear in an interview he is not talking at all about 'lifestyle proposals' but 'poetics': 'I do not harbor any such desire for a return to a perfect or original past way of life. What I am concerned with is a poetics for today and open on tomorrow' (Joris 2003: 128). In a related essay in the 2003 volume, we find a description of one technique of nomadic poetics. He notes of Picasso's poetry, its 'complete obliteration of punctuation marks. This gives his poems the feel of a wide open field, a smooth, non-striated space, or blocks of space, through or along which one can travel unchecked, free to choose one's own moment of rest, free to create one's own rhythms of reading,' a reading process that is itself described in the language of nomadology (Joris 2003: 118). Similar effects to those achieved by John Cayley's morphing screen are achieved on the fixed totality of Picasso's page.

It might be thought ironical that the central figure of European twentieth century modernism is taken as exemplar of the nomadic future, but one of the ironies of poetics is that it has to predicate the future upon the examples of the past in its quest to stake out the inaccessible inexistent ideal artistic productions of tomorrow. Joris lists what he will not jettison from twentieth century art. Amongst others he wants to keep Burroughs' exploration of inner-states, Dorn and Olson's explorations of space (rather than place), Nathaniel Mackey's sense of 'the imperfect fit of word and world' (Joris 2003: 31), Pound's inclusion of history in the poem, the syntactical play of Gertrude Stein, and the drawing-poems of Henri Michaux, for example, all of which may be found in *Poems for the Millennium*. Version 4.00 of the 'notes' includes a passage on Allen Fisher. Joris comments: 'We will take the whole of the new century to finally read Allen Fisher's vast investigation into all our knowledges, the great serial constructive *dérive* he calls *Gravity as a Consequence of Shape*' (Joris 2003: 34). When Joris informs us that '69 pages of commentaries have been deleted' we are thankful for this and for his summary: 'From the 20C we will retain everything – in memory. We will forget nothing and we will forgive nothing' (Joris 1999: 9). This ethical note, Joris's refusal of Christian forgiveness here, emerges from our sense of having passed through an era about which one might say, with Muriel Rukeyser, 'I lived in the first century of world wars. Most mornings I would be more or less insane' (Joris 2003: 36). 'Notes Towards a Nomadic Poetics' opens with a bold but generalised statement, in which we can read both Deleuzoguattarian intent and political judgement:

The days of anything static, form, content, state are over. The past century has shown that anything not involved in continuous trans-formation hardens and dies. All revolutions have done just that: those that tried to deal with the state as much as the state of poetry (Joris, 1999: 2).

While the equivalence of the 'state of poetry' and the political state may seem rhetorical, the political and ethical imperative is strongly felt if not sharply delineated. The implications of this are far-reaching into the political realm; if the 'two major modes of poesis' in the twentieth-century involved 'love (eros) & strife (nike)', then in the future they will operate as elements of the 'stasis that makes movement', as minor deviations (Joris introduces the Lucretian-Oulipean term clinamen) in 'a world where accident is rule', as Joris puts it in a poem of his own which he includes in his poetics (Joris 1999: 4-5). We need continuous transformation.

But his final word – he calls it 'the *fin mot*' – incongruously occurs on page six of the document and is a quotation from Paul Celan (Joris 1999: 6). Joris is one of Celan's distinguished translators and it is almost inevitable that any ethical understanding of utterance should turn to this austere and subtle poetic thinker. Indeed, Celan's trace may be felt – perhaps appropriately as a negative – in Joris' neologistic play of the 'noet' resting by the 'poasis'. Would not a noet write 'noems'? Unfortunately, Celan (or both of the best translators of the poem 'Weggebeizt vom') have already bagged the term 'the noem' for what Celan calls 'the hundred-/tongued pseudo-/ poem' that attempts to recreate experience loquaciously but unthinkingly (Celan 1990: 231). This warning about the use of neologism in poetics also brings us closer to Joris' central borrowing from Celan, the assertion, 'Reality is not. It has to be searched for and won' (Joris 1999: 6). As another of Celan's translators, Rosmarie Waldrop, says: for Celan, 'Literature belongs to those who are at home in the world', whereas for him, his exilic, if not quite nomadic, poetic experience, is one of alienation and of poesis within alienation (Celan 1986: viii). The real is not given. It must be strenuously sought out, and it has to be gained, fought for, possibly even captured. Waldrop says Celan

> can only talk in a simple – deceptively simple – way: circular, repetitive, insisting on the very gap between him and nature. He can only hope that out of his insistence will come a new language which can fill the gap and include the other side. 'Reality must be searched for and won' (Celan 1986: viii).

This translation of the quotation is slightly different, of course, one also given by Joris himself elsewhere (Joris 2003: 4), but in his 'manifessay' he needs the previous version to effect a suggestive substitution: 'Replace "reality" with "poetry" or "millennium"' (Joris 1999: 6). 'Poetry is not. It has to be searched for and won', by the very nomadic poetic war machine that is described throughout this poetics. 'Celan's phrase,' Joris remarks, 'is the quest, as it includes the critique of the "society of the spectacle" – & of the whole specular natures of our mis-takes on the real' (Joris 1999: 6). This, like other parts of the document, attempts to summarise too much, but it suggests that Celan's thinking is a site of resistance to late global capitalism, as theorized by Guy Dubord and others, that it offers hope of discovering an alternative 'reality' (and 'poetry', and 'millennium', through Joris' suggested substitutions.)

The millennium has to be searched for and won, and perhaps it is too early to see whether Joris' millennial poetics will become – as it clearly intends to be – more than simply the thinking behind his own poetic practice or as part of his translation theory, and become part of a zeitgeist poetics. (As we shall see it is this latter ambition that causes some disquiet.) Certainly in the era after September 11, Joris, as one who translates from Arabic, is well-placed, 'where we have to start to think a new cultural constellation that will, finally, have to include the heritage of the excluded third – Islam & Arab culture' (Joris 2003: 114).

This new, different (and unpredictable) poetics needs to be searched for and won too. Joris' bold attempt to synthesise so much of twentieth century modernism, his neologistic play, his playing off of rhetorics of movement against rhetorics of interruption and rest, his ethical appropriations from Celan, and finally his attempt to produce a poetics in serial and branching versions, points to the vitality of his speculative discourse, that situates itself neither within the confines of criticism, nor within the extensions of artistic practice (for which they may prove of variable utility).

Adrian Clarke is a Linguistically Innovative poet who emerged, in many ways, under the sign of Allen Fisher, whose poetics essay *Necessary Business* had laid the groundwork for more general poetic experiment in the post-1978 era.[5] I have written about Clarke's work elsewhere, and about his poetics, which largely consists of papers (often delivered to the

---

[5] When Clarke and I edited an anthology of London poets of the 1980s under the title *Floating Capital: New Poets from London* (1991), we placed Allen Fisher at its head, featuring work from *Gravity as a Consequence of Shape*. (We also featured Bob Cobbing for his persistence and example.)

SubVoicive Colloquia of the early 1990s) that he provocatively published in single volumes with his poetry in a refusal to separate his poetics from poems. (See Clarke 1998).[6] Most particular is his adherence to a poetics of the phrase, derived from a reading of Lyotard, whereby abutted phrases avoid grammatical and syntactic cohesion and semantic coherence in a way that keeps the discourse open; on the other hand he adopts modes of word count (derived from the example of Louis Zukofsky) that create stanza shapes of great formal austerity, so that he can play floating phrases against mathematical form, utilising enjambment to the full. Difficult to demonstrate in excerpt, Clarke's *Skeleton Sonnets* (2002, revised and republished (without poetics) in *Possession: poems 1996-2006*) evince a combative approach to the global that represents capitalist media and power as obsessed with speed rather than 'mawqif', a world of threatening connections rather than one of cross-cultural fertilisation or 'mated frames':

> global eroded celebrity spells it
> out with a black
> and white Head
> Office module in close
> up
>   choice of auto
> mated frames
> once on the running
> board at the speed of receipts (Clarke 2007: 61)

One of Clarke's poetics documents contains a partial critique of Joris' 'Notes', and is published in *Skeleton Sonnets*. It is entitled 'Introduction in the Form of an Open Letter to Robert Sheppard on Exile, Nomads & the Demon'; the appearance of my name demands an explanation. The occasion of the 'letter' was my prose piece 'The End of the Twentieth Century', which is one of the core poetics documents of my millennial project *Twentieth Century Blues*. Much of Clarke's letter speaks from his projects (the sonnets particularly and his own millennial sequence 'Millennial Shades') to my project, but at various points he strays into potting a shot or two over the bows of Joris' millennial poetics, and it is largely towards these remarks I

---

[6] See the chapter 'Creative Linkage in the Work of Allen Fisher, Adrian Clarke and Ulli Freer in the 1980s and 1990s', particularly pp. 203-8, in Sheppard 2005 and the similar 'Colossal Fragments: the work of Adrian Clarke' in *Far Language*. Exeter: Stride Research Document, 1999.

direct my attention.

'The End of the Twentieth Century' praises the anthology Joris edited with Rothenberg, *Poems for the Millennium*, as poetics in action. By making of it 'a prospectus of reading', I say, 'I have constructed a twentieth century more generous than that given to me, to give to others, into the next,' a formulation that not only predicts my adoption of the book in my teaching of creative writing but is consistent with Joris' poetics, which I had not then read[7] (Sheppard 2008: 346). Clarke will have none of it. He tells me:

> I have difficulty both with 'ethnopoetics' as copyrighted by Messrs Rothenberg and Joris, inasfar as I grasp its rationale, and with your enthusiasm for their anthology *Poems for the Millennium* – which Joris considers 'should maybe be better seen as nomadology in action' – if not for some of the work collected there. My problem is that the translations … lose much of the strangeness we might value in the source texts as they are accommodated on a plateautude of AGIT-PROP strung with dead International Surrealist light-bulbs (Clarke 2002: 6).

Clarke suspects that the Deleuzoguattarian rhetoric operates in order to level the work presented until it flattens out into an unproblematic and homogenised international avant-garde mode; one result is that ethnopoetic oral text is presented as the equivalent of Dada sound poetry for example. Rather than being released nomadically, these texts are decontextualised and lose the otherness, and thus their power, that Joris actually praises in his poetics. 'To translate is, of course, to welcome the work as an other into the same, to transform it from the foreign to the familiar,' Derek Attridge says; 'but in doing so, if its otherness and singularity are respected – if, that is, the translation is inventive – the field into which it is welcomed is also transformed in the process' (Attridge 2004: 74). Clarke suspects that otherness and singularity are suppressed in favour of assimilation.

Clarke attacks Joris' poetics head on. 'Facile notions like Pierre Joris' nomadic (cyber)poetics … fill me with rage and despair … Or at times a reluctant cynicism,' Clarke says (Clarke 2002: 3). After praising the demonstrators at the Seattle World Trade talks, Clarke will have no truck

---

[7] For an account of my use of this anthology and for the fullest account of my teaching practice see 'Experiment in Practice and Speculation in Poetics', in Peter Middleton, Nicky Marsh (eds.), *Teaching Modernist Poetry*. Basingstoke, Palgrave Macmillan, 2010.

with what he sees as a too-easy utopianism of connectivity in nomadic poetics. He sees 'circulation' as a 'key term' in debates about political power rather than drift; the faith that Joris puts in technology seems too easy an option for Clarke (Clarke 2002: 2). Additionally, he tells me:

> Joris' appropriation of the *dérive* subjects it to an accelerating and 'ever more displaced drifting'. Noting the [Situationist] movement's immediate preference for backstreet labyrinths, underground passageways and houses due for demolition – for which I am tempted to find a poetic parallel in your interlinked texts threatened by impermanence –

(Clarke is thinking of the knotted numbering and indexing of my *Twentieth Century Blues* project and possibly of its preference for the darker recesses of history and consciousness) 'Vincent Kaufmann remarks of the project Situationist hanging city above its ground-level transportation systems: "Circulation is to take place <u>below</u> the space of everyday life…."' (Clarke 2002: 6). Thus it seems to Clarke that possibilities of guerrilla action in the sewers of culture, as it were, beneath the level of 'everyday life' eulogised by Lefebvre and others, are denied by Joris' sunny armchair *dérive* and its faith in technology. Joris, we are told, 'waits for the caravan (no more oasis stops needed, boys – metaphoric or otherwise!) to a mathematical plurality in the Electronic Millennium' represented by John Cayley's e-poetry (Clarke 2002: 5). Clarke's bad-tempered charges expose a danger that the free synthesizing of Joris' poetics may end up entangled in its own rhetoric, the mawqif swiftly swapped for the latest poetic fashion.

Joris is no less uncivil in his 'Open Letter in Response to Adrian Clarke's', which is included in the 2003 book *A Nomad Poetics*, and is a response to a version of Clarke's letter. He flings the same term of abuse back at Clarke: 'facile'. He responds to Clarke's poetics as 'your rather facile strictures re "dematerialized is immaterial" which you tease out of Bruce Andrews' reflections on materiality and graphic immediacy' – which is an accurate description of Clarke's own poetics, but he adds that this is 'maybe pointing out the sleek anorexia of his/your signifieds' (Joris 2003: 139). It is odd that he says signifieds, where one might expect signifiers, since Joris is referring to what he describes elsewhere as the 'trap' of U.S. Language Poetry that 'runs the risk of remaining stuck exactly … in linguistic auto-referentiality'; he assumes Clarke's slavish adherence to this poetics or to this simplified critique of its poetics (Joris 2003: 100). (Clarke's practice is not at issue here, but it is worth recording that his poetry, while estranged and difficult, is nevertheless referential, however much it dematerialises its substance and makes its materials immaterial. One of his 'Eurochants' of 2010, a sequence which displays a plurilingual internationalism to match Joris' own, opens with a line which clearly equates the emptiness of New Labour/big business rhetoric with Joris' central concept: 'blue skies thinking "nomadic"' (Clarke 2010: 69).)

In fact, Clarke's probing makes Joris more specific about the ethics of his position. Sensing that Clarke suspects him of complicity with a postmodernity that demands ever-accelerated speed instead of finding a fixed position from which to mount critique, Joris declares that there is no home to return to in language, and that 'being' and 'dwelling', Heideggerian terms seemingly valorized by Clarke, are tainted with the Nazi brush, the very fascism his 'manifessay' warns us is capable of a strange and powerful return in the new millennium; 'being' itself can dangerously serve to aggrandise the self and belittle the other.[8] We are condemned to this unethical position 'until we become nomadic, until "becoming" is what we want' (Joris 2003: 136). Joris admits that 'the enemy (late global capitalism) has been thinking nomadically for a long time,' an assertion that could damage his claims for nomadology, but as his attitude to the uses of the internet and e-poetry demonstrates, he envisages using that techno-power against itself (Joris 2003: 137). Clarke's stridency on this point in his piece allows Joris to regard him, wrongly, as a technophobe; 'simply tuning out is not a solution' (Joris 2003: 137). Joris suspects 'sedantariness' might be an affliction of the British, and assumes a native poetics resistant to poetry's true 'desire to feel everywhere estranged, out of touch/in reach with the other – out of house and home' (Joris 2003: 140). To my mind, Clarke is one of the most adventurous and self-estranged of British poets and writers of poetics. However, taking sides (at this point) may not enrich our understanding of conflictual poetics.

Neither of these poets reaches out to the other. Their mutual 'perplexity', an account of which Joris uses to open his letter to Clarke, is more telling

---

[8] 'Poasis' finds a fellow-traveller in Badiou, who argues for a renewed 'principle of interruption. It must be able to propose to thought something that can interrupt this endless regime of circulation,' – a concept Clarke has identified as worthy of interruption – indeed establish 'a point of interruption,' born of a 'retardation process ... because revolt today requires leisureliness and not speed. This thinking, slow and consequentially rebellious, is alone capable of establishing the fixed point' of interruption that will allow, in Badiou's thought, the 'patient search for at least one truth' (Badiou 2005: 36-38).

than the actual exchanges, the incomprehension more eloquent than any connection one might elaborate in an attempt to show a relationship of poetics, let alone a fellowship of poets. Neither sees the other's position, I fear, but this is not just a lack of clarity or charity but something more fundamental about the nature of poetics itself.

The hybrid nature of writerly poetics, the very formal choices it makes, its mercurial qualities, militate against it being considered fully a discourse in the specific sense intended by Foucault, although there are enough shared characteristics for it to be regarded as a weak form of discourse. In short, poetics lacks what Foucault claims as necessary conditions, or effects, of strong forms of discourse: institutions, founding figures of discursivity, originating concepts, principles of recognition and validation. In addition, it evades principles of verification and falsification. This lack of conditions, in the case of poetics, I would argue, is fundamentally productive. The nature, or natures, of poetics, in the present examples, seems to support the case that it desires to resist finality of statement: Clarke is gnomically aphoristic where Joris is expansive and manifestic but still claims the provisional status of 'notes' for his poetics. Indeed, it is this combination which makes me uneasy when I consider Joris' text as a whole. When I think about its parts I am less concerned; for example, his notion of the 'poasis' speaks to both my criticism and my poetics. The document teems with good ideas and attitudes for the contemporary poet, but despite its fragmentary and deterritorialising forms, it approaches the assumed authority of the manifesto; as a totality, it is loud, as Caws would say.

Poets, eternal optimists in one sense, do trust that poetics might prove the last word (if only to themselves); they treat a provisional position as though a theoretical absolute (if only to produce the latest text or brave a creative crisis). But deep inside they know that the fixity is – to borrow Joris' vocabulary – but a rest by an oasis on a long journey of continual transformation. My disquiet with Joris – despite his ostentatious versioning – is that he is courting universal application and projecting that on poetic and wider reality, a compulsive nomadism, a compulsory 'becoming', that steers 'continuous transformation'. Joris' global assertion – itself a deliberate echoing of André Breton's final sentence in his surrealist novel-manifesto *Nadja* – that 'the millennium will be nomadic or it will not be', is predictive and absolute. It leaves no room for dissent, or possibly even for poetics as a developing practice of paradigm-breaking 'becoming' (Joris 1999: 1 and 29).[9] This is an unintended consequence of its manifestic 'overdose and

---

[9] 'Beauty will be CONVULSIVE or will not be at all' (Breton 1960: 160).

overdrive' (Caws 2001: xxi). Already as the twenty-first century ceases to be a novelty and becomes our reality, the irruptive poetics of 'conceptual writing' offers a resistance to many cherished notions of literary post-modernity. It will be interesting to see if nomadic poetics can encompass its assaults on originality, aesthetic facility and readerly fascination (through work which is breezily derivative, repetitive and boring). One of its central characteristics is also to reverse the relationship between poetics and product: its poetics is often more important than its work; the poetics in a sense *is* the work. Conceptual writing may offer a victory for poetics that it might have to resist.

The dispute between Joris and Clarke brings me back to the questions I found myself asking about the very different poetics of Maggie O'Sullivan: 'May one *contest* a poetics?... Can we say a poetics is *wrong*?' This examination suggests that while there may be debate over some of the terms of poetics, while one poetics may wholly or partly contradict another, or for that matter partly or wholly confirm another (where its terms are expressed propositionally), a poetics as a whole cannot be successfully contested (the more so it includes aesthetic, hybrid, formally nonpropositional or gestural moments) because there is uncertainty about the grounds of the contest.

Poetics' purposes are often practical as well as theoretical; it might provoke or conjecture as much as it argues, and it may gesture or demonstrate as much as propose, leaving epistemological indeterminacy. 'Statements' in poetics often have contextual, fiduciary currency. Poetics' terms are provisional, modified by experience (or influenced by the practice of art-making that is beyond its own terms or scope, but which it provokes). Formally it might defamiliarize content. I am not trying to exalt the discourse of poetics, to position it on an inviolable plane of expression, like a starlet hoisted above the chorus girls at the climax of a musical. This is not a question of discursive *purity* but of the various *im*purities found in what is best thought of, *pace* Foucault, as a weak form of discourse. It is a jostling crowd rather than a debating society, let alone a legislature.

Nevertheless, questions of contestation are worth exploring in a work of metapoetics (such as this), and perhaps there are more than consolations in philosophy. Lyotard developed the concept of the *differend* to partly account for the situation of incommunicability, more acute than a stalemate, between two arguments, conducted in two different language games, a contest for which there is no final, higher, tribunal. (See Lyotard 1988). Perhaps something like this – I emphasise my simile – pertains between examples and modalities of poetics (though I do not wish to push the discourse too far into Lyotard's specific arguments).[10] Because of its forms and functions, overstating cases, understating cases, not stating cases at all, offering thumbnails rather than blueprints, and often demonstrating through formal means, it is rare to find an actual stalemate in poetics, but not unknown to find mutual incompatibility that verges on incommunicability between artists. The mutual incomprehension of Joris and Clarke may be the effect of their attempting to answer poetics (in all its formal and contentual variety) with argument. They are playing incommensurable language games. It may be possible now to see why it is difficult to contest, or impossible to refute, a poetics. (One is always free to choose whether to use it or not, of course.) This is what Clarke is attempting in his 'Open Letter', as is Joris, in a lesser sense, in his response, though his exasperation at Clarke at one point breaks down into the simple request for Clarke to re-read the original document. He possesses no new terms he can use to persuade Clarke further, offers no new moves in the language game of poetics. They are left 'to register a differend', an admirable term used by Clarke himself elsewhere in his poetics (Clarke 1998: n.p.). If we remind ourselves, in the words of Richard Rorty, that 'A talent for speaking differently, rather than for arguing well, is the chief instrument of cultural change,' we shall see that the survival of poetics depends upon the registering of differences, on paradigm-breaking, not upon the provision of paradigmatic organising principles, the accumulation of universals or discursive legislation (quoted in Spahr 2001: 101). *All* poetics – Joris's, Clarke's, O'Sullivan's (and, for that matter, mine) – is nomadic.

---

[10] Lyotard's *The Differend* is a troubling volume, whose central concept is illuminating and useful at times. The book is suggestive – Adrian Clarke has found it so, even as he misread 'phrase' literally in his concoction of a constructivist poetics – more than it is coherent, at least in my reading. Like one of Gerhard Richter's grey representational paintings, from a distance it looks clear, but close to the texture of the argument, the outlines lose definition and blur.

Works Cited

Attridge, Derek. *The Singularity of Literature.* London and New York, NY: Routledge, 2004.

Badiou, Alain. *Infinite Thought.* London and New York, NY: Continuum, 2005.

Bernstein, Charles. *A Poetics.* Cambridge, MA: Harvard University Press, 1992.

Breton, André. *Nadja.* New York, NY: Grove Press, 1960.

Caws, Mary Ann. Ed. *Manifesto: A Century of Isms.* Lincoln, NE and London: University of Nebraska Press, 2001.

Celan. Paul. *Collected Prose.* Manchester: Carcanet, 1986.

Celan, Paul. *Selected Poems.* London: Penguin, 1990.

Clarke, Adrian. *Millennial Shades and Three Papers.* London: Writers Forum, 1998.

Clarke, Adrian. *Skeleton Sonnets.* London: Writers Forum, 2002.

Clarke, Adrian. *Possession: Poems 1996–2006.* London: Veer, 2007.

Clarke, Adrian. *Eurochants.* Exeter: Shearsman, 2010.

Deleuze, Gilles. *Difference and Repetition.* London and New York: Continuum, 1994.

Deleuze, Gilles; and Guattari, Felix. *A Thousand Plateaus.* London: The Athlone Press, 1988.

Joris, Pierre. *Notes Towards a Nomadic Poetics.* Spanner 38, Summer 1999.

Joris, Pierre. *A Nomadic Poetics.* Middletown, CT: Wesleyan University Press, 2003.

Lyotard, Jean-François. *The Differend.* Minneapolis, MI: University of Minneapolis, 1988.

MacGann, Jerome. *The Romantic Ideology,* Chicago, IL: University of Chicago Press, 1983.

Massey, Doreen. *for space.* London, New Delhi: Sage, 2005.

Romer, Stephen. 'Correctives', *PN Review* 27, 1982: p 63-64.

Rothenberg, Jerome, and Joris, Pierre, *Poems for the Millennium: Volume Two: From Postwar to Millennium.* Berkeley, CA and London: University of California Press, 1998.

Sheppard, Robert. *The Necessity of Poetics.* Liverpool: Ship of Fools, 2002 (new ed. 2011).

Sheppard, Robert. *The Poetry of Saying.* Liverpool: Liverpool University Press, 2005.

Sheppard, Robert. *Complete Twentieth Century Blues.* Cambridge: Salt Publishing, 2008.

Sheppard, Robert. *When Bad Times Made for Good Poetry.* Exeter: Shearsman Books, 2011.

Sheppard, Robert. *Berlin Bursts.* Exeter: Shearsman Books, 2011.

Spahr, Juliana. *Everybody's Autonomy.* Tuscaloosa, AL and London: The University of Alabama Press, 2001.

Wesling, Donald. *The Choices of Rhyme: Device and Modernity.* Berkeley, Los Angeles, CA, London: University of California, 1980.

Poetics as Conjecture and Provocation:
an inaugural lecture delivered on 13th March 2007
at Edge Hill University

I do remember, when I was a barber, the boss, after having shorn
the heads of some particularly long-haired customers, used to
say to them:
　　'Now you look like a gentleman, sir.'
　　To which, once, one of them said:
　　'And what did I look like before?'
　　'Before?' the boss said, 'before you looked like a professor,
sir.'
　　'But I *am* a professor,' the man said.

Stefan Themerson [1]

WRITING AS INAUGURAL [2]

In a citation of my book *Far Language*, Marjorie Perloff, in the introduction
to an essay upon contemporary poetic innovation, refers to me as a 'poet-
critic'. The assignation surprised me on first seeing it. Its hyphen appears
to announce an uneasy hybrid that looks dangerously as though it has
yoked by violence together two incompatibilities. It suggests that unity is
achieved by pressurised co-habitation, force of will. And yet, it is unity of
purpose and project – but not of product – I would like to emphasise in
this presentation of my work. The unity is achieved by introducing a third
term, poetics, not just as mediator between the scholarly research of the
critic and the practice-led research creative writing of the poet, although
it is also that.

---

[1] Themerson, S. (1967) *Tom Harris*, London: Gaberbocchus. Watch out for the
re-appearance of this neglected and brilliant novelist, poet and thinker later in this
piece. I write about him in some detail in *The Meaning of Form* (Cham: Palgrave,
2016).

[2] 'It is because writing is *inaugural* … that it is dangerous and anguishing. It does
not know where it is going, no knowledge can keep it from the essential precipita-
tion toward the meaning that it constitutes and that is, primarily, its future.' Derrida, J. (1978) *Writing and Difference*, London and Henley: Routledge and Kegan
Paul, 11.

Poetics has been open to a variety of misunderstandings. The first, and apparently most obvious, is that it has something to do with poetry. Or with poetry alone. I'm not going to help that impression tonight by almost exclusively referring to poetry, but that's because I am a 'poet-critic'. But I'd like to stress that while poetry and poetics share etymological roots – they both derive from the Greek verb 'to make' – poetics, as *the thinking about how something is made*, can be used with reference to all kinds of writing (and not just writing, and not even just art). Poetics is as relevant to the writer of supposedly formulaic writing, like the crime novel, as it is to the most experimental writing which involves the setting up of systems to produce unforeseen textual effects. On the one hand you've Raymond Chandler's crisply written article 'The Simple Art of Murder'; on the other John Cage's performative 'Lecture on Nothing'.[3]

While I have offered a sketchy history as well as definitions of poetics elsewhere – indeed 79 of them, and I've written another one since, you'll be horrified to learn – I want to come at the concept from a slightly different angle tonight.[4]

I want to tell you what I think poetics is; I want to show how we might begin to read one writer's poetics; I want to share *my* poetics; and I want to read some of my poetry that relates to it. I also want to suggest how poetics might become part of the English Literature curriculum.

I now most commonly call poetics a 'speculative writerly discourse'. 'Speculative' because I define it against modes of 'reflection' on works already written; its orientation is towards the next 'job'. That doesn't mean that there isn't a reflective component, but that poetics is primarily, in a definition of American poet Rachel Blau DuPlessis that is often picked up by my students, 'a permission to continue', beyond the self-evident and the already achieved.[5] It is 'writerly' because it is not a critical activity. Critics may speak of constructing a 'theory of poetry' – Harold Bloom uses this term – but that is distinct from 'writerly' poetics which will remain the concern of writers or of groups of writers. It's not impossible for critics and writers to discuss the same issues, but for writers, the questions will be as

---

[3] In Chandler, R., (1980), *Pearls are a Nuisance*, London: Pan Books, 173-190; and in eds., Joris, P and Rothenberg, J,. (1998) *Poems for the Millennium*, Berkeley, CA: University of California Press.

[4] See my *The Necessity of Poetics*, Liverpool: Ship of Fools, published in 2002, re-edited here.

[5] DuPlessis, R.B. (1990) *The Pink Guitar, Writing as Feminist Practice*, New York and London: Routledge, 156.

practical as they are theoretical. Poetics is a paradoxical theory of practice *and* practice of theory. It asks not just what kind of text is this, but how do I write one like it – or, more probably – one *not* like it? Thirdly it is a 'discourse'. By this I don't simply mean that it is spoken or written, but that – after Foucault – it is a discursive practice with a history and rules of its own. The history is demonstrable. The 'rules' are less so, because the discourse is mercurial. Writers do not often sit down and inscribe 'Poetics' at the top of a sheet of paper and then enumerate an orderly blueprint for writing a particular named text. Indeed, it is the history that shows us this. Writers' speculations appear in a variety of guises. The poetics of American poet Wallace Stevens manifests in a number of different 'genres': from formal essays, lectures and published aphorisms, in reviews of other writers' works, in his (private) correspondence, in introductions to his work and – here is the most paradoxical – in the poetry itself. Readers of poems, not just Stevens' poems, not just modern poems, will have noticed how many poems are about poetry itself – they are metapoems – and sometimes they speculate their own existence and future into being. Given this heterogeneity it follows that the discourse of poetics can also appear in hybrid forms between these recognisable genres: something I encourage students to explore, although it has its own danger of authorising obfuscation in lyrical afflatus or collage 'theory buzz'.

Poetics is the working out of difficult ideas about how writing is (to be) made, without necessary recourse to logical argument. As Richard Rorty says, 'A talent for speaking differently, rather than for arguing well, is the chief instrument of cultural change.'[6] Without ever *explaining* the creative writing it precedes, accompanies and (occasionally) post-dates, poetics can serve a number of functions, one of which might be to deliberately confuse the writer about his or her intentions, rather than to evaluate them, itemise them, convert them into a programme. Meanwhile the work can generate itself as the writer is scratching his or her head. Poetics may be an elaborate game of self-deception, rather than a deliberate manifesto. Poetics is not explication or interpretation, which are the proper jobs of a reader. Equally it might be that poetics is to come upon that which one already knows, but with the force of revelation as if discovered for the first time. (If you're interested: that's my recent 80th definition!)

How can I be sure that poetics exists, as a 'discourse', if its intermittent and mercurial nature cause it to take such strange forms and to hide in so

---

[6] Rorty, R., quoted in Spahr, J. (2001) *Everybody's Autonomy.* Tuscaloosa, AL and London: The University of Alabama Press, 101.

many genres including creative work itself? One is simply that I recognise the impulse in my own practice. Indeed, many of the innovations I claim in the name of poetics here at Edge Hill University are little more than transferences of my own experiences and experiments into generalised exercises. Neither is this a professing of my uniqueness and perspicacity. It was simply what many of the avant-garde London poets who emerged during the 1980s under the ugly banner 'linguistically innovative', *did* as a matter of course: Allen Fisher or Adrian Clarke, for example. This may come as a surprise to anyone familiar with our predecessor generation, the poets of the British Poetry Revival, Tom Raworth or Lee Harwood, for example, since they are (still) notoriously averse to little more than thumbnail indices of poetics. It is a commonplace for them that the work speaks for itself. What happened in the 1980s was a threefold influencing. One was the influx of continental critical theory which promised philosophical definitions of some of the techniques we were applying. Lyotard's definitions of postmodern knowledge – 'The artist and the writer ... are working without rules in order to formulate the rules of what *will have been done*'[7] – seemed to speak to us as practitioners. A trip to the theory basement of Compendium Books was an obligatory Saturday afternoon enthrallment. Secondly, the influence of a generation of American poets who also fed off this theoretical moment, the language poets, cannot be overestimated. Their theoretical musings, particularly from 1978 in $L=A=N=G=U=A=G=E$ magazine, encouraged poetics in hybrid forms: reviews of books that were collages of its contents, collage poems that were also reviews of books. Thirdly, this British poetry itself was beginning to be studied, by myself amongst (a very few) others, in my PhD which resurfaced in my 2005 volume *The Poetry of Saying*.[8] But all the time I was keeping my own poetics discourse alive outside of the academy: in reviews, in my magazine *Pages*, in the editing of an anthology, in the poetry itself, and in the simple keeping of a notebook, something that continues, as I shall show. It seemed natural, therefore, to encourage others to do similarly, when I arrived at Edge Hill in 1996.

What is not on my list of influences (you might think oddly) is the rapid development of Creative Writing as an academic subject. This occurred when my back was turned and I was outside the academy. Let me

---

[7] Lyotard, J-F. (1984) *The Postmodern Condition*, Manchester: Manchester University Press, 60.

[8] Sheppard, R. (2005) *The Poetry of Saying: British Poetry and its Discontents 1950-2000*, Liverpool: Liverpool University Press.

confess openly, that I was sceptical about Creative Writing, since my taking the subject on the pioneering MA at the University of East Anglia in the late 1970s. Once I had begun my PhD, I ceased to mention the 'Creative Writing' component of my MA much (whose only lesson, I thought, at the time, was that I could not write fiction, which I have recently *un*learned). I see now, and wish to acknowledge, that I am as much a grateful product of UEA as of the British Poetry Revival. Nevertheless, I regarded Creative Writing with some suspicion, because it seemed antithetical to the kinds of explorative poetry and poetics I was writing and writing about, in favour of what is known in the US as the 'workshop poem', a neat formulaic and formalist lozenge of experience, lightly spiced with epiphany or leavened with moral. This has since changed, although my setting up of the Network of Experimental Writing Tutors (the glorious sounding NEWT) was both an acknowledgement of the entry into the academy of other like-minded writers, and of the fear that we still need to stick together as potentially endangered amphibians. But, more importantly to my current exploration, early Creative Writing also seemed to downplay the function of poetics. To a great extent this was an unfair pre-judgement, and my recent research for the English Subject Centre on what I call 'supplementary discourses' – all the parts of Creative Writing teaching which are not creative: commentaries, reading as a writer exercises and so forth – revealed a variety of reflective and speculative practices, some of which I happily call poetics.[9] But the research strengthened my sense of its specificity and I argued as such in a pamphlet I entitled *The Necessity of Poetics*.[10]

Another effect of the comparatively obscured or hybrid nature of poetics is the misreading of it as though it were a variety of literary theory or literary criticism. If you still think they are the same, consult Jon Cook's excellent anthology *Poetry In Theory* – another product of UEA by the way – the contents of which fall into three broad (sometimes overlapping) categories: literary theory (written by philosophers and theorists, which is constructed at a high level of generality and, it has to be confessed, a low level of specific textual reference; it is alarming how much Lacan seems to squeeze from one line of Mallarmé); literary criticism (which is usually

---

[9] The full report, *Supplementary Discourses in Creative Writing Teaching in Higher Education,* which was written by myself with research assistance from Dr Scott Thurston, may be found in full on the English Subject Centre website, at: www. english.heacademy.ac.uk/archive/projects/reports/supdisc_cwrit.doc.

[10] I also followed another example of linguistically innovative poetry, which I pass onto my students: I published it from my own small press Ship of Fools.

textually specific around themes or authors, such as Barbara Hernstein Smith's 'Closure and anti-closure in Modern Poetry' or excerpts from Thomas Yingling's *Hart Crane and the Homosexual Text*); and poetics, an altogether tattier affair written by creative writers themselves, often in forms which evade formal academic discourse, such as Charles Olson's seminal and expressive 'Objective Verse' essay.[11]

But this still begs a question: if poetics is so specific a *writerly* response, what is the purpose of reading it, both for other writers, and non-writers? Who is its audience? And how might this discourse impact upon Creative Writing as an academic discipline and upon English Studies generally. In short: why read poetics and how to read it?

It's a sorry confession, but I think I have wasted time and energy reading poetics in the hope that it would tell me *how* to write. There is a whole species of Creative Writing handbook and textbook and workbook that claims to tell you how to write, while usually coyly disavowing such an intention. I am sceptical of these, even as I've contributed to one, and they seldom rise to poetics.[12] To misread Charles Olson's essay 'Projective Verse' as a 'how to' guide – to fixate on its emphasis on the line as breath, the use of the typewriter as a scoring device, for example – can work only if one is content to remain a second or third generation Olsonian. Fortunately, much poetics (including Olson's essay) resist being read in this way. Part of the attraction of poetics to fragmentary and hybrid form is to evade the totalising certainty of a manifesto.

One exemplary work of poetics is the notebook kept by the senior and – in my opinion – major, British poet, Christopher Middleton, entitled 'A Nocturnal Journal'.[13] A journal is one of the more obvious modes of poetics, an easy way for a writer to dialogue with his or her practice, and one we encourage in all our writing students. It can particularly accommodate 'speculation', though Middleton favours a term he uses of his polished essays as well: 'conjecture'. This suggests that every utterance is in inverted commas. Each statement can be read as a question; it's like a reversible skirt or jacket. For example, musing upon Benjamin Fondane's discriminations between philosophy and poetry, Middleton asks, 'What he certainly doesn't

---

[11] Cook, J. (2004) *Poetry as Theory*, Oxford: Blackwell.

[12] 'Try Something Different' (with Scott Thurston), in eds., Graham, R., et. al, *The Road to Somewhere: A Creative Writing Companion*, Basingstoke, Palgrave Macmillan, 2005, pp. 207-16.

[13] Middleton, C. (2004) *Palavers & A Noctural Journey*, Exeter: Shearsman Books. Future references to this text will be indicated as *P*.

consider is a rather odd fact: no, a question – Don't some poets selectively breed only those ideas which promise poems?' (*P* 127). It may matter less that the idea is true (or false) than that the idea is rephrased as a question.[14] 'The activity of writing,' Middleton continues, 'may tend less to father ideas than to *other* them, and to gainsay their power' (*P* 127). The poem as an arena for the estrangement of the violating power of ideation is itself a powerful idea and reminds us that much poetics – and Middleton's journal entries hover around the theme as its irresistible honeypot – concerns a situated definition of poetry itself.

Defining poetry is a tricky business even for a conjectural poetics. On the one hand, you have Douglas Oliver, in his book *Whisper 'Louise'*, in which poetics arises periodically, offering an essentialist definition: 'Poetry is not summed up by poems... A *poem* taps into poetry, a primordial form of knowing emanating from the "one life" that we share with animals... Poetry is a fundamental aspect of mind.'[15] In this view, an individual poem affords access to the basic life force of the universe, here defined as a mode of thinking. But the individual poem disappears under a welter of obligations to the cosmos. Another view, that of Middleton in his journal, takes on board the 'concept' – his word – of poetry as 'an extrapolation from an infinitely heterogeneous range of possible poems. Brecht's graphic poems are no less poems than Mallarmé's enigmatically involuted logocentric charms' (*P* 119). In one view the nature of poetry must be fixed a priori; in the second the nature of poetry is open to modification, that is, to history. Both views constitute poetics (though I favour the latter).

We overhear Middleton in his notes asking himself (again), after half a century of practice, to define poetry. It may be possible that the journal was kept during a period of creative fallowness; poetics is often born of moments of crisis (which might be constant) and of the perpetual need to change, in Middleton's case, as he entered his eighth decade. In short, his poetics was a provocation to himself. It speaks differently. If we are writers we read it with a related sense of provocation to move towards (or beyond) our own conjectures and speculations to enable our own art, our own 'ideas which promise poems'.

It is this sense of *provocation* I would wish Creative Writing students (or any writer) to read out of poetics, to educate them away from the

---

[14] Of course, such 'selective breeding' may be yet another definition of poetics itself.

[15] Oliver, D. (2005) *Whisper 'Louise'*, Hastings: Reality Street Editions, 162. Future references to this text will be marked *WL*.

expectations of the answers and models of 'how to' books, to the questioning of conjectures, which requires an active response, and which could either be further poetics or creative work itself.[16]

It follows from this that much poetics is read wrongly, and not just by writers looking for knack and wheeze, but by critics who are looking at it as though it is a theory of writing similar to their own, or as an interpretive tool, or even – more basely – for actual authoritative interpretations of particular texts, which they can never be, by my definitions. Critics are often slightly incredulous at the indirection, the incoherences and inconsistencies of writerly poetics.[17] But I would like to wear the glint on this badge of shame as my beacon of faith! I think that the greatest apologia for Creative Writing *as an academic study* is not that it produces writers and writing, but that it poses questions of literariness in this conjectural way, through both the production and reading of poetics, which is neither blueprint nor theory.

Poetics can heal the creative-critical split of some Creative Writing programmes, render the boundaries between them porous, or – most radically – erase the distinction entirely.

It follows that, in addition to teaching writing students how to write poetics, poetics should be studied in the academy, and that we must learn to read and use it in ways not yet developed, or only partially developed. This is miles away from calls for Creative Writing to be regarded as an adjunct to English literature teaching, to promote conventional reading through so-called 'creative' exercises. As English Studies becomes more affected by the presence of Creative Writing, with a growing student body alert to the potential mobility of text and to *speculative* ideas about textuality, then it will have – perhaps unforeseen – effects. Poetics should be at the heart of Creative Writing, which in turn should be at the heart of a reoriented English Literature, which might rediscover questions of literary value and resistances to what Derek Attridge calls 'instrumentalist' readings

---

[16] I would like to acknowledge Cliff Yates, a member of the Poetry and Poetics Research Group that has met here at Edge Hill since 1999, for emphasising the term 'provocation' in his poetry and poetics PhD.

[17] Ian Gregson is one critic who sees this. Indeed, he writes of Middleton: 'Throughout his career he has formulated theories about how a poet should ideally write but has also been aware that what actually gets written is different.' Gregson, I. (1996) *Contemporary Poetry and Postmodernism: Dialogue and Estrangement*, Basingstoke and London, Macmillan, 152. His excellent chapter 9, 'Christopher Middleton: Journeys Broken at the Threshold', is one of the best pieces about the poet.

of literature.[18] We need poetics journals, centres, conferences, networks, poetics research groups, teaching modules and further academic study to explore poetics and how to write it and to read it. Practice-based research in poetics and academic research into poetics (both of which are in their infancy under those designations) need to acquire a language to talk to one another.

MEASURING EXPERIENCE

I am going to treat Christopher Middleton's 'A Nocturnal Journal' as a series of provocations to my own habitual ways of thinking about poetry and to demonstrate how its conjectural exploration of literariness – its poetics – differs from literary theory or literary criticism.

'A Nocturnal Journal' is a 40-page notebook assembled over about a year – 1997–8 – written in various locations, and, in addition to poetics, it considers whether animals have memory; the nature of various artists – work seen in Delacroix's studio, for example – and various European and Turkish histories. There is one septuagenarian sexual epiphany and a *récit* upon bottoms in Berlin.[19]

As ever, this pan-European US resident, bemoans British artistic insularity, and the 'failure of English poets, by and large, to risk, question, challenge, subvert, conventional ways of measuring experience', a remark that motivates his attempts throughout the notebook (*P* 142). Our greatest failures are failures of the imagination in Middleton's view, and his self-disgust at his momentary 'speculation' that a litter-strewn platform might be an art installation, for example, comes from being momentarily hoodwinked by conceptual art's impoverishment of the aesthetic dimension.[20] Indeed,

---

[18] Attridge, D. (2004) *The Singularity of Literature*, London and New York: Routledge, 6-10.

[19] There is also much poetics to engage with in the journal with which I do not deal here. For example, one finds one of Middleton's old contentions that poetry is too rich aurally to be actually heard in performance, that the 'inner ear is capable of an auditory complexity which exceeds almost any audible vocalizing', that the poem can best exist as a wordless *gestalt* in our memories. (Middleton, op. cit., 92.) It is a conjecture which partly contests my enthusiasm for the poetry reading as one of poetry's provisional institutions.

[20] 'How tormented the present century has been by the decay of imagination into paranoia and mass hysteria'. Middleton , C. (1998) *Jackdaws Jiving* , Manchester: Carcanet, 2.

while his concern with aesthetics – which is the ancient theoretical twin of poetics – seems old-fashioned, it does accord with the 'aesthetic turn' in literary studies of the last few years, a 'turn' which might prove another of the avenues for poetics to be particularised for study.[21]

His refusal to use the language of literary theory and criticism much, though he borrows freely from philosophy, is one of the notable and fresh features of the journal and it gives it an urgency, as when he examines anew the conventional distinction between writers oriented towards phenomena and those (post-twentieth century) artists, like his experimentalist Oulipo friend, Oskar Pastior, who have treated the word itself as a phenomenon – those whose experience is of the world and those whose experience *is* the word, those who work to reach out into the mute world and those who dig deeply into the spoken word to find its 'latent innermosts' – and Middleton calls each disposition a *niche* (a biological term indicating a self-sustaining environment) *(P* 121). I want to concentrate on these conjectures about the role of *experience* in poetry.

Middleton is no enthusiast for self-expressive art (he mocks 'the self-juicing artist' here) *(P* 131), and has argued for a poetry of artifice against one of 'anecdote' elsewhere and often, the 'configural' against the 'confessional', in Middleton's terms,[22] the latter a version of a 'poetry of panic and egomaniacal delirium'.[23] At a less extreme level he distrusts poetry that hangs 'an edict from an anecdote', one version of the workshop poem I mentioned earlier.[24] Although I agree with this, as a writer who perhaps has justified his practices more in the 'word' niche than the 'world' niche, I am provoked – that doesn't mean convinced – by his conjectures about experience.

---

[21] The aesthetic turn may be demonstrated by volumes such as Attridge, op.cit., and Joughin, J.J. and Malpas, S., eds, (2003) *The New Aestheticism*, Manchester and New York: Manchester University Press.

[22] Ibid, 28

[23] Ibid, 30

[24] Ibid, 25. He most forcefully expresses his case in 'Reflections on a Viking Prow', which begins: 'To recapture poetic reality in a tottering world, we may have to revise, once more, the idea of a poem as an expression of the "contents" of a subjectivity. Some poems, at least, and some types of poetic language, constitute structures of a singularly radiant kind, where "self-expression" has undergone a profound change of function. We experience these structures, if not as revelations of being, then as apertures upon being. We experience them as we experience nothing else.' Ibid, 24.

Although Middleton's poetics is tinged with aesthetics, it emerges from his writerly concern for his *own* experiences; he conjectures: 'Tacit criteria for poems read: can they compete with, can they outweigh, certain experiences (aesthetic or not) which one has had?...' (*P* 103). He lists a sequence of his most profound experiences, both positive and negative. It's a heavy burden to put upon other poems, and an incalculable weight with which to balance one's own creative work. Perhaps all the writer can do is ensure that 'the poem should be full of events (linguistic or vital)' (*P* 106). These two 'events' correspond to the two 'niches' of contemporary writing: linguistic experience and lived experience. 'Event' is taken as intrinsic to the life of the poem, to its artifice, not to its pre-existent life 'anecdote'. I take the point here, but wonder how experience can be rendered without some narrational function that at least risks anecdote.[25] We can, however, appreciate that the artificial antidote to self-expressive anecdote lies in aesthetic transformation, as when we attend to the strange self-ordering of the most impressive bits and pieces of our recalled and unignorable experience, which is what Middleton is describing when he argues that

> The 'aesthetic' (*keen* perception) preserves in memory small ensembles, of feelings and objects, which have undecidable values, opalescent ensembles. But they have presence, intricacy, and from them, as stored images, flows an ordering power, a transitive power to order diffuse and scattered particles of experience in a here-and-now. The liberating transitivity, thus, of the image, in memory, in 'art', counters the entrapment of the ego in circumstance and selfhood (*P* 103-4).

The role of the aesthetic in this passage is more than that of 'keen perception', and later in the journal Middleton proffers a traditional definition: 'I mean by aesthetic... a certain deep-down urge to make (not impose) order and beauty from what you experience as chaos or horror' (*P* 114). I'm not sure what Middleton would finally intend here (if there *is* an end to speculative conjecture), because one of his conjectures here has experience ordering itself, while the other makes 'order' a part of writerly poesis. Perhaps the 'orderings' are of different kinds, of aesthetic experience and of aesthetic

---

[25] Even in Middleton's own splendid poem 'Wild Horse', he includes anecdotal asides: 'Thinking of you Ann Alberto Caroline/ And you Tsëpë Romanian clown my friend', though he adds: 'And someone else I'll put no name to'. Middleton, C. (2001) *The Word Pavilion and Selected Poems*, Manchester: Carcanet, 209.

making, but he doesn't say so. ('Aesthetic' as a term can, after all, relate both to keen sensory perception and to art.)

Middleton hopes of this transformative aesthetic experience: 'To come through, at least, with a piece of Paradise stuck to your boot' (*P* 114). After my not-so youthful absorptions of Herbert Marcuse's and TW Adorno's socialist readings of the aesthetic dimension and aesthetic theory (to allude to the titles of their influential volumes), any piece of Paradise will always be imaged as stuck to a boot that has necessarily waded through the blood of history. As Adorno reminds us: 'Even in a legendary better future, art could not disavow remembrance of accumulated horror.'[26] But Middleton doesn't take that negative turn here; indeed, elsewhere he states that Adorno's 'conceptual system ... exists to house despair, not to defeat it', which at least implies that his own aim is to defeat despair.[27] In any case, vigorous aesthetic transformation, the traditional urge to create, is political enough in what I call our 'September 12' world. 'The violence of the urge, in Delacroix, say, or Picasso, is utterly other than that of the Sultans, Despots, or calculating terrorists: theirs only leads to more violence, or to schemes which exploit, absorb, and jellify the aesthetic' (*P* 114). (This 1997–8 notebook is prescient in naming Osama Bin Laden at one point.) Middleton expresses how he conjectures jellification to occur: 'Fundamentalisms, Islamic, Judaic, or Christian are divisive and their (undialectical) intolerance of the *other* is what art... is not. Art... isn't from another world, it isn't superhuman, but it arouses the feeling that alternative worlds could be as congenial as this one at its rare best moments' (*P* 133). This reversal of metaphysical otherness, in favour of the otherness that art always brings into being through its innovations, is important to bear in mind when Middleton describes the event of that otherness coming into being in quasi-spiritual language:

> It is poetry happening when language rises to the challenge to connect a sense of the historical world as an obstacle and a sense of the numinous as a power levitating the obstacle (*P* 108).

This carefully constructed sentence alone deserves more consideration than I can give it tonight. The active verbs, 'happen', 'rise' and 'levitate', grant to

[26] Adorno, T.W. (2002) *Aesthetic Theory*, London and New York, NY: Continuum, 324. Marcuse's volume is Marcuse, H. (1978) *The Aesthetic Dimension*, London and Basingstoke: Macmillan.

[27] Middleton, *Jackdaws Jiving*, 5.

literary language the agency to 'connect' the two senses he intuits – history as an obdurate mass and the numinous as its transcendence: the event of the poem transforming the event of history into the eventless eternality of the near-divine aesthetic dimension. The two 'senses' cooperate like the parts of a musical fugue: 'There is "augmentation through contrary motion"...', he says (*P* 108). Middleton attempts to describe the 'process' and the images that arise, although it is clear that imagination (of the writer? of the reader? – he doesn't say) is the unifying principle of this 'happening' as poetry: 'The poem...is a "picture" – of process – which an individual imagination composes and decomposes, volatile, streaming, inexplicable' (*P* 108).

Literary language is obliged to be the engine that rises to the challenge of connecting history and the transcendent, releasing the historical from its determinants, the more luminously to see it. Here, where Middleton becomes technical, he also becomes tentative, and self-questioning:

> In so *doing*, language gives full and sufficient (which?) play to its own often opposing functions: to represent exactly and to suggest mysteriously; to fix the isolable specific, and to resonate with vibrant universal process. Hence the anguish embedded in aesthetic delight... (*P* 108).

I baulk at any talk of '*universal* process' until it is further defined (as it won't be in this conjectural poetics); I wonder whether it is any kind of universality at all that causes the agony and the ecstasy of art, in its dialectic with the 'the isolable specific'. However, I take joy in Middleton's multiple and suggestive account of the objects of the poet's keen perception. This is where he fires me! His poetics revitalises a sense long-lost to literary criticism that art is good for us, that 'imagination is also a source of well-being' against atavistic misappropriations by bigots and commerce (or global terror – fundamentalism – and global capital, we might say now).[28] He again qualifies the status of the 'order' that emerges from chaos, in an account of *how* artists select art's contents:

> The 'isolable specific' is *selected*, of course. It is picked out of the junk: a firefly rescued among rotting vegetables; no, real gypsy music which starts a wild dance in the sedatest tea-room (*P* 108).

---

[28] Ibid, 4.

I wish I had Middleton's eye to pick specifics out of the junk, to approach this 'poetics of difference' which he begins to sketch here (*P* 108).

Indeed, this whole poetics is curiously full-blooded and skeletal at once; it is exact and suggestive in equal measure. But perhaps this is just to detect the presence of poetics as I follow the trace of Middleton's mind moving through its speculations, scattering conjectures like spring blossom, experiencing it arriving at thoughts as though for the first time. It is unlike reading most literary theory. It cuts across my politicised sense of the aesthetic dimension, as it may cut across Middleton's own, of course (he is not an unpolitical poet).[29] His feeling for the necessary transformation of experience rather than my own sense that the transformation of language *is* the experience of the poem, taunts me as I question myself in the noisy niche of the *word* poet with his 'linguistic innovation'. I have long thought that writing should provide an experience for the reader *in* the reading; that is obviously important. This supplementary view is not that poetry should merely be about what happens to us, though both we and the writing should be *worthy* of what happens to us, a theme to which I will return. It is rather that experience – not reduced to anecdote, but disclosed as a psychic, social and environmental complex – can be transfigured into the energy we call poetry, by the energy we call poetry. The insistence in Middleton's poetics that *both* experiences are necessary – of *world* as well as *word* – provokes me towards dialogic change.[30]

Doing Poetics

What I am going to read now comes from my rather rough poetics 'notebook' – more a commonplace book – rather than a composed and elegant 'Journal', like Middleton's. It consists of unfinished thinking in glimpses and gestures, pointing and naming. It is wasteful to reproduce its dispersal and repetitions. I have therefore edited and rearranged some of its

[29] I am here alluding to his poem 'How to Listen to Birds'. which appears to be instructions to do just that, but which ends, with masterly enjambement: 'This / is not unpolitical'. Middleton, C. *The Word Pavilion and Selected Poems*, 201-2.

[30] Indeed, this is the very balance Middleton's friend Zulfikar Ghose finds in the work: 'Christopher's poetry is not so much about so-called "human experience" as it is experience itself or an instant of revelation when a fragment of experience is comprehended by the imagination receptive to specially constructed nuances of language.' See 'Christopher Middleton and *The Bare Bone of Creation*', in *Chicago Review*, 51:1/2, Spring 2005, 49-58, at 54.

parts, and have re-written short passages, in the course of which its main concerns become clearer, but it now reads very differently – to me – and I have discerned patterns of yearning of which I was hitherto unaware, and which I need to consider, perhaps, in the light of my future practice. You can hear me talking to myself and, not surprisingly, you may lose me in places. This doesn't matter. I want you to feel what it is like to *do* poetics.

Jettisoned along the way are asides on reading the 'visionary metapoems' of Paavo Haavikko and Antonio Porta, the haiku-like *dainas* of Latvia, some attempts at fresh poems, as well as plans to write a complete fictional poet's real poems (a project best left for another occasion, believe me!). Notes which lead nowhere (yet) – such as 'Idea: write 6 poems beginning with the word "Between"' – are also omitted. Curiously, there's nothing about my fiction writing, which is another story. The notes were made irregularly between June 2005 and September 2006, during which time I turned 50.

What I fear by making it public is exactly the diminution of its conjecturality, as it were, that merely by filtering a comment from the scribble, it might assume an authority it neither deserves, nor seeks, and that it will cease to be read as poetics. It follows that this poetics should not be used in the attempt to 'clarify' or 'focus' the poems that follow. These are the dangers, but it is one of my main contentions that we need to develop new ways of reading such a discourse as a conjectural and primary investigation into the nature of writing, which allow for its twisting and turning, 'duckin' and divin'', and – remember – the almost inevitable, and even deliberate, mismatch with the work for which it acts as permission.

*

Unease, and not knowing quite how to get going again, despite the success of the poetry and prose piece 'Roosting Thought'. Say, – of *how* lyrical I could become (that 'I' of course), reading Jennifer Moxley. But also *how* visually disposed upon the page (screen space, Barbara Guest), or how rhetorically flat (Mei Mei Berssenbrugge). Or indeed how to deal with enjambement. Is syntax struggling against prosody, sentence against line, as in Agamben's agonistic formulation, or struggling for their reconciliation? As Keston Sutherland rather abstractly suggests: 'Prosody is implicit cognition … manifest in poetic language as the technical and unending dialectic of transgression and reconciliation'.[31] An 'ever-compensated-for-

---

[31] Sutherland, K., 'Prosody and Reconciliation', *The Gig*, 16, February 2004, 41-

falling', as someone – Merleau Ponty? – described walking?

Deleuze writes: 'To the question, "Who is speaking?" we answer sometimes with the individual (Classical), sometimes with the person (Romantic), and sometimes with the ground that dissolves both.' Then he quotes Nietzsche: 'The self of the lyric poet raises its voice from the bottom of the abyss of being; its subjectivity is pure imagination.'[32]

But my edition of *The Birth of Tragedy* has Nietzsche saying: 'The 'I' of the lyricist therefore sounds from the depth of his being: its "subjectivity", in the sense of modern aestheticians is a fiction.'[33] Which would be a restatement of the 'Romantic'. Roll on the ground that dissolves....

*

Why should the poem be 'a form of life'? (Joan Retallack) Why a model? Such a notion may destroy its efficacy. Critique?

So in the deepest sense to discover what poetry is. To rise beyond

the technical → social → ethical

(the 'levels' of textual analysis in my book *The Poetry of Saying*). Conversely, *start* with the distinction between the 'saying' as quality and the 'said' as quality and to radiate out towards *various* textual strategies that enable 'saying', not just so-called 'linguistically innovative' ones.

To bear in mind the interrelated 'three ecologies' of Guattari:[34]

psyche ↔ socius ↔ environment

which comes back to my definition of 'Writing' in 'The End of the Twentieth Century' (1999), though there it's ironised, even comic, and quotes a poetics notebook of 1993:

55, at 53-4.

[32] Deleuze, G. (2001) *The Logic of Sense*, London: Continuum, 140-1.

[33] Nietzsche, F. (1967), trans. Kaufmann, W., *The Birth of Tragedy and The Case of Wagner*, New York: Vintage Books, 49.

[34] This is a reference (as are later ones) to Guattari, F. (2000) *The Three Ecologies*, London and New Brunswick, The Athlone Press.

Writing

both process and product, is a significant and coherent deformation of the linguistic system with the power to reorder and reconfigure individual, collective and social constructs of subjectivity, the face to face encounter with alterity, which will assist the processes of greater subjective autonomy and responsibility towards the other, as just one example of a possible aestheticisation of politics to catalyze change in the environmental, social, and psychological domains.[35]

*

I think of W.S. Graham, around 50, reaching the apparent simplicity of *Malcolm Mooney's Land* after rhetorical excess. And of his rigorous self-editing.

Or of something like this? 'The starkness of this late vision...is paralleled by an aesthetic absoluteness that replaces the earlier grammatical complexity with an uncomplicated syntax consisting largely of declarative sentences and a purified style,' as Edmund Keeley wrote of Yannis Ritsos.[36] Not those determinants in my case, of course, nor so 'late' I hope...

Or of thinking through the implications of the footnote I added to my essay 'A Carafe, a Blue Guitar, Beyonding Art: Krzysztof Ziarek and the Avant-Garde', when I surprised myself by saying, 'as a member (or past member) of one of these avant-garde groupings....':

'The reason I ponder my possible "past" membership of an avant-garde is not my fear that I've not kept up my subscription, or that a modern-day Breton has expelled me for having a bourgeois face or something, but that I feel geographically remote from the centres of avant-garde practice, and that I've reached an age when perhaps one's poetics – which is hopefully still avant-garde in some sense – is developed for the individual and less for

---

[35] Sheppard, R. (2002) *The End of the Twentieth Century*, Liverpool: Ship of Fools, np. This is republished in *Complete Twentieth Century Blues* (2008) Cambridge: Salt Publishing, 331-350.

[36] Keeley, E, 'Introduction' to his *Ritsos in Parenthesis* (1979) Princeton: Princeton University Press, xxv-xxvi.

the group, though I hope it is of use [I would mean now "provocation"] to others. I'm frankly not looking over my shoulder to see whether I adhere to the manifesto. The wolfish packing mentalities of avant-gardes are their least attractive aspects, despite the historical necessity of exclusivity and a decent supply of the drug of choice.'[37]

*

I read Douglas Oliver's *Whisper 'Louise'*… He positions his own art as non-mainstream and non 'innovative'. He talks, though, of needing a further dichotomy, that of the extremes of 'clarity' and 'obscurity' – *not* for his work to be located in the middle (a third way poetics), which is where mediocrity lies, but to inhabit *both* 'extremes' at once. (He imagines this geopoetically on a map of Paris, Heine and Celan the 'extremes'.) I'm not suggesting for one moment that there is a contradiction here, at all, but that the two go together, at least in Doug's mind.

The work neither belongs to the avant-garde nor to the mainstream; it belongs to both the extremes of 'positive … ballad-like poetry' and to 'negative opaque and complex' poetry: 'both poles … are necessary'. The positive is also 'bravery in withstanding vicissitudes' (WL 340); but is there no 'also' for the negative, the complex, no bravery there? so why that polarity at all? In any case, a sense here of an individual positioning himself.

The book is also trying to posit the positivities of Poetry: [Here I quote the essentialist definitions of poetry I discussed earlier. I continue:] And, less explicitly, but more complexly, poetry is related to an eidetic consciousness, surrounded by the 'humming', the background 'radiation' of the universe. So that:

> 'In life … the healthiest agents of a story's collapse are love, justice, mercy and hope. It takes love to understand' death (*WL* 423).

Kind. Kindness. It all ends up as a series of abstract nouns, like Stefan Themerson's 'decency of means'. (Indeed both are trying to avoid the fanatic's monomania… Philip Roth's *I Married a Communist* is arguing something similar. Like Oliver, he sees personal heroisms amid both personal and public stupidities (on both sides), the McCarthyite witch hunts not too different a historical mess from the Paris Commune in

---

[37] 'A Carafe, a Blue Guitar, Beyonding Art: Krzysztof Ziarek and the Avant-Garde,' *Avant-Post*, ed. Armand, L., published by Litteraria Pragensia (Prague), July 2006.

Oliver's reading.). Yet neither of these is a 'slogan'.

What impresses me is the long-term/large-scale working out of these things. But with the openness to know that he hasn't the answers to some of the questions he posits, whether his residual materialist scepticism about 'eidetic consciousness', or about the 58 items on his list of undeniable 'potentially disastrous pathways' for humanity.

What is interesting is the sense of measuring all this against one's death, though he didn't know he was dying when he began the book, out of some ethic for the only life, the 'one life', the only earth. I think of *The Three Ecologies* of Guattari – but I remember that he (or Deleuze, or both) is called a 'bigot' by Oliver in one of the few bigoted moments of the book. I read that accusation sitting opposite Patricia reading Deleuze [indeed, the influence of her researches are felt throughout this notebook]. A post-Deleuzean definition of the purpose of art hangs upon my study wall:

> Artworks ... are not there to save us or perfect us (or to damn or corrupt us), but rather to complicate things, to create more complex nervous systems no longer subservient to the debilitating effects of clichés, to show and release the possibilities of a life (John Rajchman).[38]

'Release' is suggestively dynamic here.

Also in that article on Krzysztof Ziarek and the avant-garde is some address to Utopianism. I know! I've run hot and cold on that for a couple of decades. Doug only has the utopianism of his 'subject', Louise Michel, in his sights, as self-delusion. She was an anarchist and willing to destroy human life to achieve her aims, like Blair even. But unlike Oliver, or Levinas, or Ziarek, who have a basically pacifist ethos or like Themerson, who sees only tragedy ('Factor T') facing the decency of means.[39]

But Ziarek's aesthetics – how he would hate that word – is a utopianism of sorts: 'predicated on its ultimate success but guaranteed only by its inevitable failure' as I put it. I mean utopianism *in*, within, folded into, art.

---

[38] Rajchman, J. (2000) *The Deleuze Connections*, Cambridge, Mass and London: The MIT Press, 138.

[39] See Themerson, S. (1972) *Factor T*, London: Gaberbocchus. One example of Factor T is our dislike of killing being matched by the necessity of doing it. I promised in footnote 1 that Themerson would re-appear.

Which perhaps makes utopianism more powerful, so long as we remember with Adorno that 'Art's utopia is draped in black'.[40]

*

qualities of

lucidity

(with its connotations of
shining /transparency/easily understood /intellectually brilliant

and

complexity

(with its connotations of
infolding/being composed of many parts/intricate

rather than – say – 'lucidity' and 'diversity', as in Lyotard's binary, borrowed from Malraux's borrowings from Valéry: 'It befalls consciousness to assemble and unify diversity while lucidity mercilessly trains a *flash* of light on the worst of it all.'[41]

Or Oliver's poles of 'complexity' and 'obscurity', or even Christopher Middleton's attractive dyad for the poem during composition, of 'effervescence' and 'distillation' (*P* 22).[42]

*

---

[40] Adorno, TW, *Aesthetic Theory*. I have been unable to re-locate this quotation.

[41] Lyotard, J-F (2001) *Soundproof Room*, Stanford, Stanford University Press, 46.

[42] I find that Borges, in one of his introductions to a volume of his poems, *The Self and the Other*, puts his finger on both the question of writerly development and the nature of the preferred model of complexity: 'The fate of the writer is strange. He begins his career by being a baroque writer, pompously baroque, and after many years, he might attain if the stars are favourable, not simplicity, which is nothing, but rather a modest and secret complexity.' Borges, J. (1999), *Selected Poems*, New York: Viking, 149.

Christopher Middleton's best poems

Stage their own meanings as they unfold
The rhythm and lineation enact the unfolding

They are joyful in their very processes (like the singing of Sarah Vaughan,
that sudden high-octane octave-leaping swoop on 'I'll Never Be the Same')
They mediate matter and mind; consciousness
The language is precise but never bookish (despite his reputation as a
difficult writer. He's written some of the best poems about cats). Vernacular.
Spoken

Most of Middleton's poems begin in the quotidian, from 'starters', technically speaking, but end somewhere else, elsewhither, elsewise. In short,
that is their purpose, as embodied ecstasies.[43]

They are splendid – in the full sense of the word – articulations of the
human attempt to access Being, something visionary, that integrates
experience through experiences articulated. Many of them unfold that
articulation in their own artifices. The result: beauty as well as splendour,
even with negative experiences...

[I paused from my notebook for a moment to play my audience a recording
of Middleton reading his poem 'Old Bottles'.[44] It is an early work, first
published in the 1960s, demonstrating *some* of the qualities I list in the
notebook. It seems to be an oneiric poem, or a hypnogogic-into-dream
poem, but somehow it gives access to deeper levels of dream that embody
the deadliest moments of twentieth century European history, especially
through the resonant 'isolable specific' of the striped pyjamas. Indeed, one
of Middleton's 'negative' experiences against which he will measure any

---

[43] I am pleased to find Jeremy Hooker expressing it thus: 'If Middleton's poems are
journeys or voyages of imagination, they also move by "turns" or "leaps".' Hooker,
J. 'Habitation for a Spirit: The Art of Christopher Middleton', *Chicago Review*,
51:1/2, Spring 2005, 60-70, at 68. This article is one of the best pieces of writing
on Middleton. It comes from a special feature on Middleton's work in *Chicago
Review.*
[44] The recording may be heard on, and the text may be read in, (1995) *CD Poets 2*
London: Bellew Publishing. The text appears in Middleton, C. (2001) *The Word
Pavilion and Selected Poems*, 140-41. In the former, the word 'They'll' in line 27 is
given – and read – as the less-effective 'they'.

poem is his 'first sight of a person recently liberated from a KZ' in 1945 (*P* 103). It represents, I suppose, 'lucidity mercilessly train(ing) a *flash* of light on the worst of it all', in Lyotard's phrase, but I find it a curiously haunting and uplifting poem, possibly through the narrator's final deep-sleep habilitation and escape.]

*

Multitopics

Deleuze says, in *The Logic of Sense*, 'Either ethics makes no sense at all, or this is what it means and has nothing else to say: not to be unworthy of what happens to us.'[45] Not to be the 'creature of resentment' (Nietzsche again) but 'the free man who grasps the event, and does not allow it to be actualised as such without enacting.'[46]

Muslim resentment shouldn't drive British foreign policy, neither should it be ignored. It's disastrous in its own right, needs changing because it is immoral.

The free enquiry into culture/ language/ text/ science/ art not tied to theocracy in any form (whose paradox is that it is man-made, illusory, my last laugh). To create more complex nervous systems. Enlightenment and post-enlightenment values alike. Against the meganarrative.

An ethics of responsibility to the Other, as in Levinas' thought. 'And I say we should all be conditioned and educated to regard violence in any form as something to be ruthlessly mocked' (Muriel Spark).[47]

Not to be unworthy of what happens to us, to not curtail our civil liberties, or academic freedom and democracy, for example, to not answer terror with error. The greatest defence is the free use of the faculties that are being defended.

A commitment to the only earth we have. The three ecologies. Multitopia:

---

[45] Deleuze, op. cit., 149

[46] Ibid, 152

[47] Muriel Spark, quoted in Cheyette, B. (2000) *Muriel Spark*, Tavistock: Northcote House, 73.

'there is always another town within the town' (Deleuze).[48] Velopolis. Dissensus as well as consensus.

The necessity of Atheism? Brightness is all. In the face of William Empson's 'Torture Monster' and his death suckers. Religiomania *as* a mania. At its outer limit: 'Fundamentalism is a kind of necrophilia, in love with the dead letter of a text' (Eagleton).[49] The last recorded words of a suicide bomber, his fear of historical and human contingency: 'If I sit here I will commit sins.'

Species solidarity and a dispersal of subjectivities, subjectivation. A sense of humanness that has to come from a shared 'awareness of human frailty and unfoundedness' (Eagleton)[50] – of potential wounding – and hurt, and sexualities, and not from 'humanism', as that has evolved. We must 'keep faith with the open-ended nature of humanity, and this is a source of hope' (Eagleton).[51]

*

This is, remember, a spring-cleaned and tidied-up version of my intermittently written notebook. As I understand it, it offers speculations on, conjectures about, the effects of finding myself an older writer with an avant-garde heritage, and with a deep sense of a damaged utopian project for writing, as well as claiming a more generalised neurological function for art; a writer with an uncertain sense of how questions of prosody, lyricism and the lyric 'I' will play out in his future writing. It re-discovers my older definition of 'Writing' itself, which is consonant with a more recent formulation (though they are not the words I would use now). Remember my 80th definition of poetics: to come upon that which one already knows, but with the force of revelation as if discovered for the first time. Preferred qualities of writing – emulating the binary thinking of Oliver and Middleton and others – are expressed in terms of tensions between complexity and lucidity. Other qualities are detected in the work of other writers, as is common in poetics, in this case, in Middleton's, and, although I don't say it – don't need to – I am weighing these qualities against my own

---

[48] Deleuze, op. cit., 174.

[49] Eagleton, T. (2004) *After Theory*, London: Penguin, 207.

[50] Ibid, 221

[51] Ibid, 221

practice. Merely stating them as kinds of provisional benchmark may alter my poetic trajectory.

But the last section, 'Multitopics', is different. Again, the tidying up for you has hardened the outline of the conjectures, softened the fuzzy logics of poetics, and it's not possible to tell whether that is productive or not for the actual poems. In this case, it projects, in an unusually direct way, the still-to-to-be-written fourth sequence of 24 poems called *September 12* after the frozen state of emergency we are living through at the moment. [The title was finally 'Warrant Error', in my 2009 volume of that name.] These notes probably test out the *content* of that sequence – I can't imagine *not* using the quotation from the suicide bomber, or the rhyme of 'terror' and 'error' – and perhaps they exceed my definitions of poetics because of that; they are about *what*, not *how*, writing is made. All I can say is that the limits of poetics, the limitations on its scope, is yet again one of the projected areas of study for those of us involved in Creative Writing as an academic discipline.

Poems [52]

don't normally wear a suit   don't normally wear a tie   not at a reading
        (laughter) *not when I'm reading poems   that's all*   All poems   (single catcall from audience at disrobing) *I knew you'd say something*   All poems stage their meanings at a critical remove from their occasions, sources, influences and poetics. Sometimes poems subvert such complex and lucid notions as 'complexity' and 'lucidity', to produce poems that are anything but complex and lucid in an attempt to re-define   *those things*   In any case, poems… run ahead of the conjectures we make   *the conjectures run ahead of the poems at different times I'm going to read   I'm going to turn this into a brief poetry reading   partly because I believe that the poetry reading is one of the provisional institutions of linguistically innovative poetry or whatever you want to call it   and one of the functions of it is to flog books   I thought I'd do that   I have some books here and there's one thing free   and also there's something else that's common with poetry readings   that's a   that's a trip to the hostelry afterwards   I know there's a bun-fight immediately after this   but there could be an after after   I think I will simply delegate the Buck I' th'Vine as a possible   venue   so here are*

---

[52] I have attempted to transcribe the verbal introductions to the poems I read (in italics), which includes me reading and abandoning prepared text (in ordinary type) before the lecture transforms into a poetry reading. I have borrowed a number of transcription conventions from the 'talk poems' of David Antin.

five poems   they're all metapoems   they do what I was talking about   this is what I wrote for the Alan Halsey reading here as part of the series Ailsa (Cox) and I run from the writing department   I decided to do a kind of introduction for him I kind of see this as you know when you go home and you find three answerphone messages from the same person   it also rhymes and   I tell students 'rhyme is a crime'   but they never quite get the irony of me saying that   so I've got the maximum number of rhymes

[I then read 'The Hello Poem', 'Another Poem', after which I announced: *what I was attempting to do was to write something that was neither poetry or prose nor a critical article but it's a response to that book but I'm not sure you need to know that book* and read 'Not Another Poem', followed by 'As Yet Untitled Poem', which I told the audience was dedicated to John James and composed after his visit to Edge Hill. These four poems are from *Berlin Bursts*, but I concluded with 'Reading the Poem', which was later the untitled penultimate poem in *Warrant Error*, the work I was projecting in 'Multitopics' above.]

thank you   (applause)   *thank you*

Critical Tuning: Radio Interference
and Interruption as a Poetics for Writing

> Mayakovsky dreamt of a radio station for poets.
> *Shklovsky*

When I appeared on Rob Holloway's radio show *Up for Air* in November 2003, the engineer at Resonance FM noticed how many references to radio there were in my poems. While one of my chosen records was playing, we set up a microphone for him to repeat these remarks on air. It was true, I admitted, there were references to radio (or wireless) in a number of my poems. For example, Book 2 of *The Lores* is a narrative of a fascist traitor who broadcasts for the Nazis, a fictional analogue of the real Lord Haw-Haw, the man I mention elsewhere for having broadcast the news that my father – Bomber Command rear air gunner – was a POW in 1944.[1] Perhaps – deeper than this – there was a serious analogy to be teased out. I spoke a little of the importance of mass communications in the twentieth century, but that was only half the story.

I said that I'd always been fascinated by radio, that I was a DX-er as a teenager. DX is code for (long-)distance. In other words, I listened to radio broadcasts from around the world. The log I kept contains entries such as these:

> Quite a few weaker hams.
> Radio Nordsee International doing old Caroline thing of flashing headlamps from shore.
> Radio Denmark's last broadcast badly jammed on 19 mts.
> Radio Kiev (from Russia's Ukraine) answering questions and playing music from the USSR.
> Radio Prague from hidden base at 113 – fairly clear.
> Radio Pyongyang – or DX prog on 9 – not in English – very bad reception – the 41 metre band unusually workable.

---

[1] This points to another (dual) thematic focus of my work: war aviation and prison camps, which met in the long poem 'Schräge Musik', *Complete Twentieth Century Blues*, Cambridge: Salt, 2008: 20-36. (*The Lores* may also be found in this volume: 168-217, with Book Two located at 172-177.) Recently reading Ian Patterson's concise book *Guernica* (London: Profile, 2007) I suspect that this material is not exhausted.

Radio Tirana: the people who bend the news.

S.B.C. Call sign.

Sun Radio, a pirate broadcaster playing last hours of Radio London and the going illegal of Radio Caroline.

From amateur radio, which didn't interest me at all, since there was no content – the operators were expressly forbidden to discuss politics – to medium wave pirate stations playing rock. In some cases these were off-shore, in others, Sun Radio for example, it broadcast from a house round the corner every Sunday afternoon, louder than any other station on air! From short wave liberal democratic soft-propaganda to Soviet and Chinese hard-propaganda. Radio Tirana was the (literally) loudest Maoist mouthpiece on air. Such was the Babel I frequented.

The log shows that I listened intently between 1968 and 1970. Occasionally, I caught world events. The covert operations of Radio *Free* Prague (an incident from the Russian invasion of Czechoslovakia that turns up in my short story 'Tropp').[2] Or Radio Moscow rather solemnly announcing that Apollo 11 had landed on the Moon, the Russians throwing in the towel in the Space Race. This is preserved still on the hours of media source plus independent commentary that I recorded for myself on cassette tape on the moon-landings, my own private radio documentary.

In short, radio was ubiquitous, and was suffused with ideology and historical questions of its own legitimacy, and sometimes legality. A whole history is encoded in my bland log entry on Radio Kiev. Amid the whistles, static and distortion of the short wave bands (25, 32, etc.) a plurality of *voices* spoke to me. If I wanted music, on the other hand, that required a more consistent reception, not one that made all songs sound like the phased ending to Hendrix' 'Little Wing'! I listened to the medium wave pirates and the BBC for music. Although I remember tuning in to Emperor Rosko's Radio Luxembourg (French) programme on long wave with his Franglais catch-phrase, 'Maximum de musique; minimum de blah blah!' VHF (or FM) I disdained for being merely 'local'. Indeed, I marched on BBC Radio Brighton with the Campaign for Free Radio to demand the repeal of the Wireless Telegraphy Act 1968 that had banned the pirates which local radio had inadequately replaced in our opinion, a sentiment that missed the moral dilemmas posed by unregulated Capitalism. It was sometimes fun to tune into the police on VHF too, which I believe was

---

[2] In *Short Fiction* Issue 1, 2007: 136-163. Reprinted in *The Only Life*: Newton-le-Willows: Knives Forks and Spoons, 2011.

illegal but I knew that they couldn't track me.

It was strange and distant voices, in many languages, but predominantly in accented English, that drew me to short wave radio, for long hours, for many an evening. You didn't listen in one location for long. Once identification was established, you moved onto another station, tuning this way and that within the designated bands. The scramble around the top of the hour was particularly intense. The stations would then briefly identify themselves and offer their versions of the news. I didn't need lessons in Communication Studies to teach me about selection, bias, gatekeeping and ideology. Later, I always thought my own A Level students rather slow in picking this up. I was adept at recognising call-signs: the jaunty Swiss, the funereal Albanians, the confident Americans. The Voice of.

The lone speaker in the radio studio became my unacknowledged image of a kind of isolated heroics, even of authenticity of being. The single voice, possibly in the night, in a distant country, from a secret location, from a ship on the waves, or from a North Sea platform. I remember an episode of *Danger Man* set on a pirate station, possibly the platform that housed Radio Essex, the one that became Sealand, an attempted independent state. (I am still awaiting a reply to the letter I sent them in 1967.)

It's not too much of a mental leap to see here an image of the poet. A solitary voice – I've always read my poems out loud when composing them, and revising them, even now, on tape – finding its pitch among the dialogic babble, uncertain whether there's anybody listening. As Frank O'Hara said, 'It is good to be several floors up in the dead of night wondering if you are any good or not', particularly if you imagine you're in a radio studio: dead acoustics, thick glass, gleaming equipment, anonymous listeners of indeterminate number.[3] An image reinforced by the single-handed 'broadcasting' I inflicted upon my parents, via microphone, record deck, amplifier, a long flex from my bedroom to the living room, and loudspeaker, as Radio Slugwash International. I invented a world-wide media empire with such implausible names. No wonder the last time I was on live radio, interviewed about *Twentieth Century Blues* on Radio Merseyside, I felt the unshakeable conviction that I was on the wrong side of the desk.[4] But

---

[3] Frank O'Hara, quoted in Allnutt, Gillian, et. al., *The New British Poetry.* London: Paladin, 1988: v.

[4] Perhaps I felt something like that too, when in 1969 I was interviewed about Student Power of 3A, those of us who tried to take over our Secondary Modern School, though I would have been sniffy about merely being part of a local OB (outside broadcast). I could more or less do that myself with my tape recorders. It's

I have never thought of the poet as a radio set, as impassive medium, a metaphor famously taken up by Jean Cocteau and Jack Spicer.

It's an obvious image, of poet as radio-voice, but for me it's flooded with these memories, like strong radio signals seeping into and blocking the one you are trying to listen to. To those who've not heard it, it's difficult to describe the shifting of the signals and their relative strengths as they jostle for prominence, distorted as they bounce off the ionosphere. The sudden switching on of a transmitter somewhere knocks all the others off-balance. Even Radio One on medium wave on the South Coast of England had to contend with an underbelly of call signage from Radio Tirana from the other side of Europe. You can hear it on the BBC Soft Machine concert I taped in 1971. By that time, such interference was simply interference, as my interests shifted towards music, and tape recording engendered the skiffle-like 'splod' music which my friends and I invented and recorded passionately. The image of radio became a submerged metaphor for the act of writing, the speaking of the poem into a transmission device, its encoding and decoding, and reception at unknown sources, to use the simplistic Communication model of Shannon and Weaver that was itself derived from radio, but which includes the interference of 'noise'.

I'm not sure that the equation between broadcasting and writing is an analogy, since analogy implies a consciously worked-out correspondence. It's actually an experiential transference, of one of my experiences, temporally speaking, into another. It happened along with other pastimes, such as the use of that early cassette tape recorder, that itself had writerly consequences: the tape poetry magazine I edited in the mid-1970s, called futuristically *1983*, and possibly the training of my voice for performance. And another, such as the taking of photographs, and the ingenious and impoverished use of an antique bellows camera as an enlarger for developing negatives, possibly led to the recurrent use of photographs as writing material. But I've never believed that writing poems is like taking snapshots, as some writers do. I don't *describe* photos; I squint at them, steal from them, riff on them. That simple recording of reality is the opposite of the act of radio broadcasting, which is already *in* the medium of language and, at best, is a potential intervention or interruption of the real.

In the late 1980s, I developed radio quite consciously into a political analogy. I was reading of Félix Guattari's association with the Italian radical radio station Radio Alice in 1970s Bologna, and I conceived a series of poems,

---

no wonder that, when the opportunity arose, I took to teaching radio journalism like a bird to air, taping and splicing mini-packages.

'Radio Anna', in which Anna stood for: ANarchism, Noise and Autonomy (I mistakenly thought Alice was an acronym). I conceived of the writing of poems as a radical radio station broadcasting avant-garde programmes: not programmes *about* the avant-garde, but noise (interference, jamming) *as* the message itself. Think: John Cage's 'Williams Mix', which uses radios anyway. Think: William Burroughs' tape experiments described in 'the invisible generation'. (I'd read Burroughs' suggestive piece by 1974 and I was sceptical. I knew from my own use of tape recorders that you couldn't fool anyone that there was an actual riot going on by playing a tinny cassette player in a crowd!) In his article 'Millions and Millions of Potential Alices', Guattari says (or quotes): 'The viewpoint of autonomy towards the mass media of communication was that a hundred flowers should bloom, a hundred radio stations should broadcast.' His neo-Maoist talk of 'The guerrilla war of information, the organized disruption of the circulation of news' seemed an appropriate and quite conscious analogy for my poetry of the time.[5] The original 'Radio Anna' poem – never published, though I notice all of its best lines were cannibalised for later texts – reads:

> noise/each light flashes a voice/open
> women's voices between men's language/
> uncertain elements/distributive informatics/
> speech act therapy/chora music/groundless
> voices plot music footprints/vary call signs
> catch desire/ANarchism/Noise/Autonomy/
> magnetic storm tapes/demolition music/
> noise imagination/culture belts/mistake
> identities/internal exile/networks
> and feedbacks feed in lines/flashlight
> opinions/sexist blackspots/critical tuning/
> deliberate fading/troubling wholes/
> imaginary news/government building
> towers of voice

It's a poetics for the writing of that time that didn't quite find its way into the poetry itself, and it hangs around long enough to show up, as irony, in the poetics piece 'Rattling the Bones (for Adrian Clarke')', from 2002–3, in which I say: 'We interrupt/ This broadcast which is a broadcast of/

[5] Guattari, Felix, *Molecular Revolution*. Harmondsworth: Peregrine Books, 1984: 236.

interruptions', though its renewed purpose is 'to bring you/ *more complex nervous systems*'.[6]

The radio analogy – if that's what it still is – is on the edge of antiquation, of course. Already with the development of push-button pre-programmed radios and with the advent of DAB radio, the *frisson* of straying off-message (to use a loaded phrase), the attractions of tuning away from the mainstream to find an unscheduled alternative, straining the ears to hear a weak but rare message, becomes an enthrallment of the past. DAB is no more satisfying than closed-circuit hospital radio that I recorded some poetry programmes for in the late 1970s. The internet, of course, with its blogs and sites, offers wonderful alternatives to, advances on, this technology, but the internet is also the instrument for the downloading of radio programmes out of their temporal sequence, with facilities such as iPlayer, a term that one day will be as incomprehensible as QSL card. Even when broadcasting is not literally live, the feeling (illusory perhaps) of the formal necessity of listening in real time, at a particular moment, the sheer contemporaneousness of the act of reception, is paramount. There is nothing like hearing a station going on air for the first or last time, like Radio Denmark. Or hearing DJs on the now-forgotten early 1970s pirate Radio Nordsee International asking listeners in cars parked along the Essex coast to flash their lights out to sea towards their ship simultaneously. Both are recorded in my log extracts quoted above. All of that is lost in the multiple temporalities and slick convenience of instant playback. Radio Alice was lost in the end to the interventions of the state, according to Guattari: 'The police got rid of Radio Alice – its perpetrators were pursued, condemned and imprisoned, and its premises ransacked', but, Guattari optimistically predicts, 'its work of revolutionary de-territorialization goes on unabated....'[7]

The antiquity of the analogy arguably gives it renewed energy, and not just as revolutionary nostalgia. The nostalgia for valves that needed to be warmed-up before the sound of radio emerged provides echoes of its own. My radios were all old, built by my father from bits or bought from jumble sales where I also acquired piles of 78s and eclectic tastes in

---

6 'Rattling the Bones (for Adrian Clarke)' was published on the *Softblow* website, but was reprinted in *Berlin Bursts*, Shearsman, 2011. The italicised passage is a quote from John Rajachman's *The Deleuze Connections*, Cambridge and London: The MIT Press, 2000: 138.

7 Ibid, 241. This was also the fate of the canal boat of Radio Free Amsterdam, the fictional counterpart of Radio Free Prague, in my 'Tropp' story.

music: Frank Crumit to Frank Sinatra, Pinetop Smith to Les Paul. The image of the voice in the night, the image of noise interfering with reality, is a pregnant one. It's not an image, actually, but an echo, or like the pre-echo that you can hear where magnetic tape has been wound too tightly and stored for too long, a ghostly impression. Or where the stylus picks up a vibration through the wall of a groove on a record. I think of Little Richard's 'Tutti Frutti' unintentionally cueing itself like this in the opening hiss of the brittle shellac of a long-broken 78. I am again diverted from the force of argument towards the signals of memory, broadcasting forever on wavelengths I keep flicking over on my way to authorised channels.

Echoes, the very acoustic repetitions that are banished from radio and recording studios by soundproofing. Echoes of these engagements with vanished technologies provide material for writing, already have, in this account, a radio talk with no station to transmit it, an echo of these echoes.

What is required for my poetics is a newer kind of formal interruption than I imagined in the late 1980s, though it is actually the globalised, capitalised mediatised flow that radio is part of, the 'media's inconsistency of images and commentaries' as Alain Badiou puts it, its 'temporal carnival', that needs to be stemmed.[8] With the advent of what Guattari called Integrated World Capitalism, this is all the more urgent. Thus radio has lost most of its romance. With no old-style ideological divide to drive propaganda, I doubt whether there *are* stations broadcasting on short wave now, though I haven't the technology to check. I do know the BBC is frantically countering both Al-Qaida and Al-Jazeera on world-wide satellite TV, but that's a subject upon which I've uttered my own tape-'spliced' provisional 'last words' elsewhere.[9]

Badiou argues for a renewed 'principle of interruption. It must be able to propose to thought something that can interrupt this endless regime of circulation,' indeed establish 'a point of interruption,' born of a 'retardation process ... because revolt today requires leisureliness and not speed. This thinking, slow and consequentially rebellious, is alone capable of establishing the fixed point' of interruption that will allow, in Badiou's thought, if not in mine, the 'patient search for at least one truth.'[10]

---

[8] Badiou, Alain, *Infinite Thought*. London and New York: Continuum, 2005: 36.

[9] I am alluding to the final poem in 'Warrant Error', which ends: 'You receive my wild meanings/ and divine unfinish in his spliced last word.' See *Warrant Error*, Exeter: Shearsman Books, 2009: 116.

[10] Badiou, op. cit. : 36-38. This move, according to Badiou, also hails the end of the prevalence of the linguistic analogy in thought and the end of postmodernism.

From this point of view, the counter-language of Radio Anna (and Alice, even) runs the risk of *replicating* the form of the mediatised flow of Capital(ism), while merely contesting its content, in a breathless onslaught of anti-slogans and counter-images. We must interrupt this broadcast of interruptions anew, but still with the aim to create more complex nervous systems (which, I take it, is the function of art).

However, it is with three 'images', one of broadcasting, one of recording, and one of what I call 'human unfinish', that I wish to end.

Imagine an alien being out there in space, with Jodrell Bank ears attuned to radio signals. He hears nothing for centuries. Then suddenly he catches Marconi's mouse heartbeats in Morse. Within alien-seconds he hears Peter Eckersley's irritating 'Writtle Calling' test broadcast from the BBC. By the time Harry Lauder is singing 'I Love a Lassie' and Stanley Baldwin is talking about the War Loan, these voices are beginning to drown in a cacophony of words and music and sound: Goebbels, Arthur Askey, Alistair Cooke, Patrick McGee performing *Krapp's Last Tape*, John Peel, Marcus Brigstocke, all more or less at once. This is interruptive interference well beyond the dream of any of the operatives of Radios Anna or Alice, but it's complete chaos that cannot provide radical interference, because it is a homogenised homeostatic field.

A Roman potter – 30 B.C., say – is spinning a pot, scoring in the still malleable, spinning clay a continuous groove from top to bottom around the bulb of its wobbly body with a taut stick. The potter is singing very loud, as is his habit, and the stick is picking up vibrations from his voice and recording them on the body of the pot as solid sound waves. The pot, if it survived intact, *could* be played like a Victorian cylinder to recover the sound of ancient singing, of value since there are but 24 seconds of music preserved from the whole of the Roman era, a fragment from a play of Terence. But the equipment upon which it would have to be played would need to minimise noise to a remarkable degree. It will never be invented, though it may be imagined.

In my third, final image, radio and poetry apparently cohabit. Both Marconi and Dante have tombs in the same church in Florence, the Santa Croce. Shadowy recesses into which the eyes, afflicted by the dust and silver glare of the sweltering piazza outside, seek carved shapes and memorial

---

Salt, pinch of. Of course.

inscriptions. But whatever you see here cannot obscure the knowledge that Marconi's tomb is occupied, whereas Dante's remains vacant.

15 July 2008

Ekphrasis and Anti-Ekphrasis: Undelivered Talk for the Open Eye Gallery, Liverpool, for the Ideas Lab on Writing and Photography

Ekphrasis: I've always hated the word, because it seemed to mystify something that seemed to me second nature, because it seems to me to ennoble, with its Hellenic majesty, the act of doing something ignoble. There's a whiff of euphemism about it. One of the widely used definitions of ekphrasis only heightens my disquiet; James Heffernan calls it 'the verbal representation of a visual representation' (Miller 2015: 11). This evokes the fear that it is unnecessary at best, parasitic at worst. There are great poems 'about' (or roundabout) images, but the best carry a transformative twist, such as Michael Davidson's 'The Landing of Rochambeau', which turns out not be a verbal representation of an historical painting, but is the representation of a representation of a representation; it's about a postage stamp featuring the painting; the postmark obscures significant details. Unless the act of forming involves such transformation it seems invalid as art.

Although I make use of photography – or rather, photographs – there are very few straight ekphrastic exercises in my poetry; the one recent example I carried out under the guise of a Czech fictional writer, Jitka Průchová, whose *Poems Ekphrastic and Plastic* re-write the imagery of the tragic photographer Bohumil Krčil and the surrealist photomontagist Jindřich Štyrský. My fictional poems, published in *Twitters for a Lark*, are mostly about doing what I don't let myself do under my own name.

In simple terms, and ignoring differences of medium, my practice seems to have been blithely to take a lot of details from lots of photographs from both selected and random sources, and to use them in literary collages that are analogues for the photomontages these scraps might have made, in acts of what I call 'creative linkage' (when I'm writing about the kinds of accelerated collage one finds in the work of a poet like Allen Fisher, for example).

It's not always easy (though it's also not always impossible) to trace words back to image, but it will be an equivalent verbal fragment for a visual fragment, to parody the definition of ekphrasis itself. An example of 'selection' is 'Shutters', in *Complete Twentieth Century Blues*, which I wrote for the dancer Jo Blowers, which used the ectoplasmic mist of early photographs, Lady Hawarden's well-known images of her daughters in diaphanous interiors. The poems deform the perceived or remembered images. An example of 'random' – by which I mean less motivated, 'found' – is my long exploration of sexual politics, 'Empty Diaries', one poem for each year of the twentieth century, also in *Twentieth Century Blues* (and beyond), and which was a creative linkage using (amongst many other stretches of language) writings drawn from squinting at – literally, using them as flash cards – photographs of all kinds, from photojournalism to art photography, related to the appropriate year. I remember Bill Brandt furnishing images of the 1930s, and Cindy Sherman (to whom one diary is dedicated) for the 1970s. 'She's an appointment that'll not be missed', the latter concludes.

This is an extensive project, but I have domesticated and tamed the method for an intermittent series of recent poems, 'Burnt Journals', that I make for people's birthdays, usually poems knocked off in a bit of a hurry. It's easier to demonstrate the method and the source: I make pragmatic and singular use of Tom Phillips' wonderful year by year collection *The Postcard Century*. I use the postcard images – they are mostly photographic – in a montagist way to produce the short poems; images bleed, are read and then written as superimposed. Here's the opening of 'Burnt Journal 1939, for Lee Harwood at 70', a not particularly disruptive collage:

The sergeant under the umbrella splashes
Bovril as he carries a cup to the private on duty.
It's all part of the service of the services,
it seems, in this dream that you're marched into.

In none of these cases would I want the images to be presented with the poems, even if there were any clear descriptive correlation left, which there is in this example. This makes me guilty of what Andrew D. Miller calls 'suppressed ekphrasis' (Miller 2015: 6). I don't always feel the need to acknowledge the sources, although another recent sequence, 'Out of the Way' from *Warrant Error* (my 2009 book dealing with, as the title suggests, the war on terror), fully acknowledges its sources, and says it 'owes to the photographers Marieke van der Velden, Rodribo Abd, Stephanie Sinclair, Newsha Tavakolian, featured in the exhibition *Risk,* at Fotografiemuseum, Amsterdam,' which I saw and bought its catalogue to use. But even here I pick and choose from more than one photograph. In 'Afghanistan', a poem which has subsequently been re-articulated by the American calligrapher Thomas Ingmire (so it has a long collaborative life) its grim details are the grim details of the photographs; the rest is my imagining.

Like a figure in a dream of perfect falling
Like something from somewhere like hell

You were the dark-eyed girl who crept out
Before the pink meat dawn to spy
The growling machines while the whole town
Still dreamt of exactly what she saw

Mesopotamia was written in 1985 and first published with images, the photocopymontages of Patricia Farrell, one of our many Ship of Fools collaborative publications. The text used found images and my great uncle's contact prints from the First World War that were too faint for Patricia to collage into her images, but other photographs were used (we shared some, but not all) for both image and text, but they possess a relative autonomy in the final product. The prose text, though, is extremely collaged:

One step backwards, and you're gone, waking to a dream of dawn, over which wild cat's eyes, carved into the arm of the chair, close her head. She turns away to reveal a veined neck, set between the cool brass. No, that was somebody trying to locate the morning – my chest covered with flies – a history of sensation on the streets. You're here because that same courtyard, or so I fancied, was the studied flight of stairs until I can take only one sentence at a time. The peep show stilled at the word halting.

My daily practice of writing – it either gathers notes for poems or remains as an exercise in keeping 'writing fit' – usually uses photographs, and to simplify, one source has been returned to regularly, the German artist, Hans-Peter Feldmann's book *Voyeur*, a collection, now in several reshuffled editions, of all kinds of photographs, indeed, all the types I've habitually used elsewhere: from art photography to vernacular snapshots, from pornography to advertising. Like Tom Phillips' book it saves me work but acts as an explanatory tool, and introduces minatory caution. This daily practice throws up the dangers of ekphrasis, even of repressed ekphrasis, the flash-card squinting, or the flick book approach to images, the long naïve gaze that either reads materials as reality or fantasy, that I favour: that is, the freezing in language of the decisive (or indecisive) moment, the danger of static description, often indicated by the use of persistent present tense, the focus exclusively ocular and suppressing the other (necessarily to be imagined) senses. The answer lies, for me, in my certainty that to be formed, an ekphrastic text might fragment, unform, deform, re-form, equivalent or non-equivalent verbal fragments and linkages and assemblages, but, to succeed, it *must* transform the given, or transcend its sources. Even if the photographs – photography itself – becomes invisible. Miller even talks of 'anti-ekphrasis' (Miller 2015: 6-7).

Miller also says that Heffernan states that there is a 'representative friction between the ekphrasis and materials of the ekphrastic object' (Miller 2015: 11). If so, I wish to make fire from that friction, to go much further – his model of the literary is more conventional than mine. 'Ekphrasis…is dynamic and obstetric,' he comments, beginning well. But when he adds that 'it typically delivers from the pregnant moment of visual art its embryonically narrative impulse, and thus makes explicit the story that visual art tells only by implication', he may be descriptive of others' practice, no doubt, but not mine, with creative linkage working against narrative if not narrativity (Miller 2015: 11). But my poetics can only be indicative about this.

I have collaborated a good deal – I have used the photographs Patricia and I took of North London to produce the Ship of Fools booklet, *Looking North,* and those taken by Pete Clarke of the buildings around Liverpool docks; some of my words appear in his prints and paintings – but I had never worked with a photographer per se, until recently. A friend of 42 years standing, Trev Eales is a well-known photographer specialising in images of performing musicians. We collaborated, using some of these photographs, but copyright problems derailed the publication of a sumptuous joint image-text volume. I salvaged a shorter sequence from the wreckage, 'Sound on the Lip of Silence: from the photographs of Trev Eales', which contains unashamedly 'ekphrastic' poems as well as some collages of materials drawn from several of his images.

2016/2022

CRITICAL WORK CITED

Miller, Andrew D. *Poetry, Photography, Ekphrasis: Lyrical Representations of Photographs from the 19th Century to the Present.* Liverpool: Liverpool University Press, 2015.

MATERIALS + PROCEDURE

an account of the writing of The Given (*Knives Forks and Spoons*: 2010),
now the *first part of* Words Out of Time (*Knives Forks and Spoons*: 2015)

This work began as a project – out of an existential dilemma – to deal with particular MATERIALS: the piles of journals, diaries, and less categorisable autobiographical writings that I have accumulated since 1965 when they began, and that I have periodically attempted to use for writing. In its opting for PROCEDURE it is thus a conceptual project, but is perhaps not quite an example of 'uncreative writing' as that term has come to be used, but is a creative 'unwriting', to adapt a term I have used to describe my earlier texts refunctioned or re-moulded from others. Perhaps the work might be thought of as an 'unwriting through' of the MATERIALS, but such proliferation of terms is only useful if it assists a gloss on PROCEDURE.

Part one began with a simple notion: that I would list – in an ironic reference to Joe Brainard's influential anaphoric *I Remember* – all the events that I did *not* remember as I read through these records anew. I anticipated a ten page work covering 34 years. Instead, I amassed 34 pages but I only reached 1979 (the end of 'The Hungry Years' and the beginning of 'The Drowning Years' in my personal periodisation)! Before beginning this project I had an unjustified belief in the accuracy of my memory; now I felt like Confused of Hippo, whose words I used as an epigraph to that first draft:

> When then I remember memory, memory itself is, through itself, present with itself: but when I remember forgetfulness, there are present both memory and forgetfulness; memory whereby I remember, forgetfulness which I remember. But what is forgetfulness, but the privation of memory?[1] (St. Augustine).

The re-discovery of a series of autobiographical fragments written in 1989, 'Voices in White Noise', provided a series of sharply delineated memories (some of them lost over the intervening 20 years) to counter the record of forgetfulness. I combined and selected from the two texts, using a stochastic method, aiming at concision and counterpoint, although the 'I don't remember' sentences dominate. The simple PROCEDURE

---

[1] *The Confessions of St. Augustine*, Airmont: Clinton, 1969.

had thus begun to grasp the complexity of the MATERIALS with scant regard for autobiographical shape. The text is allowed to make its own history, to become the biography of a practice of writing rather than my autobiography, or 'My Life' to refer to the title of Lyn Hejinian's text that had both inspired and hindered me over the years. So much for memory.

Part two has a simple PROCEDURE – to ask one (difficult) question of the 'hero' of the text after reading each page of the MATERIALS, an intensely written lengthy, detailed journal. It thus distorts the passage of time, since only 1979–1982 are 'covered' in this exhausting paragraph. Not all the questions were finally selected and the order again resists, but does not obliterate, temporal sequence.

Part three deals with the most transformative years of my journal writing and the most rapid development of my poetics. The PROCEDURE adopted is largely that used in writing *Letter from the Blackstock Road*, which was written during this period (1983–1993) and is referred to in the writing: the accumulation of text and the working of that through a stochastic method of using guided chance, liberated choice, dice and eye, hand and mind, a kind of improvised textual performance at the desk.[2]

The final section posed different problems. The diaries which stretch from 1994–2009 (supplemented by a few notebooks) are written in a deliberately non-literary style and often record banalities. I decided to settle on the months of May – season of elections in particular – and to account for each one (we had now moved into 'The Age of Irony' and 'September 12', but not yet into the 'Era of Immiseration'). I was thinking of the 'mayday' strand (1997–99) of *Twentieth Century Blues* which intertextualises these writings.[3] An early draft – one paragraph accounting for each May – appears in *Erbacce* 18 (2009), but I wanted to disrupt chronology further to allow the MATERIALS to speak in their own new-found voice, and did so by re-adopting the PROCEDURE of one of the 'Mayday' texts themselves, 'Report on Seaport', which was written around the 1997 General Election and whose MATERIALS (sentences) were arranged in alphabetical order. (This is referred to in the text and thus it describes its constraint.)

These writings, even down to finding a title, have been the most troublesome that I have attempted. (At one point I intended to interleave

---

[2] 'Letter from the Blackstock Road', in *Complete Twentieth Century Blues*, Salt: Cambridge, 2007: 48-58.

[3] In *Complete Twentieth Century Blues*: 'Report on Seaport, mayday 97': 243-9, 'A Dirty Poem and a Clean Poem for Roy Fisher, mayday 98': 315-6; 'The End of the Twentieth Century, mayday 99': 331-50.

between the sections other writings: the autobiographical piece 'Malcolm Lowry's Land',[4] the critical article 'The Colony at the Heart of the Empire: Bob Cobbing and the Mid 1980s London Creative Environment',[5] and the meditation 'Critical Tuning'.[6]) As the text attests at various points, this is not my first attempt, nor my second, at such a project. Despite the boldness of PROCEDURE, the processes of editing have been as arduous – if not more so – than in other, less conceptual unwritings.

2009

Note: The demonstrative use of the capitalised terms throughout derives from the classroom demonstration Adrian Clarke once provided for my students, when he wrote on the board the glyph 'MATERIALS + PROCEDURE = ?'.

---

[4] In the event, it 'appears' as a footnote reference in *The Given* to 'Malcolm Lowry's Land' in eds. Bryan Biggs and Helen Tookey, *Malcolm Lowry: From the Mersey to the World*, Liverpool: Liverpool University Press, 2009, although the text is gathered in my book *Doubly Stolen Fire*, Llangattock: Aquifer Books, 2023.

[5] In ed. Louis Armand, *Hidden Agendas: Unreported Poetics,* Litteraria Pragensia: Prague, 2010. Reprinted in *When Bad Times Made for Good Poetry.* Exeter: Shearsman Books, 2011, and the focus of the first piece in section three of this volume.

[6] Published in this volume (and 'appears' as a footnote reference in *The Given*).

Three

Took Chances in London Traffic

My critical book *When Bad Times Made for Good Poetry* (Exeter: Shearsman Books, 2011) is really a hymn of praise to the poetry scene in London from the 1970s to the mid-1990s, just before I came to Liverpool. The chapter 'Informing the Nation: The Manifesto of the Poetry Society (1976)' deals with the well-documented events at the Poetry Society (and with the poetics document mentioned in the title), which I saw at first hand only a couple of times, once to see Peter Redgrove reading in the mid-1970s, and another to drop by a poetry workshop at which Bob Cobbing read an early poem of his and one of the 'Reform Group' read what I thought he'd called a 'socialist' poem. (I quickly realised he'd slipped the word 'national' in front of that description.) I'd met Bob Cobbing already, had visited his house in Maida Vale in November 1973 – while I was still at school – and stayed all day, learning about the politics of the poetry world (Poets Conference had met the day before) and about concrete and sound poetry. The effect of the radicalism I learnt was immediate but intermittent in its after-effects.

By the time I moved to London in the autumn of 1983 I was completing a PhD which concentrated upon the relatively critically-neglected work of Roy Fisher and Lee Harwood (the latter I'd met in London in 1974, just before I went to university in Norwich, at a reading in the Enterprise pub (organised by Paul Brown) that I recorded for my tape magazine *1983*). I was concocting a poetics of discontinuity and indeterminacy with respect to this work but in Norwich and Manchester where I had worked on it I'd yet to apply that poetics to my own work, which, apart from a few false-starts, was free and lyrical, but not yet imbued with the radical pressure I suspect I could only have discovered in London.

Discover it I did. My chapter 'The Colony at the Heart of the Empire: Bob Cobbing and the Mid-1980s London Creative Environment' outlines the readings and performances I witnessed or of which I kept evidence. It's a fulsome but not comprehensive account, particularly of the two weekday fortnightly reading series: King's College readings, organised by the scary blasting and bombardiering Eric Mottram, which included more established writers, such as Lee Harwood, Peter Riley or Iain Sinclair (though I had read there in 1981, as a visiting guest, probably at the urging of Steven Pereira, the co-editor of *Angel Exhaust* which had featured my work); and Subvoicive, organised by the non-coercive and anecdotally-gifted Gilbert Adair (one of Mottram's research students) and by the shy artist Patricia Farrell. Emerging writers tended to read here, Gavin Selerie, Maggie O'Sullivan and Adrian Clarke, for example, though Allen Fisher and Geraldine Monk read at both venues. Reading styles were performative but non-dramatic, musical rather than theatrical, a major part of the work's 'publication'. Subvoicive format was occasionally experimental: another chapter, 'Ken Edwards and *The WE Expression*', focuses on Ken's reading-presentation at which he dared to present poetics (around the first-person plural and its use and mis-use, poetically and otherwise). Even at that stage I found it odd that there was little discussion of ideas among writers, although there were exceptions and extremes: Mottram intellectualised excessively; Cobbing eschewed discussion entirely in favour of performance and example. My commitment to poetics as a speculative, writerly discourse proceeded from this perceived lack.

Weekend events included the Cobbing-inspired New River Project, held in the cavernous interior of the London Musicians' Collective, which allowed for every kind of performance from single voiced readings, to multi-voiced and instrumental pieces. My 'Colony' article exhaustively catalogues the artists and events, from the themed Spring Festival of the Alphabet (Cobbing's seminal *ABC in Sound* received its annual revival), to packed programmes of various inter-art experiences. The Association of Little Press bookfairs were also Saturday events, with readings and displays of many of the small presses which were operated by poets themselves (Paul Brown's Actual Size or Cobbing's own Writers Forum, for example). All these events, as my accounts tell in some detail, were chances for poets, publishers and reviewers (often one person was all three) to meet. Nobody had invented the term networking – and there were very few courses in Creative Writing to teach such skills to student writers. Which was just as well: it's unlikely that the radical forms of artifice being nurtured in London would have been taught much in higher education. The whole relation of this poetry to the academy is a fraught one. Mottram's readings seemed semi-detached from any actual teaching or research at King's. My own PhD was unusual, as was my possession of an MA in Creative Writing, I realised, comparing myself to my peers, who were learned and well-read, but often only academic in other spheres. We made our own networks.

Perhaps that brings me to the implications of my title 'The Colony at the Heart of the Empire'. The British Poetry Revival (I was using the term in my critical work) or linguistically innovative poetry (Adair had yet to offer that term in 1988) was an active, self-supporting world of creative artists, pushing ahead often with no regard to mainstream poetry (few cared to lampoon 'Britpo' as I had in my Wayne Pratt spoofs). Readings were often attended by a small number of people (a dozen at best out of a city of millions!) but it was a knowing, attentive audience. My teaching colleague Rob Brown was astonished at the level of concentration he observed at the White Swan during a Subvoicive reading. On the other hand, there were very few women on the scene (I married one, Patricia from Subvoicive!). It was more like a colony than a capital. Presses and readings seemed unable to access London Arts money, whereas in the provinces (notably in the North East and South East) there was local funding. Pamphlets and magazines circulated within London (via readings) but seldom reached beyond. Poets from outside London were often neglected for readings and events (a by-product of the paucity of funding, of course, after the death of the National and London Poetry Secretariats, which had supported readings until the early 1980s). Excited by itself, there was a psychic M25 even then encircling the city.

I am a diarist, which is why I possess a generally accurate but intermittently detailed account of this time. What surprises me about my early London days (I was busy with my post-graduate teaching certificate) was how long it took me to access what was going on. Through Tony Baker – I'd published in his *Figs* and we'd friends in common – I met John Welch and David Miller and these kind people introduced me to others. It must have been through John that I ended up at Anthony Howell's 40th birthday party, at which the host danced extraordinarily, and it was David who recommended my work to Rupert Loydell's Stride Publications in Exeter. I met Adrian Clarke, co-editor of *Angel Exhaust* and, with me, of the 1991 'London' anthology *Floating Capital*, at a reading at Islington Town Hall, organised by Geoffrey Adkins, at which Frances Presley (another poet I'd known before in Norwich) read too. But the central London crowd around the reading series seemed a little sniffier if not distinctly frosty. The offer of a reading one week could be forgotten the next; I shared this sense of alienation with the one writer of my own age that I met at this time, John Muckle, who, as general editor of the 1988 anthology *The New British Poetry*, would do so much to publicise innovative writing, established and less so. I needed to demonstrate that I could write work to the general consensual liking (I would never have admitted it thus at the time) and this I did at my two Subvoicive readings in 1985. (They were single-author affairs, so one had to prepare two sets of about 30 minutes, the entire output of a fledgling author!)

Witnessing a lot of varied work probably had an unconscious effect on me, but seeing Allen Fisher read the first *Gravity* poems in 1983 at King's, *consciously* brought a new (and politicised) dimension to my theories of indeterminacy and discontinuity, the development of an accelerated form of collage (I'd call it creative linkage a decade later): cutting across syntax, but preserving the forward-thrust of syntactic articulation, and the energy, but not necessarily the coherent content, of narrative. It seemed a form of disruption and interruption rather than an atomising fragmentation of forms. (In that sense it was the antithesis of Fisher's first long project *Place* and excitingly new.) My literary-critical concepts developed into the poetics that permitted my 'coherent deformations' of earlier pieces of writing, 'The Hungry Years'. They are dated 6–12th August 1985, and I read them, and similar later pieces, at that second reading in December 1985. They are also described as 'Unwritings 1985-1978' as though in London I was playing catch up with my cut ups.

2016

Negative Definitions:
Talk for the SubVoicive Colloquium, London, 1997

'Linguistically innovative poetry' as a term had humble beginnings in a March 1988 issue of the British magazine *Pages*. Not then dignified by capital letters into proper nounhood, it was Gilbert Adair's way of describing the kinds of British poetry we believed had been 'operating since 1977' in 'fragmentation and incoherence'. The result had been a 'public invisibility of the poetry' and 'ditto of a theorizing discourse' in Adair's words. Its definition is not to be found in the terms of its name: the argument that all good poetry is linguistically innovative doesn't invalidate its particularity, but suggests that its meaning is its use. If anything, it is a term to magnetically constellate certain practices. Yet it has been used recently to speak of British Poetry Revival work as well as American language poetry in a way well beyond Adair's use: a buzzword for a fuzzy set of poets outside his temporal and cultural determinants. I want here to attempt not what I hoped I'd be able to attempt at this stage, an outline of the *positivities* of such recent (and now not so recent) British work which Gilbert complained I was *not* addressing 9 years ago. I want to begin to define this term (which I'd gladly drop like Wittgenstein's ladder, not because it had no further use, but because it has been put to unhelpful uses) rather negatively. The differentials I wish to draw, firstly, with the British Poetry Revival are paradoxically the most contentious, yet the least revealing; secondly, the differential with North American language poetry is more obvious but more illuminating.

The conditions Adair identified as the post 1977 condition of the poetry – e.g. 'decreasing publishing opportunities; wide gaps in continuations of public... discussions; a one-way "dialogue" with oppositions that largely expunge us, ... movement in a less visible, less real poetic community' – contrasts with Eric Mottram's celebratory survey (note the dates) 'The British Poetry Revival 1960–1975', which catalogues reputations, achievements and opportunities. (See Hampson and Barry, *The New British Poetries*.) Yet this carries an appendix, dated 1978, which makes sorry reading: the story (again!) of the end of the Poetry Society Era (and the demise of *Poetry Review* and *Poetry Information*). This was the 'fragmented and incoherent' backdrop to the despair of the early 1980s, one echoed by Allen Fisher's identification in his 1985 introduction to his *Necessary Business* essay of those wound-licking years as 'a period of entrenchment and awe… speaking in a considerably small room' (*Spanner* 25, 163). A small room, it is worth reminding ourselves, that Thatcher was crusading to empower somebody to buy. A bumbling 70s social democracy had been replaced by an ideology that wanted to change human consciousness, and nearly succeeded, 'a culture fascinated with change, ruthless curtailment of job reliabilities, share-owning, and the legitimating *professionalism*', as Adair put it in language which is only just (and arguably) a period piece, post 1997!

The most positive aspect of *Necessary Business* I've outlined elsewhere with an 'awe' of my own: the attempt to articulate a poetics, drawn from three already active writers, which we might see as a poetry of a new pertinence that shifted the poetics from the Revival interest in Olson to activating readers through habit-breaking unpredictability and plurivocal structures. I believe that Fisher's essay should have been better known, and I still see it as the paradigm shift it was intended to be. But the moment has gone.

The increasing willingness of poets to operate theoretically, in terms of post-structuralist and other theory, to even expound poetics more coherently, was a change that seems not yet historical enough to comment upon (but magazines like *Fragmente* and *Parataxis*, and earlier, *Reality Studios*, had promoted the 'public discussion' of which Adair lamented the absence). The result of this may have been the willingness to work in terms of conceptualized projects, whether Fisher's *Gravity*, Clarke's 'Trio', or Adair's *Jizz Rim*.

My unwillingness to name names here, to deal with lists of in/ex/clusions does not just derive from restrictions of space, but from an awareness that many British poets, like Fisher himself, belong to both 'moments', that active poetic careers stretch decades, as Mottram noted of his 70s Revivalists: 'Poets in their twenties or early thirties (have) their careers largely ahead of them.' Many excellent poets, like Bill Griffiths, do not fit the schema well at all. Neither should my insistence upon differentials be taken as a denial of continuities. I'm willing to concede that my differentials may come to little more than a ruthlessly circumscribed 'scene', and a rising interest in theory and poetics, but even that is bound to be of significance, as are, of course, revisionist readings of the Revival.

The differential with language (or language-oriented or -centred) poetry seems more obvious because 'linguistically innovative poetry' could be a synonym for those terms; in its weakest formulation it could be little more than a sprig of Americana which could never be grafted on

British soil (the official view of much of the Revival work, remember). More positively, Bruce Andrews in his introduction to *Floating Capital*, 'Transatlantic', demands we should forget national differences and speak of 'this more inclusive field of so-called English language writing', which evidence the 'same *barriers* being dismantled' (*Paradise & Method*, 247). Much that follows is speculative, and an attempt to show a corner of that inclusive field that will be forever British!

Several commentators (including Barrett Watten at the New Hampshire conference, *Assembling the Alternatives*) have remarked the influence of the Vietnam War on the post-68 generation of the Post-War baby boom language poets. Questions of 'ideology, discourse, social rules, & epistemological paradigms of intelligibility or opacity or "sense"' raised by Bruce Andrews' academic work on US foreign policy naturally found a place in his poetic practice.(*P & M* 79). Protest at this War had been present in British Poetry Revival work, of course, but the 1980s in Thatcherite Britain was a very different situation with different answers to the same questions. The F111s were taking off to defend the council house they had sold you. A foreign policy dominated by manufactured wars and by a frantic last minute cold war before the Wall fell, was combined at least with a politicized, antinuclear official opposition in Parliament. To be engaged in Leftist politics in Britain in the 1980s was not the act of despair it would have been in 1970s America. The enemy and the evil was identifiable in all its absurd manifestations: 'colourless nation/ sucking on grief/ a handbag / strutting between uniforms/ such slow false tears/…the state as/ the status/ quo/…while the homeless stare/ at nightlong lights/ in empty offices' (Tom Raworth, *Tottering State*, 214).

Language poetry seems opposed, if not in fact, then by stance, to such empiricist strands in US Poetry as the works of Williams and the Objectivists. No such Oedipal hold can swerve the British writers, and a strong, often Situationist-derived, sense of the *everyday* invades British poetry, as in the Raworth quotation, as in Fisher, as in cris cheek, whose work is often a translation of the real: 'a primacy/ of sight/ in blinkered/ place culture' (*Talus* 5/6, 128). The exception is Ron Silliman in works such as *Tjanting*.

Early language poetry theory (before about 1982) was necessarily very strict to keep the object of its attention clear. Reading the 1970s pieces in Andrews' *Paradise & Method* its structuralist model of language seems almost nostalgic. His three-part argument contrasts a mainstream aesthetic of linguistic transparency with the structuralist analytic of opacity and difference, and extends this theoretically to a '*third* paradigm' (26) in which the linguistic system is worked over to produce 'a political writing practice' that avoids complete opacity, 'that unveils or demystifies the creation & sharing of meaning…to stress (words') use value & productivity in the face of mechanisms of social control' (19). While British writers have at times developed a similar straw man Mainstream Poet, few have seen themselves operating exclusively in the area between the signifier and signified, to produce sense while defying reference (to borrow a distinction of Ricoeur's). Perhaps, and I am by no means sure about this, there is some value precisely in a distinction between language-centred, as a mode of poetic investigation inside the sign, and linguistic innovation, as a mode of experimentation between the signifier and its referent, one which better reflects British work.

Indeed, this seems the direction language theory developed, itself. By 1987, Barrett Watten in 'Social Formalism' (*North Dakota Quarterly*, Fall 1987), was arguing that Andrews' linguistics were archaically 'scientific' and 'objective', and that a social dimension to the linguistic theory, the notion of language as a social semiotic, as it were, was lacking. (I don't share this view, but let it stand as a critique of Andrews' *early* poetics, which he constantly revised and socialized.) Watten plumps for Bourdieu as a model for language's socially communicative gameness. (See 'Poetic Sequencing and the New' for my take on this.)

Bourdieu stands here as an analogue for Theory in the 1980s, to indicate that by the time British poets were developing linguistically innovative poetry, they were responding directly (and indirectly) to a range of continental theories not available to the Americans in the 1970s: a vast, sorted, body of knowledge, ranging from Bourdieu's sociology to Lyotard's delineations of the postmodern, to Deleuze and Guattari's proliferating machines, and, more recently, on to Derrida's turning towards ethics – all beyond the structuralist beginnings. The poets also had the works of the Americans: *The Language Book* and essay collections by Watten and Bernstein.

Adair referred to both Fisher *and* Guattari to develop a view of linguistic innovation as social experimentation, intervention in concepts of value: 'Allen Fisher calls attention to art as "necessary business" – posing absolute challenges to the essential separation between "exchange value, use value and desire value" (Guattari). Cutting across formations categorized as discrete, "discontinuity" *is* so only if it makes *other* relations: or else it is mimesis of actual informational chaos.' This parallels Andrews' desire for a third paradigm, but posits new continuities in social (informational) terms (remember the delineations of Thatcherism in Adair's piece), and in terms of techniques of radical artifice, as Marjorie Perloff would put it, of creative linkage, and not in terms of the by then tarnished 'linguistic analogy'.

(Doubts about Andrews' early *poetics* are not doubts about his poetry, or the later socially-oriented poetics. Poetics are a permission, not a description, a strange self-involved discourse. Work should not be judged on its conformity to poetics, or vice versa, nor on any 'unity' thereby achieved. Indeed, Adair's Deleuzoguattarian assertion that Andrews' work 'apes but contests the shit-machine' remains a powerful description, one which implicitly proves much I'm saying here (*Reality Studios* 10, 108).)

Without outlining in detail the convergences and divergencies of the British Veronica Forrest-Thomson's *Poetic Artifice* (1978) and American Charles Bernstein's 'The Artifice of Absorption' (1986), it is clear that language poetry itself moved towards a more open notion of artifice as 'devicehood'. Some opacity could be used for antiabsorptive purposes. Here the straw man version of The Mainstream is given a third dimension. This is an approximation to Forrest-Thomson's notion of 'naturalisation', which she defines as 'an attempt to reduce the strangeness of poetic language and poetic organization by making it intelligible, by translating it into a statement about the nonverbal external world, by making the Artifice appear natural' (xi). This concept is active in some British discussions of poetic language. If 'good naturalisation' dwells on the levels of Artifice, it holds open the way for this disruptive work between the signifier and the referent (or wherever it is located), for the new continuities Adair called for, for creative linkage, in work of more radically artificial structures than Forrest-Thomson herself countenanced, and in work different in orientation from language poetry.

To come up to date, and to quote from my *PN Review* account of the New Hampshire conference, Barrett Watten attempted to set a new agenda for American writing, an

historicist delineation of language poetry as a situated post-1968, post-Vietnam, discourse that now faced new challenges and the need to change, not into an easy intelligibility, but into a mode of negotiation for the text as social, and the invasion of the text by a wide range of materials, to engender productive encounters with the world – including history which American poets have largely turned their backs on in a reaction, I have always thought, against Olson and Dorn. This plea had an odd ring to British…ears: with a poet of the distinction of Allen Fisher at the conference we didn't need to look far for a poet who could influence the Americans.

The thought of influencing the Americans is an interesting one, one raised at the conference itself by Keith Tuma. It strengthens, by reversal, the case for differentials here, my sense of a poetry with characteristics of its own. But any invasion of the text by new materials must heed the words of Bernstein in his 1990 formulation: 'Content is more an attitude toward the work *or* toward language *or* toward the *materials* of the poem than some kind of subject that is in any way detachable from the handling of the materials' (*APoetics*, 8; my emphases).

The insistences of those *or*s, the repetition of the word 'materials', suggest where formally *and* linguistically innovative poetries worldwide might be going.

Linking the Unlinkable: an answer to the question 'Why Do You Do What You Do?'

Such questions as 'Why Do You Do What You Do?' require one set of answers no individual writer can access about him or herself, in a personal history that is far from personal often, or in a genealogy of some profound but obscure disposition towards language or one of its substrata.

Aesthetic allegiance, from this point of view, may be no more than a position for this disposition to be situated. By this time, this *doing* can no longer be questioned. It is so far from a *why*, so ingrained perhaps in the individual's consciousness, that it requires the jolt of history to shake this intensity free of its occasions.

The question eventually becomes – or became for me – 'why you *continue* writing'. The pre-disposition to write (for me) seeks a justification, in poetics, in the processes of a resistant practice, a negativity that balances the affirmation of the originating impulse. My project *Twentieth Century Blues* is a 'net/(k)not-work(s)'. One of its current aims is to link the unlinkable.

In 'Discussions, or phrasing "after Auschwitz"' (*The Lyotard Reader*, 1989), Lyotard considers this name that, for Adorno, risked overstamping all human endeavour, including, famously, and relevantly to my current purpose, poetry. For Lyotard, 'Auschwitz' is 'a model for'… 'the incommensurability between the universe of prescriptive phrase (request) and the universes of the descriptive phrases which take it as their referent'. The '*agon* of phrases is perpetual'. The just action can only be to effect 'the linkage "that suits" in a particular case, without there being known what the rule of suitability is'. One can only '*invent* rules for the linkings of phrases'.

Derrida responded to Lyotard's lecture and revealed himself less interested in phrases, than in the processes of the essential linkage.

We have, he says, 'to make links, historically, politically, and ethically with the name, with that which absolutely refuses linkage'. It is the ethical imperative that I find both profound and resonant in these remarks. He continues: 'If there is today an ethical or political question and if there is somewhere a *One must* it must link up with a *one must make links with Auschwitz.*' But this necessity could be broadened, both ethically and technically; for me, it demands a writing practice that must link the components of the daily catastrophe, along with all its ecstasies, that we live. 'Perhaps Auschwitz prescribes – and the other proper names of analogous tragedies (in their irreducible dispersion) prescribe – that we make links.' These remarks have haunted (indeed, have been linked in) my recent work *The Lores, Twentieth Century Blues 30*, to offset the Adornoesque negativity that also haunts it. It implies a practice: 'It does not prescribe that we overcome the un-linkable, but rather: because it is unlinkable, we are enjoined to make links.' Any apparent unlinkability, I would generalise, requires creative linkage for a writer, a kind of investigative experimentation. The writing practice will determine that such linkages be articulated at times on a surface which is like the skin of delirium, with simultaneously *more* disruption than would be connoted by the term 'juxtaposition' – and also *less*, where the links are so melted into the materials that they disappear.

This derivation for Derrida is different, though allied, to Adrian Clarke's fortuitous blending of Lyotard's poetics of the phrase with his own phrasal poetic practice to form the poetics of his *Listening to the Differences* talk (*RWC Extra*, 1991). Clarke himself integrates the theory and his practice and demands 'a subversive plurality that many of the rules available to link phrases may also be used to sustain, short-circuiting the connections that might combine to pronounce a sentence, but not necessarily those constitutive of a critical judgement whose force is less than absolute.' The rules of this subversive linkage, I believe, have to be invented to counter absoluteness with plurality. The disruption of the authority of the sentence by the micro-judgements of the phrase is one way. There may be others, as linguistically innovative writers momently create new 'rules' for linkage, for what suits the particular 'case': the disparate materials in need of procedural linkage. Lyotard has previously described the paradox of this process in *The Postmodern Condition* (1984): 'The artist and the writer...are working without rules in order to formulate the rules of *what will have been done.*' Indeed, 'short-circuiting' is an interesting analogy for a wholly unexpected and deregulated linkage. As Lyotard notes: 'To link is necessary, but how to is not.'

Asking myself, again, the question 'Why Do I Do What I Do?' evokes the necessary response:

To link the unlinkable.

January 1995

Working the Work:
notes towards and beyond *Internal Exile*[1]

January 1987:

The role of the reader is, of course, paramount to the construction of a text – yet to totally allow the reader control (this old conundrum rolled out again)…is to go too far, to abdicate responsibility (I am always responsible for my works, if not their severally generated meanings). But what I've not faced yet is: *how* does indeterminacy affect a reader? how can I gauge the effect? is my aim – in the broadest sense – political? Do I follow Marcuse and see in the aesthetic dimension (and in the reader's involvement therein) a critique of society that is necessarily Marxian (I've answered that – NO! –) and in the *images* of sensuous freedom an *image* of the utopia (I've answered that one in 'Utopian Tales')? (Sheppard 2008: 38-41). Up until now I think I may have. But to see the distortions of form as the representation of the ideal is indeed perverse. Lyotard – in *Driftworks* – says it is to make it 'a *representation* of representation…This leaves politics as representation uncriticized'. He adds, 'The system, as it exists, absorbs every consistent discourse; the important thing is not to produce a consistent discourse but rather to produce "figures" within reality. The problem is to endure the anguish of maintaining reality in a state of suspicion through direct practices.' The poet holds language 'under suspicion, i.e., to bring about figures which would never have been produced, that language may not tolerate, and which may never be audible, perceptible, for us'. The 'truth of art' equals 'the destruction of social forms' (Lyotard 1984: 78, 79, 83).

Practice: working, important terms too.

These ideas struck me as important (as did his description of Klee working between *representation* and formal devices to free himself of phantasy and desire: See 'Looking North' (Sheppard 1987, np; Sheppard 2015: 26-27).)

I bought the book yesterday, after going up to the Registry Office to register Stevie's birth. Strange sensations on the tube: of the rule of privacy and hermeticism. It's almost as if Aids were a symptom of pervasive mass solipsism. It's a world of spies and disclosures, secret dealings and paranoid

---

[1] 'Internal Exile' was published in *The Flashlight Sonata*, and collected in Sheppard 2008: 42-47; reprinted in Sheppard 2015: 28-32.

security: the only transcendence of privacy must be a media event: awful blind-date TV programmes, couples being filmed fucking, intimate record dedications, – soap opera manipulations of representation…

Is the ultimate aim, now, to change the consciousness of the reader, to change the consciousness of the people of the world – is this a utopian fantasy? To make the reader 'let go' of consciousness, in Lyotard's c. 1970 construction?

'Desire is caught in phantasy: being caught in something, it is compulsive, but it also has the force to make this phantasizing turn, and this force makes desire wander over different objects' (Lyotard 1984: 73). This is the 'profoundly revolutionary function of art': to make the *un*known, not the known, to turn. Turning the compulsive phantasy of representation, for example, as Klee turned the page. Create a 'coherent deformation' of language, through restless technique(s).[2]

These scraps of philosophy hold together just long enough to base a poem upon them, and constellate, re-form, re-constellate.

To make a reader *stop* his or her fantasizing. The 'critical reversal' (Lyotard 1984: 78).

Capitalism and mass media: to fulfil desire, therefore to kill it, pseudo-satisfaction. Art finds non-'realist forms at the level of perception, not signifiable within an articulated discourse.' Art 'disconcerts', disturbs: as Lyotard has said recently at the ICA (Lyotard 1984: 81).

Poets such as John Ash and – at times – Roy Fisher offer defamiliarisations as *images*, or representations of utopic states (e.g. Ash's 'urban pastorals'); poets such as Allen Fisher and – at times – Lee Harwood offer a *transformative* programme, whereby it is *not* the crystallisation of a moment of vision (of showing what is no longer/not yet *expressed*), but a continuing process, unfolding its meanings without a political goal, yet being political in intent. Woodcock says that anarchism, because it is dynamic, cannot bear the stasis of utopias. It is something like this distinction I am beginning to sense, for the dynamism. What Lyotard says of *Driftworks* one might wish for one's own works: a meaning of a text is not so important as 'what it does and incites' (Lyotard 1984: 9). It 'does', a 'charge of affect'; it incites 'the metamorphoses of this potential energy into other things – other texts' etc…, promotes more *working*, both artistic and in the lifeworld (Lyotard

---

[2] The term 'coherent deformation' is drawn from Merleau-Ponty, though the phrase is not his. Source long lost.

1984: 9).

It's not a question of waiting until one's work is 'accepted'; it's a question of saying: *This work stands at the very centre of the culture I dream of; a culture which doesn't yet exist. Therefore the work cannot represent* images *of a future utopia, it must begin to construct the culture around itself in its* working: *as Milton, Blake, and Pound attempted to build a* paradiso...

No! The images have gone static and utopic once again. There never will be the final thing: a process of becoming-being-becoming better... There is no perfectibility in human temporality, scraped across the grain of history. Only the *working*. With an ethic – not too strong a word – of *working* (the opposite of a limiting 'work ethic')...

I suddenly feel I'm moving quickly. Create in the hiatus before the leap is possible.

The negative side of this desire to begin building a new culture around a poetic work – as potential revolution – is that it has often been a reaction to a loss of a coherent culture (as was the 1970s' emphasis upon 'place'): Milton after the failure of the English Revolution; Blake after his radical hopes; Pound after the 'myriad' had died in the War; Allen Fisher after May 1968 and the failure of various revolutions of the everyday lives. The affirmative side is all in the waiting...Allen Fisher's eclecticism, his grabbing at sources before they're assimilated, does have an air of desperation; it's not just an exemplary plurivocity, the creation of inconsistent subversion.

Possible to do these things without hitting the 'political' head-on. Value, here, for aestheticism: the playfulness that baits consistency.

Utopianism, then, only as a working thought, *not* as a worked-out image: the drifting of mist and sunshafts over a never fully revealed terrain, *not* the crystal city...

July 1987:

I've been reading EP Thompson and Raymond Williams on Utopianism, re-reading Marcuse... As opposed to 'static' models of Utopia (criticised by Lee Harwood in 'The "utopia"') the two men propose the category 'heuristic utopia'; Thompson comments on, and quotes Abensour: 'And we enter into Utopia's proper and new-found space: *the education of desire*…it is …to open a way to aspiration, to "teach desire to desire, to desire better, to desire more, and above all to desire in a different way".' It 'liberates desire to an uninterrupted interrogation of our values and also to its own self-interrogation' (*NLR* 99: 97).[3]

Yet how can this be enacted in writing?

The affirmative moment can never wholly be divorced from the critical function of art. The two, it seems to me, can never be heard apart – the cry of despair and the cry of hope –; they can only be made to either sound in harmony (offering *images* of Utopia), or in dissonance (working to produce irreducible *figures* of possibility). The latter is more conducive to 'the education of desire': the necessity for the reader to participate in the construction of meaning.

WORKS CITED

Lyotard, J.F. *Driftworks*, New York: Semiotext(e), 1984

Sheppard, Robert. *Complete Twentieth Century Blues.* Cambridge: Salt Publishing, 2008

Sheppard, Robert. *History or Sleep: Selected Poems*, Bristol: Shearsman Books, 2015

Sheppard, Robert. *Looking North* (with images by Patricia Farrell), London: Ship of Fools, 1987

Thompson, EP, and Raymond Williams, unidentified writing, *New Left Review* 99.

---

[3] I have lost the full reference for this suggestive piece, suggestive because *The Education of Desire* is the title I chose for a pamphlet about reading linguistically innovative poetries for A Level students, reprinted in my *Far Language: Poetics and Linguistically Innovative Poetry 1978-1997*, Exeter: Stride Research Documents, 1999; second printing 2002. I refer to it in the talk 'Invite! and Incite!', and it appears in *net/(k)not/works*, both of which follow.

Invite! and Incite!

No one listens to poetry:
SubVoicive One Day Colloquium 20ᵗʰ July 1991, University of London

Statement: New forms of poetic artifice and formalist techniques should be used to defamiliarise the dominant reality principle in order to operate a critique of it; poetry can use indeterminacy and discontinuity to fragment and re-constitute text to make new connections so as to inaugurate fresh perceptions, not merely to mime the disruption of capitalist production. The reader becomes an active co-producer of the text. Reading can be an education of motivated desire, not its naturalisation by means of a passive recognition.

Since we have never had a forum of this kind, it is tempting to talk about everything, but I have at least decided to deal with some area of my own poetics and practice in terms that address the concepts of Audience and Technique: two out of three of Gilbert Adair's suggested concerns [for the colloquium]. I want to talk, fairly personally for once, about the connection between textual strategies and 'readers', the real people who use the texts. (Audience, I take it, is a more global, perhaps sociologically de-fined category. 'Addressee' is a device of the rhetorical structure of the text.)

Firstly, I am struck by one irony of my position, as expressed in my opening statement. This theory privileges the role of the reader in the construction of the meaning of the text. Such an approach is, of course, increasingly conventional in its weaker forms: reader-response critics such as Wolfgang Iser and Stanley Fish are widely read and even at A Level English Literature the rather ill-thought-out concept of 'informed personal response' guides the assessment of students' work. But the irony is not that time has caught up with us – but that I have – many of us have – this respect for the readers' productive energies, this education of desire, if you like, and there doesn't seem to be much of an audience! Part of my desire to talk today comes out of the experience of recently having found my work read, an experience in part unsettling to some tenets of this poetics. But if, as Rachel Blau DuPlessis says, a poetics is a 'permission to continue' then it is necessary to stop the poetics fossilising, which could only 'permit' dishonest repetition or conscientious silence.

In 1988 I wrote a short piece, *The Education of Desire*, for my A Level students to supplement *The New British Poetry* which they were studying.

Christopher Beckett wrote a response to the Ship of Fools pamphlet of *The Education of Desire* in *First Offense* 5. While recognising the particular audience for the piece, he was severe on my lack of definition of the term 'desire'. Did I mean desire as in Lacan's theory? Or did I mean a conscious political impulse towards societal change? I've still not resolved this, though I suppose I still stand behind my response at the time that I meant both, and that one would lead to the other: deep desire activating surface desires. I suppose underlying this there is a Deleuzoguattarian conviction that poetry is motive as well as e-motive.

I wrote a response to Beckett's piece called 'Re-working the Work' in which I expanded upon some of my thoughts. My starting point was Lyotard's short essay 'The Critical Function of the Work of Art', which is in *Driftworks*. It is a kind of manifesto for formally disruptive poesis that subverts the representational and social, that activates desire rather than earths it. The true artist, Lyotard writes, is not self-expressive, does not simply represent his or her phantasy. The true artist 'undertakes to free *from* phantasy'. Paul Klee painted by operating an abrupt and effective critical reversal.

> By turning his drawing around, he reverses the relation between the represented and formal system, he is *working*, and if he reverses representation, it is in order not to see the figurative, not to be the victim of phantasy any longer, in order to be able to work upon the plastic screen itself, upon the page, by producing strokes that have a certain formal relation between themselves (Lyotard 1984: 74-75).

The cinema of Renais similarly

> obliges the public to stop phantasizing. The spectator finds himself in the reversing, critical, function of the work and his desire collides with the screen, because the screen is treated as a screen and not a window (Lyotard 1984: 75).

In short, it did not fulfil desire; it activates desire without providing resolution or dissolution. In this case, Lyotard insists, 'the critical reversal is brought about by its cutting and editing'. It is possible to see the formal techniques of the most pertinent of contemporary British poetry – say, Allen Fisher's *Gravity as a consequence of shape* – effecting this critical reversal. Reading such a poem should be an active education of desire, not a fulfilment, and therefore killing, of desire.

I have believed that the entry of an active reader into the poem is the poem's affirmative moment at which its technique, so often involving modes of indeterminacy, or its foregrounded poetic devices, invite the reader to participate. This affirmative moment can never wholly be divorced from the critical function: the cry of hope and the cry of despair are heard together. Dissonance. In the act of constructing its meanings, the readers share in the poem's state of becoming; in doing so, they discover that it is what a text can be made to do, as well as what it is made to mean, that is micro-revolutionary. The poem, as it is read, projects a future in its very refusal to completely mean *this* world.

The formal techniques of the text may effect this desirous reading, but it is precisely these techniques that engender Christopher Beckett's instructive 'anxiety'. He senses a connection between the anxiety of living in a time 'of undoing and untying' and the more textual anxiety 'that the disjunctive poem of the eighties may simply be a regressive "mimesis of actual informational chaos"' – he's quoting Gilbert Adair there. It has been my hope that the text will be open enough for the reader to be able to participate; capitalist informational chaos exists partly to stop such participation. Another of Adair's assertions should be taken as a warning: 'Cutting across formations categorised as discrete, "discontinuity" *is* so only if it makes *other* relations' (Adair 1988: 68).

Before moving on to some tentative conclusions I want to look at some attempts to write in ways that activate a reader, through techniques of indeterminacy as well as those of discontinuity, ones that don't entirely work.

My first acquaintance with such a theory was in the work of Lee Harwood. He commented, 'I want the poem to be like a beautiful object, a box that's all slotted together; then I leave it on the table and leave the room, and you come in and pass it on' (Bockris 1970: 8). A poem is thus not primarily self-expressive; it is only completed by the reader, though here Harwood does not have in mind the ideal reader of reader-response theories, but the multitude of readers who engage with the poem-catalyst; it causes various changes within different readers without itself altering its objective form. Nevertheless, the reader's responses must fuse horizons with the text as he or she 'reacts to the play of the stimuli' and to which 'the individual addressee is bound to supply his own existential credentials', as Umberto Eco puts it in 'The Poetics of the Open Work' (Eco 1959: 49).

In the late 1960s, particularly in *The Sinking Colony*, Harwood's use of indeterminate forms and discontinuous textual lacunae and fragmentation was precisely to activate the reader. One poem, 'Linen', ends:

> touching you   like the
> as soft as
> like the scent of flowers and
> like an approaching festival
> whose promise is failed through carelessness
>
>   (Harwood 2004: 144)

Harwood glosses his own text by pointing out that 'each of us has got a different concept of what touching is like … And so I should respect your view … So we've got to leave this room for people, and here it's very consciously half-lines and areas of doubt' for the reader's intervention (Bockris 1970: 9). But the text is not a blank page for the reader to inscribe his or her self, as Eco reminds us. The lacunae are underwritten, as it were, by Harwood's own concluding similes, which create a necessary context. Eco writes, 'The *possibilities* which the work's openness makes available always work within a given *field of relations*' (Eco 1959: 49).

I've written about this Harwood poem a number of times yet it was only the other day that I realised that I'd never once undertaken the task of filling in the gaps. The problem with suspended textural lacunae is that the reader may simply read the utterance as incomplete. The point is: it invites too little. It is, in fact, a generous gesture of such an aesthetic, a calculated metaphor for such respect.

My second example is personal. Last year I read my poem 'Daylight Robbery' at the Torriano Meeting House; it is perhaps the most impacted and difficult of my texts.

> Whitewashed thought
> Flashing articulations
> Those transparencies
> Into the daylight modern
> Intermittent outbursts of unique
> Movie mind flying skating on
> Nobody's dream
> This dodge into synaesthesia
> Writing provides feet core

Tremble and
Skating on a frozen world
I speak rest my thoughts speak at war with
Video rhyme
Too brilliant to bear
Out contemporary
Blocks a Chinese reading... (Sheppard 1990: 19)

Whereas Lee Harwood had left his text open, I had presented a closed text that I felt a reader's engagement would open, as it were, working through the indeterminacies and discontinuities. One reader, Alison Orbaum, an ex-student of mine, did what not enough of us do: she told me what she thought of it. For her, the text was hermetic; 'selfish' was her word. And that charge (whether justified or not) has rung in my ears ever since, as has my strong counterclaim that the text deliberately *refuses* to mean *this* world.

My response to Christopher Beckett and the book from which 'Daylight Robbery' was taken – also *Daylight Robbery* – were reviewed together by Norman Jope in *Memes* 5. Given the material conditions of 'our' poetry, such an intelligent review is actually a rare pleasure and makes a change from the 'incoherent-ramblings-of-a-crazed-consciousness' kind of review which I suspect many of us have suffered from – unless we're reviewing each other.

> It is clear from *Daylight Robbery*, as this essay, that Sheppard is working from a context that is broadly socialist and anti-auth-oritarian – and it would be cruelly dismissive to label him as just another 'cashpoint situationist', raiding the image-store of London-in-the-eighties as a means of fabricating something that seems both artistically and socially 'relevant'. So how does his intended strategy manifest in 'Daylight Robbery' and does it *work*? are the essential questions. My reading of it, firstly, discovered texts that were palimpsests, lacking final resolutions and liable to shatter and disjoin before my passage...The terrain is ours. BUT...for me, at any rate, it is not always the desire to act, to realise social change that results. I am brought into the language;...but then I am bogged with Adair's 'actual informational chaos' which I didn't need Sheppard to tell me was chaotic in the first place! So, in con-clusion, I have to say that this worked for me in obsidian flashes-one-liners, getting up the bourgeois nose, rather than in totality (Jope 1991).

Christopher Middleton, in his 'Notes on a Viking Prow', theorises the process of a fruitful reading of a text as 'a re-ordering' of the reader's 'perceptual schemata (which) releases mental energy'.[1] Clearly, my work has not been entirely successful in the case of Jope (though it has in the case of others). His perceptual schemata – the sets into which the brain sorts and selects from its perceptual field – have been stirred but not shaken.

My concern here has not been so far with the difficulty of texts but with the extent to which their formal techniques offer an invitation to the reader. But I'd like to consider the question from the point of view of two terms that occur sometimes in discussions of some of the language poets (most recently a transcript of a discussion of a paper by Bruce Andrews, 'Poetry as Explanation, Poetry as Praxis'.)[2] The two terms are 'the opaque text' and 'the transparent text'. I doubt whether either could exist in a pure form, as it were, but as models I think they shed light on my central concern. Briefly: the transparent text is automatically read through; it is noise-free. The act of reading produces the opposite of the micro-revolutionary effect I have been talking about. It is reading as immediate consumption. In fact, very few creative writers, I suspect, would want this possibility in which their artifice would disappear.

At the other extreme, and I know that I simplify, a text might be so utterly opaque that there seems to be no coherence with which to organise a passage through the work. Lexical, semantic, syntactic, grammatical, even conventional levels of the work would be either so dispersed or so condensed that, in Communication Theory terms, everything in the text is noise. Speaking personally, some of the work short-handed as 'language poetry' strikes me in that way. Whereas I want to be invited and incited by a text in proportion, I experience a bafflement that ironically can engender a very similar sensation to that of pure transparency. It offers a kind of pleasurable surface over which the mind skates. It's like reading a book in a state of extreme tiredness: just going along with the lilt of its form.

Both extremes deny active reading. In both cases the reception of a text offers instant solutions, not a raising of questions. In both models, the text almost vanishes. What Allen Fisher calls the reader's 'desire in production' is denied its productivity. Coming back to Christopher Middleton's formulation for a moment: opaque texts may dis-order but they don't *re-*

---

[1] These quotations probably come from the second part of Middleton's essay, which is less known (and I have long lost my copy of it).

[2] The paper, but not the discussion referred to here, was later reprinted in Andrews 1996: 49-71. Andrews is *not* one of the 'language poets' criticised later in my talk.

order perceptual schemata; they don't release mental energy. Repeating Gilbert Adair's remark too: discontinuities must create new continuities for the reader.

I want to tie up this argument by introducing another term that I have found useful: Naturalisation. This, Veronica Forrest-Thomson, in her *Poetic Artifice*, defined as the

> attempt to reduce the strangeness of poetic language and poetic organization by making it intelligible, by translating it into a statement about the non-verbal external world, by making the Artifice appear natural (Forrest-Thomson 1978: xi).

This process of moving from word to world is, it is worth stressing, an inevitable one, according to her theory. It is what all reading, finally, has to do. It is the function of poetic artifice to delay this for as long as possible, to make texts complex structures, its devices collaborating in a classic act of defamiliarisation. The problem with transparency is that naturalisation is immediate, unsensational; the reader's desire is left unengaged. The problem with opacity is that naturalisation cannot begin, the text's complexity cannot be drawn out in the process of reading. It is uninviting – and similarly fatal to the desire I would wish to incite.

In conclusion, although I feel perhaps less committed to the exclusive use of techniques of indeterminacy and discontinuity, and I'm trying to explore other ways of disordering a reader's habitual responses, *I* still feel the need to activate the reader, to re-order schemata and release energies, to incite the reader's desire in production, to invite through formal means. In short, to provide structures, whatever they variously might be, for an education of desire. On the other hand, naturalisation has still to be a distended process in reading, and is neither to be avoided by opacity nor by-passed by transparency. Not – as I put it in 'Sharp Talk and Amended Signatures' – 'commentaries in which the zeitgeist is ordinary perception, just things. A disruptive poetics is called for until morning's potential high tunings re-define themselves' (Sheppard 2008: 8). A poetics which is a permission to find the changing means of inviting and inciting.

It seems, finally, that all the laudable attempts to widen the *audience* for the kinds of poetry offered with tenacity by SubVoicive – I think cris cheek has got something to say about this later – might fruitfully be based upon an aesthetic of the *reader*. Readers might find themselves offered structures they can respond to (so long as appropriate strategies of response are acquired – I know that's a separate and large problem involving a consideration of social and educational determinants). Our texts might then become 'intertexts', part of a proper network of exchange: voiced marginalities, not voices from around, or beyond, the margins.

July 1991

Two Questions

GILBERT ADAIR: Surely to 'dis-order and re-order' is the *sine qua non* of virtually *all* poetic techniques? – although sometimes (eg Herbert's 'The Collar') at the service of a (threatened) ruling order, sometimes (eg Williams's 'Defense', *Collected Poems II*) against a complex anti-aesthetic consensus. So this alone doesn't explain writing in extreme discontinuities. Suppose that many *other* intersecting reasons for such writing are in danger of being supplanted by a false political rationale which grows increasingly entrenched the vaguer its ambitions. Then theoretical disputes would be conducted over forms with the demand that they effect what *no* poetry *can* (cf Andrew Lawson's uncomprehending assault on 'indeterminacy' in *Pages 65-72*). Without trying to deny the political informants of our poetry, do you not think what we can and are doing with them should be more precisely defined?

ROBERT SHEPPARD: Yes.

GILBERT ADAIR: Another (connected) supposition: the 'reader', 'ideal' or not, is a red herring. You can write only for yourself – so that it doesn't die on the page in front of your eyes after one or two readings. If it does – if poem or technique go belly-up stale – *then* is the time to try to make something else. To change your writing because of the imagined require-ments of hoped-for readers can only be disastrous. It sacrifices writing to the failures of education.

ROBERT SHEPPARD: Perhaps my use of the term 'invitation' is unfortunate in its social connotations of the casual. I am *not* advocating that writers adopt a deprecating or slavish attitude towards the reader. What I understand as the 'education of desire' does not have a notion of requirement. It is more like that problematic chestnut of attending to people's *needs* rather than their constructed *wants*. The audience, in this model, is being activated, not being told what to do in a passive lecture or through a parade of moralised images. My attention is largely on the issue of the possibilities of numerous poetic *structures*, not on the censoring of content to fit the perceived (dis)abilities of the reader. Your final sentence is provocative, but we all know that education disables. The text is written, not necessarily with a reader in mind, but all poems (even ones destroyed by their authors) are inserted into a culturally defined history of reading which influences production. Don't operate as rules, but as horizons for actual work to be done. I'm not arguing for ease. A node of previous practice and theory, half-conscious decision, that cannot be jettisoned, and yet it amounts to a context that need not be apprehended and need not impose upon the 'passion-scribble/of origin', as Prynne puts it. I nearly gave this talk an epigraph from Brecht. The only experience we can have of others' poetry is reading it. Spots of indeterminacy bounce before my eyes. Vary call signs, catch desire. It is in accord with Allen Fisher's statement that the meaning of his work is the use to which it may be put. The spoilt brat pushes his half-eaten dinner across the table, says: 'You finish it.' It argues for the use of difficulty, in or out of Fisherspace. In the shop, I stood reading Beckett's last poem. Then: Cowboy Poetry by writers with names like 'Chuck'. Re-reading the earliest material, I find nothing I would write now. The changes happened, as I turned from writer to reader. A woman walks from her house at the sound of a car horn, wearing only one trainer. You can only write for yourself: to whom can such a statement be written? This patch of me has been dented. In both models, text (almost) vanishes. This, for example. I wrote this sentence for you. I wrote that sentence for me. Who's this, for example, during the bit of her life when she riles against biography? You melt into a chocolate advert, and will do so, until the morning's potential high tunings re-define themselves. You can be thought about in attitudes of static sex, or simply tenderly sensed as a possibility by someone, a fragrance. You wipe your arse and flush the lavatory. The axioms cease to operate at certain moments of working the work. Write fear into the job description, put anxiety on your c.v. Should you forget about the text, your delight is free. I would have arrived if I'd dogmatically stuck to my procedures. Cheeky new 1 to 1 Hot Line. If Guattari were invited to talk to a group of *British* writers by the British Council, would Allen Fisher or Gilbert Adair or any number of writers whose work is analogous to the micro-revolutionary act at the heart of language systems that Guattari describes, be invited? No one listens to poets? How shall

I say you best? Who overhears, halfway between a theory of poetry and a poetics? My subjectivity enunciated, Was the oily rag an artwork? Our care is after all the sociality of general freedom. Can you guess at which point I gave in and went back and read this through from the beginning? Or do you think the whole thing has been designed to trick you with a rhetoric of (dis-)continuity while the text was actually written – sentence by sentence – on record cards, and then shuffled? Or do the atomistic, pulsed, fragments into which the poem is divided reflect the barrage of data coming from the TV screen: along with the viewer's fantasies and reactions? Purist or selfish? Or the sound of Gilbert's voice outside as I read this text on the tape recorder, to check it? Mirror them no faces. Hoped-for writing sacrifices something else. Change the requirements of disastrous readers. Are you a red herring? Hood is remanded. I want to be your reader, don't I? Optionally gendered, I step from my smithereens, smell burning air. The codes can only be re-coded. If the mass is large enough, the projectile will change course. Suddenly, there were new human beings. They'd read the poem?

1992

net/(k)not//–work(s)

PRODUCING NOW

To summarise a 'poetics', as I first thought I'd be able to, would be, in effect, to revise it, since each attempt here, each 'essay' (and I include those listed in the 'Acknowledgements' as part of a larger network) is a fresh move in a game of worrying at certain concerns. The terms used are not like those of the Law, but function as enabling structures to open up spaces for poetry. The very filling of these spaces ensures the necessity for future shifts in emphasis, and confirms Rachel Blau DuPlessis' projective definition of poetics as a 'permission to continue', which is different from a retrospective theory of poetry or literary criticism.

Part One is the most recent, and most personal, piece. Part Two consists of older pieces, [the marginal marks A-F referring to other parts of the texts (with *+ marking beginnings of passages and =* marking their ends) to be read as interpolations, if wished. The pieces in Part Two may also be read linearly] as a sequence of deliberately various responses to similar issues, moves that already have been tried.

The Appendix [which also may be read as either interpolation or appendix] contains a piece of exposition which has been broadcast too widely, despite its explicit narrowcast audience and purpose; its privileging of the 'doing' of the text over its 'meaning' seems like an unfruitful move in the game. Today, I would stress a certain doubleness in poetic focus, which allows for a greater informational complexity – reference and formalism in tense relation, not simply refusing to mean, but refusing to mean *this* world. A poem is a coherent deformation of the linguistic system, which is also signifying – has a semantic core – and which, when actively engaged with, formally disrupts the reader's perceptual schema, and effects a coherent realignment of these in terms of the transformation of a recognisable world.

Again, what began as summary ended in revision, the terms reconstellating to form patterns that suggest rather than describe. The relation of theory to practice is uncertain.

8 May 1993

net/(k)not//-work(s) is dedicated to Allen Fisher

PART ONE

POETIC SEQUENCING AND THE NEW: *TWENTIETH CENTURY BLUES*

1

Works I've 'numbered', rather than named, *Twentieth Century Blues* have been appearing over the last two years. Never the title of a piece, this apparent subtitle (for example, 'Sharp Talk and Amended Signatures, Twentieth Century Blues 2') implies a sequencing of some sort. The text the reader has is clearly part of something else. How it relates to that something else and how that something else is disposed towards its own development, past and future, is my active and personal way of dealing with the question of what poetry might become.

A rejected title for this sequencing was that of Beuys' affective instal- lation, *The End of the 20th Century* – now happily in the Tate Gallery where it will be widely seen. It's a profound and resonant title, but I didn't like its suggestion of finality or ambiguous teleology (all denied by Beuys' work itself, of course). Moreover, a voice in a dream warned me not to use it. Less portentous and more fitting to my sensibility – to refunction kitsch – was 'Twentieth Century Blues', a song of Noel Coward that I once owned on a 78 but haven't heard for years: 'Blues, Twentieth Century Blues, are getting me down./ Who's escaped those weary Twentieth Century Blues?' Since I'd just then started to sing blues again in a band, it also seemed a pertinent red herring. The first 'Twentieth Century Blues' begins:

> Let it all go. As I sing, I drive my
> dynamite for some strange machine
> of this nearly spent century.

Clearly I had my eye on the end of the twentieth century – Beuys' sarcophagi could also be seeds, packed with the fat of decay or regeneration – but I wanted to avoid the millennial slip. The vast majority of the population of the world will not be celebrating the year 2000, not just because of starvation, war, and AIDS, but because they run their lives on different calendars. The twentieth century is an invention of the Christian West.

I wanted a 'title' that would allow me to order, re-order and disorder a text or a series of strands of texts in sequences, something that could be read in a number of ways. Allen Fisher's organisation of *Place* (1971–1980), it is often forgotten, is premised on a similar complexity, and was an inspiration. (See *Unpolished Mirrors, Serial H* (Spanner, 1981), for six possible ways of reading the work. Nevertheless, Fisher has always maintained that a reader can join the project at any point, becoming the 'loci of a point on a moving sphere', though the reader should respect the work's mutual cancellations and contradictory cross-referencing between its carefully numbered parts.)

The index of *Twentieth Century Blues* includes entries like this (titles in bold, strands in italics):

Blues 1: Smokestack Lightning

History of Sensation 5

3: Codes and Diodes are both Odes

Codes and Diodes 7
The Magnetic Letter 2

5: Killing Boxes

Melting Borders 2
Mesopotamia 2

7: Empty Diaries 1913 – 1945

This work includes:

Empty Diaries 1914-1919

Killing Boxes 2

Empty Diary 1917 (part iv of above)

Mesopotamia 3

Empty Diary 1924

Labour – Part One

Empty Diary 1926

For John Seed 1

Empty Diary 1929

Labour – Part Two

Empty Diary 1936 The Proletarian News

For Charles Madge 1

Empty Diary 1941

Voices Under Occupation 2

Empty Diary 1943-1945

Schräge Musik 2

9: Weightless Witnesses

Empty Diary 1991
Killing Boxes 3

'Mesopotamia 1' is, for example, 'History of Sensation 1'. 'Empty Diaries' is a long sequence of poems, one of which is 'Mesopotamia 3'. [You can see the same with the 'Killing Boxes' numbered 'blues' and its 'strand'.] Therefore, to read *Twentieth Century Blues* linearly, which is almost chronologically, causes it to double back upon itself. Many texts belong to more than one strand. New strands, even retrospectively, can be added to the weave. Some related texts, such as *The Cannibal Club*, 'History of Sensation 2', are not part of *Twentieth Century Blues*; its own borders melt. *Twentieth Century Blues* is essentially not about anything; it is a form to hang things on, to weave things through, albeit knottily. I have toyed with Deleuze and Guattari's term 'rhizome' in my hunt for the adequate metaphor, but I'm not sure that's what I'm producing, exactly. In a way, I would say that this schema organises continuities I've often sensed between texts of mine, the feeling of one poem continuing, even in contradiction, another.

Reading one of the resultant strands – even for me – is an oddly unsettling experience. For example, 'The Materialisation of Soap 1947', written in 1988, is part of *The Flashlight Sonata*, 'Twentieth Century Blues 6' and is also 'History of Sensation 4'; it clearly belongs to more than one strand. The second 'Materialisation of Soap 1947', was written in 1992 and belongs to the *Empty Diaries* 1946–1966 sequence, 'Twentieth Century Blues 17'. They therefore belong apart as much as they belong together. But to take them as a strand, they are stylistically dissimilar and what results is more of a network than a work, a dissonance, a difference born of identity (they use the same materials and share something of the same poetic focus). The first opens:

> Suspicion in the capital: the ecstasy
> Of austerity rationing the uniforms.
> It must be like air, natural and free,
> But there's a shortage of nature in this
> Land of torrents and the surrounding seas.

The second begins:

> Big Ben froze. British grit flies from
> bus wheels sticks to flesh queues do
> not waste brick dust Pearl's face silk
> through a wringer he licks her finger

There could be a third poem, different again, or one which would knot this strand into another. Or there might not. [There is indeed a third poem, 'The Sacred Tanks of Dagenham, Twentieth Century Blues 63', which knots the strand; it is numbered 4 in the strand, 3 being a particular gathering of all the existing strands into a bunch, as well as forming 'Articulates 10' and 'Impositions 3'. It opens:

> once Pearl pricks the two chops in the sizzling pan restaurant
> music she says

crouched towards the postcards outside the tobacconist's George
lives and loves it all though iceless

A

All three poems, with their different styles, use the same ekphrastic sources.] I realise that a reader's aesthetic preferences may privilege one text over another. This suits me. It activates the reader, though in a different way from my previous poetics of indeterminacy: the reader completing the author's fragments in an expansive education of desire. (See, for example 'The Education of Desire' and 'Ignite! and Incite!' in this volume.)   **B***

Whichever poem is privileged, it still has to be read against its apparently less convincing companion. The satisfaction of closure might be delayed as effectively as in an indeterminate text; the principle of discontinuity hangs *between* the texts not, necessarily, *within* them, though that's often still the practice. The aim, however, has not changed: to activate the reader into participation, into relating differences, to sabotage perceptual schema, to educate desire, not to fulfil it in a merely entertaining emptying of energy. To create, above all, new continuities.   **D***

The politics of this, though, becomes less utopian, less the text opening horizons of possibility, Marcuse's Aesthetic Dimension glittering with its pre-figurations. It becomes more strategic: a denial of what we presently are, as Foucault would have it, more a question of emphasising the text's 'capacity to promote active, procedural ruptures at the core of significatory tissues and semiotic denotatives, from which to set new worlds of reference to work'. (Félix Guattari, 'Text for the Russians', *Poetics Journal* 8)   **F***

The epigraph for the *Twentieth Century Blues* project – the chance of there being a *book*, a single volume of that title at the head of which it could stand is remote – comes from J.M. Coetzee's *Waiting for the Barbarians* (1980). The disgraced imperial magistrate, who is the novel's narrator, is forced to explain his archaeological interests (in particular, indecipherable texts he had collected) which have alerted his authoritarian captors' suspicions.

> They form an allegory. They can be read in many orders. Further, each single slip can be read in many ways. Together they can be read as a domestic journal, or they can be read as a plan of war, or they can be turned on their sides and read as a history of the last years of the Empire – the old Empire, I mean (p. 112).

His 'explanation', which stands at the head of the project [at last], is ironically barbed but his sense of the subversiveness of the marginal or of that which cannot readily be decoded into the violent simplicities of bureaucracy is affective, and provides me with a useful analogy for *Twentieth Century Blues*. We can all read the object, assemble, re-assemble, it in our own way(s). This will, of course, be affected by our acquired knowledge, our perceptual schema, and by the means of the text's availability, not an irrelevant question for the non-canonical poet, relying upon fugitive small presses. We all have to start reading with what we can get, as Allen Fisher realised. [Of course, the 2008 volume *Complete Twentieth Century Blues* did fulfil that 'remote' 'chance', much to my surprise.]

The long poem's ambition toward inclusiveness, its grasping for totality, with all its attendant drifts into dogmatism as well as stale repetition, has been, at least in this century, its most negative condition. I believe that my notion of sequencing, with its mercurial shifts, may avoid some of these traps. It is not necessary to let it go stale for the sake of titanic ambition. Although I don't wish to analyse his essay in any depth here, Barrett Watten's description of Zukofsky's *A* in his 'Social Formalism' essay (*North Dakota Quarterly*, Fall 1987) seems pertinent. His use of Bourdieu's theory, at the very least, provided me with the term 'generative schema' to describe poetic sequencing.

> The poetics I am trying to describe might be called 'process' but that would misunderstand them. The rhetoric of process describes a formal procedure given an equal value at all points; it is an imposed order, a naming from the outside of a temporal development. While these poetics involve a process, they work it out from the inside – involving a wide and indeterminate range of feedback that enacts a refiguring and transformation of Bourdieu's 'generative schema' over a long duration.

The morphogenetic poesis has a

> logic of development that creates the necessary conditions for its own 'next move in the game'. These moves are transformative – both of experience as it is understood and of the possibilities of the poem. The poem enacts a strategic argument of forms, rather than a rhetoric of process, and this temporality occurs in a tension with time outside the poem, with history and with the events of the poet's life.

The aim is that the writing – the working on rather than the working out – of *Twentieth Century Blues* should constitute such an aesthetic journey, fracturing into the new, a poetic changing by stages and confronting the changing world. There are no jumps, just swift transitions.

The fourteenth 'Twentieth Century Blues' is a short prospectus for this 'working on'.

2

Untitled

Twentieth Century Blues 14

net/
(k)not

     -work(s)

April 17 1992

3

A network but not a work, a knot of works, not work as labour, but as 'necessary business'. Several networks. *Net*: the shape of a 3D figure laid flat. Subject to no further deductions. The take home pay. *Network*: system of units, stations for broadcasting the same programme. *Not*: a word expressing denial, negation, refusal. Adv. Same as naught, nought. *Knot*: Interlacement. Twisting. In some particular form. A bond of union. A difficulty. The main point of a tangle. A complex of lines. A measure of speed. A node or joint in a stem. *Knotwork*: ornamental work made with knots. Granny knot: a knot like a reef knot, but unsymmetrical, apt to slip or jam. A tangle or a careful design? Slip knots let the world through. The net works to capture, the knot works to hold the net. *Work*: Working the Work, earlier notes on poetics. Working on. Effect directed to an end, that on which one works, the product of work, a literary composition, a book.

Works: walls, workshop, an action in its moral aspect. To produce effects. To sail in a course, to put in motion, to purge. To provoke. To excite.

Or *not* any of these.

4

What I shall be writing next may well be another 'Twentieth Century Blues'.

What I have been writing now, I realise, is itself 'Twentieth Century Blues 18' [and appears, updated a little, from this version, in *Complete Twentieth Century Blues*.] The generative schema allows for a proliferation of strands and an almost cellular splitting of new sequences. Perhaps *Twentieth Century Blues* will suddenly stop and other titles emerge from it as the 'real' work. The scheme announces only its potentialities, its host of whispered qualifiers; the strands could become, or include, music (there is one 'song' so far), performance, works by other artists in a variety of media, non-aesthetic events. One of my idle dreams has always been to write an entire literature, to become a sort of Pessoa gone fake omniscient.

The title *Twentieth Century Blues* does provide a temporal scope for my working, a moment at which, after having changed throughout, it will have to change utterly, into silence. And if silence isn't reached before that, it's a limit enough, the last years of the Empire and its calendar or not.

At Cambridge recently a group of poets eager for debate held a conference on 'Twenty first century poetry', a pre-emptive strike used, in the one paper I have read, to assert that the poetry of the next century will be – more or less – work I have written about as 'the poetry of the 1970s'. (See ed. Moore-Gilbert, *The Arts in the 1970s: Culture Closure?*, Routledge, 1994.) Such arguments, logically, lead only to the past, because it is the only known thing apart from the present. The future belongs to the unknown relation of a not yet unfolded world and the, at present, slenderly formed practices of those who will work in it, and against it. You cannot see into the granite hearts of Beuys' sculpture. But it might be possible to provide structures that can transform in terms of poetics and poetic focus as the world transforms itself. The one necessary result of *Twentieth Century Blues* should be that its future units, within strands and across the entire schema, will look like nothing that I am producing now.

July 1992

PART TWO

NEW BRITISH POETRY IN THE EIGHTIES

E+

Blake Morrison in 'Young Poets in the 1970s' grudgingly acknowledged two strands of the inventive poetries of Great Britain. One was the group of writers around J.H. Prynne, the Cambridge school, since collected in the anthology *A Various Art* (ed. Crozier and Longville). However, the genuinely young poets of that grouping, John Wilkinson (*Proud Flesh, Equofinality/Delires*), Rod Mengham (*Glow Worms,* Many) or Wendy Mulford (*The ABC of Writing,* Torque) are not to be found there. The other strand had 'been associated with and promoted by Eric Mottram'; in *Pages* 1-8, I conjectured that the withdrawal of that 'set' from the Poetry Society in 1977 was the loss of an effective power-base. I certainly feel that this marks off the poets who around that time emerged under the aegis of Mottram – Ken Edwards, Allen Fisher and Bill Griffiths, all three *Pages* contributors – from those who followed, and who had to operate in fragmentation and incoherence. I have sensed the difference myself, since as a publisher, I've experienced both periods; as a writer, only the latter. There have been enterprises for which one can be thankful, Ken Edwards' campaigning magazine *Reality Studios*, and the anthology *The New British Poetry* (ed. Allnut, D'Aguiar, Edwards, Mottram), and, in London, the tenacity of Gilbert Adair's *Subvoicive* reading series.

However, it seems to me, in or associated with London, there was, around the mid 1980s, the emergence of a number of writers who had reached independent maturity but who lacked the sympathetic context that might have existed a decade before. Editing *Pages* has only strengthened this conviction.

As a mentor figure of some distinction for these poets in the immediately preceding 'generation' – rather than in the 60s generation of Bob Cobbing, Roy Fisher, Lee Harwood, J.H. Prynne and Tom Raworth – I would point to the local presence and example of Allen Fisher. However, they point not to the 70s Fisher of *Place* – and its Olsonian fragmentation with its excuse for imitators to produce 'open field' pastoralism – but to the Fisher of *Gravity as a consequence of shape*, with its exemplary forward-thrust and lateral shiftings, and its sense of poetic production as transformative process and self-interference. Indeed, it was with a passage of this work that I deliberately launched *Pages*.

Since then, fortunately, some of these London-based writers I have in mind have been published in *Pages*: Gilbert Adair (*Hot Licks*, Subvoicive), Adrian Clarke (*Ghost Measures*, Actual Size), Virginia Firnberg (poems in *Pages*), Peter Middleton ('Portrait of an Unknown Man', in *Temblor* 7), Maggie O'Sullivan (*States of Emergency*, Magenta), Hazel Smith (*Threely*, Spectacular Diseases), and I would hope my own long text *The Flashlight Sonata* (published in separate books, Oasis, Torque, Ship of Fools [Stride and Salt]) would constellate with these works. Outside London, associated *Pages* contributors – this list is not exhaustive – included Kelvin Corcoran (*Qiryat Sepher*, Galloping Dog), Alan Halsey (*Five Years Out*, Galloping Dog) and Andrew Lawson (*Reality Studios* 10).   *A*+

The writers hold at least some of these operational axioms in common: that poetry must extend the inherited paradigms of 'poetry'; that this can be accomplished by delaying or even attempting to eradicate a reader's process of naturalisation, by using new forms of poetic artifice and formalist techniques to defamiliarize the dominant reality principle, in order to operate a critique of it; and that it may often use indeterminacy and discontinuity to fragment and re-constitute text to make new connections, to inaugurate new perceptions, not merely to mime the disorder of capitalist production. The reader thus becomes an active co-producer of these writers' texts, as he or she is drawn into the invention of the poem. Reading the poem will be an education of activated desire, not a passive recognition, fulfilment or killing, of desire.

=*A*

=*E*

August 1989

B+

In recent discussions on art and poetry, the word 'desire' is privileged, in my discourse as much as any: *The Education of Desire* (Ship of Fools) is the title of a small introduction to avant-garde poetic practice for A Level students. ***C*** The phrase itself, lifted from E.P. Thompson on Morris, is transposed and appears in a number of my reviews and articles, including my 'Flashlight Propositions' (*Far Language*, Stride Publications, 1999).

=***B***

D+

It is true that *The Education of Desire* simplifies, as Chris Beckett says in his 'Anxiety and Desire in the Poetic Machine' (*First Offense* 5), a 3 page piece which deserves to be widely read as an attempt to state a contemporary British poetics (and I'm glad he noticed the documents of Gilbert Adair and Andrew Lawson that I published in *Pages*). It is true that I simplify, necessarily I hope, but I don't think that 'there is a conflation in this argument between a desire for a more equitable and liberated society and a more fundamental sense of desire...derived from Lacan's notion of "an incessant sliding of the signified under the signifier"...This desire *precedes* representation, and its want cannot be slaked by language. This desire is not so much a want for something as want itself.' I agree, but I think that there still continues to be a possible and necessary connection between the two senses of desire and this is precisely the *education* I was attempting to sketch out. This is a question, not of theory, but of conviction.

Part of the problem is, as Beckett says, that the works of various French theorists which deal with 'desire' are 'not without some conflict' and whereas his definition derives from Lacan, my use derives from Lyotard (particularly 'The Critical Function of the Work of Art', *Driftworks*) and, to a lesser extent, from Guattari.

Bad art, for Lyotard, is simply self-expressive, is the representation of an artist's phantasy; the true artist 'undertakes to free *from* phantasy' (74). Klee paints by operating an abrupt and effective critical reversal: 'By turning his drawing around, he reverses the relation between the represented and the formal system, he is *working*, and if he reverses representation, it is in order not to see the figurative, not to be the victim of phantasy any longer, in order to be able to work upon the plastic screen itself, upon the page, by producing strokes that have a certain formal relation between themselves' (74-5). The cinema of Resnais similarly 'obliges the public to stop phantasizing. The spectator finds himself in the reversing, critical, function of the work and his desire collides with the screen, because the screen is treated as a screen and not a window.' In short, it does not fulfil desire; it activates it in the viewers. 'In the case of [Resnais'] film, the critical reversal is brought about by its cutting and editing' (75). It is possible to see the formal techniques of contemporary British poetry – say, Allen Fisher's *Gravity as a consequence of shape* – effecting this critical reversal. Reading such a poem should be an active education of desire, not a fulfilment, and therefore killing, of desire.

I have believed that the entry of an active reader into the poem is the poem's affirmative moment at which its technique, so often involving modes of indeterminacy and discontinuity, or its foregrounded devices, invite the reader to participate. This affirmative moment can never wholly be divorced from the critical function: the cry of hope and the cry of despair are heard together. Dissonance. In the act of constructing its meanings, the readers share in the poem's state of becoming. In doing so, they discover that it is what a text is made to do, as well as what it is made to mean, that is revolutionary.

When I first formulated these thoughts I had little of Lyotard's work of the 1960s. Lyotard himself in *Discours, Figure* apparently attempted to define desire in such a way as to allow for both a negative function and an affirmative one. 'Desire thought under the category of lack, of the negative; and desire produced in words, sounds, colours, volumes, under the idea of positive processes. Desire as that which models in the void the double (phantasy, counterpart, replica, hologram) *of* that which it lacks, desire as work, metamorphosis without aim, play without process' (Peter Dews, *Logics of Disintegration*, 1987, 132).

But in art, I re-emphasise, hope and despair are found together in the participation of a reader in the invention of the poem. The reader's desire, in terms of fluxes of objectless energy, is activated by the formal techniques of the text, but is not fulfilled, not even cynically as in advertising. The reader's desires, in terms of societal awareness, perhaps not even hitherto recognised, are hopefully aroused during this affirmative moment. The poem, as it is read, projects a future in its very refusal to mean *this* world. It still does not, as Lyotard rightly insists, present a coherent programme nor is it tied to a particular revolution.

These 'formal techniques of the text' are also the location of Beckett's important 'anxiety'. There is – and I certainly feel this – the anxiety of living in a time 'of undoing and untying' and the more textual anxiety 'that the disjunctive poem of the 'eighties may simply be a regressive "mimesis of actual informational chaos" (Adair)', which can only be countered – using a different work of Adair's – by 'coupling quantity with the quality of each linguistic item' (*Reality Studios* 10). It has been my hope that the text be open enough for the reader to be able to participate. Capitalist informational chaos exists to stop such participation. As Ornette Coleman put it: 'Information becomes information so we stay the same.' But 'open' for me has in the past always implied that the 'formal techniques' should involve indeterminacy and discontinuity.

Another of Gilbert Adair's related assertions is relevant here: 'Cutting across formations categorised as discrete, "discontinuity" *is* so only if it makes *other* relations' (*Pages* 68). What might these relations be? Are they only located in an active reader's participation? Are indeterminacy and discontinuity the only means of effecting this participation? Need the text always fragment and re-constitute to make new connections, to inaugurate new perceptions? What is the role of being directly affirmative, of hinting at a programme? Have I placed too much emphasis on the text doing as above meaning? Is it better to ape and contest the 'shit machine' than to operate a metalingual commentary? How can I afford Deleuze and Guattari? When will the *Lyotard Reader* be published? *E*

These are some of my new anxieties as I pause to consider what the poetry of the 80s might have been doing, and as I ponder what I might write next. =*D*

27 August 1989

F*+

CODES AND DIODES ARE BOTH ODES

for Bob Cobbing

Codes and Diodes 7
The Magnetic Letter 2
Twentieth Century Blues 3

Invent icicles dripping interference
and discover structural lift
in emergent interchange
opening like a clam – multiply coherent
shoals of desire. Flashes classic Hollywood shot
in erotic slippage exhaustion,
scorched doors for release. Desire
dances in the polyphonic
sentence, means a world, slips through
the signified, refunctioned
in our critical hold: jigsaw
scales, particle syntax admitting
intertexts and music of rhizomatic
diodes. Overlay of systems,
enough revealed delight to design
us all, while
magnetic words twin the
reader swiftly across echo's edge.

28 December 1990

=*F*

Appendix: The Education of Desire

[A text written for A Level students of English Literature]

I have set out to write as simply as I can what I believe is happening in the kind of poetry I write and in the kinds of poetry I believe to be really important today.

Secondly, I want to try and explain why I think this writing is revolutionary.

Today's Poetry and Advertising

It is impossible for anybody who wants to write a poetry that is politically revolutionary to write in the way most poems in Britain are written.

This poetry no longer works, though it wins poetry competitions.

If you think of all the things that are said to make poetry what it is – things like rhyme, rhythm, alliteration, etc – then you will today find them on any list of tricks used by advertising agencies in making adverts.

What once belonged to poetry has been stolen.

Some poets don't worry about this.

But it means that a lot of poetry today will look like adverts. It sells not a product ('Right for baby; right for you') but a moral ('What survives of us is love').

It is often in the form of a little story that moves towards its catch phrase. It may use flashy comparisons.

Think of adverts on the TV: so many of them are like that.

It is impossible to write revolutionary poetry like this.

Revolutionary Poetry

The writer who wants to do something different has to write in new ways.

The poetry may seem strange. It may be difficult to understand.

There may seem to be bits of it missing. There may be problems in putting all its parts together; things may not seem to follow on.

It may be difficult to see who's speaking.

It may seem as though there should be a story there, but there isn't.

There are lots of other new ways of writing.

The kind of difficulty I'm not talking about are difficulties that can be solved with the dictionary or the encyclopaedia.

I'm talking about difficulties that stop the process of reading, or upset your reading habits.

The very use of all these odd ways of writing will be an attack on the simple ways of thinking you see in adverts, for example, but which seem to go on everywhere.

It is a way of criticising the way society uses language, the way it thinks.

This is not the same as writing a poem about pollution. The poem about pollution might end up looking like an advert by Greenpeace, full of 'tricks' of persuasion.

Not all advertising is bad. But the poem that tries to look like an advert is bad.

What the Reader Has To Do

Adverts are easy to read, even when they seem strange at first; a lot of poems written today are easy to read. But most of the poetry I am thinking of is not easy to read. You can't consume it in one go.

This makes the reader work harder.

It does something else too: it makes the reader's work as important as that of the writer.

It is the reader who makes the poem – or rather: each individual has to make the poem, to complete it, for his or herself.

The reader is no longer a passive consumer. (Again, think of adverts: although you can analyse them, you don't usually have to work to understand their main message, which is usually: *Buy this Product* or *Stop this Pollution*.)

Some readers don't like this.

They prefer a poetry that they can immediately understand, that exhausts itself in one go (or seems to). This sort of poetry wins poetry competitions.

Another result of the poem not being written in the language of advertising or the language of our society is that it is a thing apart from it.

It exists independently of the controls of our society.

It must start out from the world, because that's where the writer is, where language is. He or she must create with bits and pieces of the world.

But the writer will rearrange everything so that out of the bits and pieces of this world, he or she will make a new world.

This is not easy to explain but it's as though the writer is breaking up a jigsaw puzzle and making a new pattern from it (but not the nice ordered picture on the box!).

This new world might not be a better world. It might only exist as a few disconnected words making a new combination.

But by saying something new, by making another world from out of the bits and pieces of language found in the real world, that is a way of criticising the way things are.

In a way it says, things must change.

Or perhaps it just says: things could be different.

This is also what the revolutionary says.

So therefore this way of writing will be a little bit revolutionary, although it will never tell you *how* things might change.

What Happens to the Reader

This poetry may be an attack on society as it is, on its ways of thinking.

But it can also have a positive aspect.

This is linked to the notion of a more active reader.

At first sight it may seem hard on the reader to make everything so difficult for him or her.

But I think it can also be a delightful thing to be allowed as much freedom as the writer, to read creatively, to fill in gaps, to be left to decide who is speaking, etc.

It is no longer just what a poem means that is important. It is also what a poem does to the reader.

The poem may tell you a lot, but it won't tell you everything. It will leave you working.

Adverts and most poems try to tell you everything. This is important because what they are trying to do is to fulfil your inner desires. In the advert's case you'll have to buy the product of course. Such and such beauty product will make you perfect.

Romantic fiction tries to fulfil desire. So does pornography.

They leave you apparently satisfied and no longer needing to think. They are full of old ideas.

The new poetry doesn't fulfil you. It leaves you with still a lot of thinking to be done. There will always be more and more to think about.

Poetry is the education of desire.

It might make you confused, mixed up. But that's all right. When you're trying to understand something difficult you do get confused for a bit. And people are all mixed up when they feel an emotion they've never experienced before: like sexual desire, for example.

At best, the poetry will change the reader, make him or her think in new ways, not simply what the society wants you to think.

Or even what the writer thinks.

Reading is no longer a guessing game to find out what the writer thinks; you do the thinking.

This is part of the positive, revolutionary function of this writing: let's repeat it: the education of desire.

To change the wants and desires of the people of the world would be the beginning of a revolution of sorts.

Writing has its small, but significant, part to play.

11 September 1988
=*C*

ACKNOWLEDGEMENTS AND FURTHER READING FOR
net/(k)not-//work(s)

[*net/(k)not//-work(s)* first appeared as a booklet from Ship of Fools, 1993.] 'Poetic Sequencing and the New' first appeared in *The ?Why? Project*, ed. Thomas Taylor, Anabasis, 1992 [and was posted online at *Jacket* and later appeared in *Complete Twentieth Century Blues*, Salt Publishing, 2008]. 'New British Poetry in the Eighties' first appeared in *Patterns/Contexts/ Time: A Symposium on Contemporary Poetry*, eds. Phillip Foss and Charles Bernstein, Tyuonyi, 1990. (For accounts of the poetry of the 1960s and 1970s, see 'British Poetry and Its Discontents' in eds. Moore-Gilbert and Seed, *Cultural Revolution?* Routledge, 1992; and 'Artifice and the everyday world: poetry in the 1970s' in ed. Moore-Gilbert, *The Arts in the 1970s: Cultural Closure?* Routledge, 1993. [See *The Poetry of Saying*, Liverpool University Press, 2005, for later incorporations of this pair.] But see also 'The British Dissonance', *PN Review* 44, 1985; 'Commitment to Openness', *Times Literary Supplement*, 10 March 1989. [The latter is reprinted in *Far Language*, Exeter: Stride, 1999.]) For more on the 1980s, see 'Recognition and Discovery in the 1980s', *Fragmente* 2, 1990; and (with Adrian Clarke), 'Afterword', *Floating Capital*, Potes and Poets, 1991. (For further discussion of the work of Allen Fisher, see 'Irregular Actions', *PN Review* 1986; and 'The Necessary Business of Allen Fisher' in *Future Exiles*, Paladin, 1992. [The former is republished in *Far Language*.] 'Re-Working the Work: Pausing for Breath' first appeared in *First Offense* 6, 1990. (In addition to the texts listed in the opening paragraph, see also 'Reading Prynne and Others', *Reality Studios* 2:2, 1979; 'The Bathwater and the Baby: A Formalist-Humanism', *Reality Studios* 3:3, 1981; 'Interview', *Angel Exhaust* 7, 1987; 'Disbelief', *PN Review* 1988; 'Flashlight Propositions' [appears in *Far Language*, as does 'Reading Prynne and Others'. 'The Education of Desire' also appears in that volume, but was also a Ship of Fools pamphlet, 1988]). 'Codes and Diodes' first appeared in *Codes and Diodes* (with Bob Cobbing), Writers Forum, 1991; and is reprinted in *VERBIVISIVOCO*, eds. Bob Cobbing and Bill Griffiths, with Jennifer Pike, Writers Forum, 1992 [republished in *Complete Twentieth Century Blues*, 2008, and in a box, in facsimile, as part of *Collaborations* (with Cobbing), Veer, 2021].